Professional and Practice-based Learning

Volume 36

Series Editors
Stephen Billett ⓘ, Griffith University, Brisbane, Australia
Christian Harteis, University of Paderborn, Paderborn, Germany
Hans Gruber, University of Regensburg, Regensburg, Germany

Professional and practice-based learning brings together international research on the individual development of professionals and the organisation of professional life and educational experiences. It complements the Springer journal *Vocations and Learning: Studies in vocational and professional education.*

Professional learning, and the practice-based processes that often support it, are the subject of increased interest and attention in the fields of educational, psychological, sociological, and business management research, and also by governments, employer organisations and unions. This professional learning goes beyond, what is often termed professional education, as it includes learning processes and experiences outside of educational institutions in both the initial and ongoing learning for the professional practice. Changes in these workplaces requirements usually manifest themselves in the everyday work tasks, professional development provisions in educational institution decrease in their salience, and learning and development during professional activities increase in their salience.

There are a range of scientific challenges and important focuses within the field of professional learning. These include:

- understanding and making explicit the complex and massive knowledge that is required for professional practice and identifying ways in which this knowledge can best be initially learnt and developed further throughout professional life.
- analytical explications of those processes that support learning at an individual and an organisational level.
- understanding how learning experiences and educational processes might best be aligned or integrated to support professional learning.

The series integrates research from different disciplines: education, sociology, psychology, amongst others. The series is comprehensive in scope as it not only focuses on professional learning of teachers and those in schools, colleges and universities, but all professional development within organisations.

Please contact Grace Ma at grace.ma@springer.com if you wish to discuss a book proposal.

Stephen Richard Billett • Anthony Leow
Anh Hai Le

Continuing Education and Training

Purposes, Practices and Futures

Stephen Richard Billett
School of Education and
Professional Studies
Griffith University
Mount Gravatt, QLD, Australia

Anthony Leow
Centre for Educational Development
Republic Polytechnic
Singapore, Singapore

Anh Hai Le
Griffith University
Mount Gravatt, QLD, Australia

ISSN 2210-5549 ISSN 2210-5557 (electronic)
Professional and Practice-based Learning
ISBN 978-981-97-2929-6 ISBN 978-981-97-2930-2 (eBook)
https://doi.org/10.1007/978-981-97-2930-2

© The Editor(s) (if applicable) and The Author(s), under exclusive license to Springer Nature Singapore Pte Ltd. 2024

This work is subject to copyright. All rights are solely and exclusively licensed by the Publisher, whether the whole or part of the material is concerned, specifically the rights of translation, reprinting, reuse of illustrations, recitation, broadcasting, reproduction on microfilms or in any other physical way, and transmission or information storage and retrieval, electronic adaptation, computer software, or by similar or dissimilar methodology now known or hereafter developed.

The use of general descriptive names, registered names, trademarks, service marks, etc. in this publication does not imply, even in the absence of a specific statement, that such names are exempt from the relevant protective laws and regulations and therefore free for general use.

The publisher, the authors and the editors are safe to assume that the advice and information in this book are believed to be true and accurate at the date of publication. Neither the publisher nor the authors or the editors give a warranty, expressed or implied, with respect to the material contained herein or for any errors or omissions that may have been made. The publisher remains neutral with regard to jurisdictional claims in published maps and institutional affiliations.

This Springer imprint is published by the registered company Springer Nature Singapore Pte Ltd.
The registered company address is: 152 Beach Road, #21-01/04 Gateway East, Singapore 189721, Singapore

If disposing of this product, please recycle the paper.

Series Editor's Foreword

A central purpose for the Professional and Practice–based Learning book series is on understanding further and supporting the learning and development of working age adults, and as directed towards their working lives. Consequently, a volume on Continuing Education and Training (CET) is a most welcome addition to this series. As the authors emphasise, CET is now a necessary educational provision for working age adults albeit given different titles and taking different forms in different industry sectors, occupations and countries. The kinds of changes that are occurring in occupational requirements and work performance make maintaining occupational currency an ongoing project. The completion of occupational preparation that often occurs in the transition from school to working life is merely the starting point on a journey of learning across working life. This is because that ongoing learning is required for being employed, staying employed and making positive contributions to sustaining the viability of the workplaces in which they are employed. All of this suggests that CET needs to be recognised as an important educational sector as it is preparing people for their occupations. Indeed, the point made by the authors is that rather than being an appendage of or an appendix to an existing educational provision, CET requires to be understood and practised in its own terms and with a particular focus on how it can address the needs of working age adults who have overlapping responsibilities and commitments beyond work and study.

The authors refer to the need for an educational system whose elements comprise tertiary education institutions, workplaces, working age adults and the contribution of friends, family and other familiars in providing support for adults to participate and enjoy success in their programs. Some of the important considerations arising from this volume are that, unlike young people's education that is compulsory or mandated, most participation in CET arises from individuals' initiatives and interests. Yet, there are some occupations that have regular professional development requirements, but in the main, ultimately, it is up to adults whether they participate or not in these provisions. That means those provisions need to be aware of what motivates, engages and addresses the needs of working age adults. The contributions of this book are structured across its chapters, but with a summary chapter early in the volume (Chap. 2) providing a synthesis of what is advanced across the book and individual chapters. In all, what is proposed in this volume is a data-driven and theoretically framed accounts of what a national CET provision or system which addresses the stated premise of having an approach to CET that is made distinct through its purposes and requirements.

Beyond the specific focus, there are aspects of this volume that make it particularly relevant to the book series. Firstly, it presents a country-specific case study through a range of data gathered from diverse informants that together offer a comprehensive approach to understanding what constitutes an effective CET system from the perspectives of working age adults, employers, teachers and administrators in a way that commences with considerations of those who are the primary focus of these educational provisions—working age adults—and then continues from there. Secondly, this study is from a country which clearly has a more mature approach to CET than many others and for good reasons. That is, with economic and social goals been dependent upon the skills of the workforce, which is ageing, Singapore is embracing the need for this educational provision in terms of policies, practices and engagements with workplaces and the community. Thirdly, some will question the relevance of a study based in this country, which offers a perspective from Asia which is as legitimate and important as those from Europe, Scandinavia or North America. Yet, this is a key strength that adds to the diversity of perspectives and orientations to the contributions made in this series. Too often, what is advanced from European, Scandinavian British or North American contacts is expected to be applicable elsewhere. Yet, when perspectives come from outside of those countries, their relevance is inevitably questioned. The authors make clear that while setting out the country context, the findings are drawn out and synthesised in ways that suggest the broad applicability that may be as adaptable to other countries as studies conducted elsewhere. Fourthly, a thematic approach is taken across the sections of this volume providing a review of what the literature is saying about the continuing education of adults, and then overviews of the project and findings, then a set of perspectives drawn from the data that inform about the views of working age adults, graduates from programs, employers, as well as those who teach in and administer CET programs. A chapter on working women and their perspectives is to follow and to finish, a chapter on older workers. This is a particularly germane contribution given the age profile of the Singapore population. However, again, this has relevance to other countries that have ageing populations.

In all, this volume makes a particular, helpful and very timely contribution to this book series, and in doing so offers insights, propositions and findings that are likely to be helpful across the broad field of adult learning and development, regardless of whether it is undertaken wholly within tertiary education institutions or within practice or community settings.

University of Regensburg Hans Gruber
Regensburg, Germany

Paderborn University Christian Harteis
Paderborn, Germany
March 2024

Preface

In the current era, the importance of continuing education and training (CET) has evolved from being peripheral and discretionary to increasingly being seen as an essential element of learning across lengthening working lives. Workers are increasingly aware that they need to maintain their skills' currency and occupational competence to remain employed as the requirements for practising those occupations and workplace demands necessitate ongoing and continuous learning. In the past, the concept of professional development was largely constrained to its namesake: the professions. Yet, the ability to remain currently competent, to demonstrate that competence and remain employable, there alone the quest for advancement or changing occupations are all now premised on ongoing learning, participation in structured programs and securing certification that verifies currency and competence. Moreover, although much of CET provisions are those organised through tertiary education institutions, specific requirements of remaining currently competent and adaptable as work and occupational requirements change demand other ways of securing upskilling and reskilling. In particular, considerations for how workplace settings can be used as sites for this ongoing learning are increasingly becoming a focus, not the least because there is a need for scalable approaches that are able to accommodate entire workforces.

More than merely constant change caused by accelerated technological innovations, new ways of working and widening participation within workforces which require processes of further developing skills, there are new and emerging imperatives. Perhaps first and foremost is an increasingly globalised economy means that workforces at the national or enterprise level increasingly require that working age adults need to be adaptive and open to ongoing learning to produce and provide the goods and services that are required within their communities, and beyond. So, this globalised competition necessitates focused considerations that national workforces need to be both export oriented and import competing in their practices, the least they be displaced by goods manufactured and services provided elsewhere. Yet, a new dimension of this imperative has arisen with emerging geopolitical tensions and disruptions that are leading nation states to find ways of becoming more self-sufficient and self-reliant. Hence, there is a need for constant upgrading and innovations, both of which are directly aligned with continual learning.

Much societal attention, investment and effort are directed towards the education of children in schools and then young adults in tertiary education institutions in preparation for engagement in the world of work. Yet, given the need for ongoing learning across lengthening working lives in most nation states with modern economies, the importance of having a dedicated focus on the purposes, processes and outcomes of CET are now becoming more mainstream and orthodox. Importantly, these processes and outcomes are often quite distinct from those that tertiary education institutions provide for younger adults, most of whom are able to study full-time and focus their efforts on their education, and also socialise with peers. In many ways, these learners are naïve having, usually, limited or no experience in the world of work. Yet, for students attending CET programs, there is often distinct purposes and processes by which they come to engage. For many, and perhaps most working age adults, their participation in CET programs comes at a cost to other activities and commitments as perhaps most of them are balancing the demands of work, family, community as well as participating in continuing education programs.

Hence, there needs to be provisions of CET that are comprehensive, systemic and scalable, which this volume seeks to inform about and suggest means by which they can be enhanced. One feature of this monograph is that the practical enquiry conducted, data gathered and workshops facilitated were all in Singapore. In many ways, this is a worthwhile and pertinent choice. This country with its relatively small size and population relies very much upon the skills and capacities of the working age population. Lacking access to primary industries that harvest natural resources or are even self-sufficient agriculturally, the policy agenda for CET is very high because of their dependence upon the quality, skilfulness and adaptability of its national workforce. Also, as the Singaporean population ages, this necessitates considerations for how that working population can remain currently competent and participating in working life far longer than earlier generations. Thus, all of this come requirements for skills development, and often from students who may not have excelled or enjoyed compulsory education.

However, there is no reason to be dismissive of or downplay the findings and conclusions reported here because they were based upon data gathered in Singapore. Instead, the readership is reminded constantly that each country has its own specific approaches to, orientations of and means of enacting CET. Yet, lessons learned from this study have the potential to inform both the purposes and processes of continuing education in other countries. Certainly, the findings here are necessarily no less informative than those arising from countries in North America, Europe or Scandinavia. Indeed, the structuring of the volume is deliberately intended to address key themes that are likely to be germane to any nation state's considerations and enactment of CET.

Structure of the Monograph

The monograph is structured into three parts. The first part—*CET Imperatives, Practices and Policies*—provides an overview of the contemporary national, workplace and personal imperatives for CET and why these make it an important focus for informed inquiry. This includes considerations of factors that need to guide and support policy and practice in this field. Hence, this first part sets out the premises for how such an educational provision might be considered by national governments, albeit situated within tertiary education systems and supported by local enterprises and communities. These premises then also advise about how CET provisions can be designed, enacted and evaluated. These contributions both comprise and are informed by a focused review of the extant literature and the multi-parted and large-scale practical inquiry that comprises a national case study from Singapore that informs much of this monograph.

The first part comprises three chapters: Chapter 1—Supporting Learning Across Working Life: Premises for Effective CET Provisions—sets out the rationale for a focus on CET and outlines the review and practical inquiry that comprises the multi-parted case study from Singapore. Chapter 2—Practice and Policy Implications for CET: A Systematic Approach—draws on the findings of the review and the phases of the practical enquiry to offer suggestions for policy and practice. In many ways, this chapter presents a synthesis of the contributions of other chapters to offer suggestions on the ways in which CET systems might be organised, enacted and evaluated.

Chapter 3—Continuing Education and Training: The Quest for Effective Provisions—comprises a focused review of the extant literature and its contributions to the effective provision of CET. It focuses on the imperatives for adults to learn across working life, both for personal (i.e., employability) and institutional (e.g., government, workplaces) purposes. It highlights the importance of partnerships amongst tertiary education sector, workplaces and working age adults to develop effective CET provisions. In particular, the contribution of workplace learning is generative of important learning outcomes. It considers approaches for organising, ordering, supporting and guiding this intentional learning through CET provisions. It also discusses the Singapore CET landscape to contextualise the phenomenon under investigation in this research project.

The second part—Singaporean Case Study—comprises three chapters that describe and justify the method procedures used in the national case study from Singapore, and present and discuss general findings from the interviews of recent CET graduates and employers about the motivations of working age Singaporeans to participate in CET programs and their perspectives on how they were guarded and supported in making decisions about participating. These chapters also report and discuss these informants' perspectives of the quality of the experiences of the CET provisions, and those provided by the educators in the tertiary education institutes in which they undertook the programs. In addition, data from a national survey undertaken to secure insights beyond the cohort of graduates and employers who were interviewed for the project. That survey provided a large database of working age Singaporeans that the interview findings can be considered and validated.

Chapter 4—Investigating Effective CET Provisions to Promote Employability: Method and Procedures—provides a detailed overview of the practical inquiry, which, as the title suggests, describes and justifies the kinds of research procedures selected for gathering and analysing the data through interviews, surveys and focus group activities. It sets out the context, framing, procedures and broad outcomes of a three-phase research project that sought to identify what constitutes effective CET provisions for working age adults. The practical inquiry was enacted through interviews with CET graduates and their employers in Phase 1, followed by a survey in Phase 2 administered to Singaporean working age adults in a range of employment and industry sectors to validate and advance the interview findings. In Phase 3, the consolidated findings from the first two phases were presented to CET educators and administrators who engaged in co-construction of the implications and generation of guidelines for curriculum and pedagogic practices.

Chapter 5—Motivations and Affordances for Engaging CET—presents and discusses the project's findings about what motivates working age adults' participation in CET and the kinds of affordances for supporting their engagement in CET. The findings indicated that the recent CET graduates were motivated personally and professionally to take CET courses/programs. Yet, there was a mix of personal and institutional factors that support as well as inhibit their participation and engagement in CET. These findings inform how a provision of CET needs to be positioned to make it attractive and accessible for working age adults.

Chapter 6—Effective CET Provisions: A National Survey—reports and discusses the findings of a national survey that engaged working age adult respondents including those who had participated in CET programs and those that had not comprising Phase 2 of the research project. It illuminates and elaborates responses from 860 working age Singaporeans who may or may not have participated in a CET program. It was found that many of them claiming on-the-job training was the most effective way to acquire skills, thereby questioning an assumption that this could best be achieved through CET provisions offered through tertiary education institutions. Nevertheless, there was seen to be a great value in these kinds of provisions to promote further the development of Singaporeans' capacities for both personal and professional purposes, and usually a combination of both.

As the title of the third part suggests—Stakeholder Perspectives—it comprises four chapters each of which introduces, describes and discusses the perspectives of specific categories of informants and respondents. They offer specific perspectives to understand what constitutes effective provisions of CET and how these are present in existing arrangements and, from that perspective, how they might be enhanced and advanced for the future in responding to their particular purposes, needs and requirements.

Chapter 7—Effective CET Provisions: Perspectives from Graduates and Employers—analyses responses from graduates of CET programs and employers. It discusses the perspectives of a selection of diverse kinds of working age adults who have recently completed CET programs, and also small sample of employers about how their employees' employability can be sustained through participation and engagement in CET programs and the ways in which these might need to change to more adequately realise important personal and societal goals. Findings indicated that there are similarities and differences in their views about how to effectively acquire and develop further occupational capacities and specific competencies required for workplace performance, what constitutes effective CET provisions, and qualities of effective educators and learners. In some ways, these can be seen as complementary views about the efficacy of CET provisions.

Drawing upon a series of workshops conducted online with practitioners, Chap. 8—Advancing CET Provisions: Perspectives of Educators and Practitioners—reports and discusses the third phase of the project. In this phase, the consolidated findings from the first two phases were presented to CET educators and administrators who engaged in co-construction of the implications and generation of guidelines for curriculum and pedagogic practices in tertiary education institutions. Overall, it was indicated that there is a need for collaboration and engagement with different partners and between different levels of CET. This collaborative approach not only enhances the practical relevance of the education provided but also opens avenues for networking, skill application and real-world problem-solving, and subsequent opportunities for employment. Importantly, a systemic approach to such collaboration and engagement is essential for enacting effective CET provisions.

Given this and the demanding roles in which they engage, Chap. 9—Working Women and CET: Enablers and Barriers—provides an analysis on the purposes, experiences and needs of women who are seeking to balance their studies with other aspects of their lives. This chapter illuminates and appraises the experience of working women through interviews with female CET graduates. Overall, it was found that the working women, just like their male counterparts, were driven by both personal and professional reasons to participate in CET courses/programs. These female informants reported that work and family commitments were key barriers to their full engagement. Understanding of these female gradates' perspectives and experiences is pivotal to respond to the quest of what constitutes effective CET provisions for working women.

Finally, Chap. 10—CET Journey: Experience of 'Older' Working Age Adults—offers a range of perspectives from mature age or older working age adults through interviews with CET graduates aged 50 and above. It was found that these graduates' participation in CET was driven by both personal and professional reasons, the mix of which were shaped by individual needs and goals. Noteworthily, the majority reported being motivated by occupational or work role changes, which is central to their sense of self as working age adults and is also important in their transitions across working life and the ability to remain employed.

Brisbane, QLD, Australia	Stephen Richard Billett
Singapore, Singapore	Anthony Leow
Brisbane, QLD, Australia February 2024	Anh Hai Le

Acknowledgements

The authors would like to acknowledge the range of institutional, personal and professional contributions that have supported the review of literature and practical investigations that were highly instrumental in informing and directly contributing to what is advanced through this authored monograph. Firstly, we would like to acknowledge the source of funding that supported the enquiry in Singapore, which was provided through nationally competitive scheme in Singapore hosted by the Ministry of Education's Workforce Development Applied Research Fund. This funding supported the employment of research assistants in Singapore. In addition, the support provided by Griffith University, Australia, and Republic Polytechnic, Singapore, which hosted the project, made the organisation and enactment of the project possible. This included the in-kind contributions provided by these institutions that permitted the authors to undertake the research and then prepare this volume.

We would like to acknowledge the research assistant work that was undertaken by Cheryl Low, Gwyneth-Ann Khoo and later Shuyi Chua. These research assistants were largely responsible for organising and undertaking most of the interviews with CET graduates and employers. Moreover, colleagues at Republic Polytechnic in Singapore, Shufen Po and Mark Chia also provided support in advising and assisting the development of the instruments being used in the project, as were colleagues from Ngee Ann Polytechnic (Sara Zaman and Yew Kong) who engaged in the first phases of the project.

Research projects such as the one described and elaborated across this volume rely upon informants providing data and being generous with their time and contributions. This project was no exception. We were fortunate that 180 working age Singaporeans who had completed continuing education and training (CET) programs agreed to be interviewed and provided rich data, as did the 40 employers who also gave up their time and made helpful contributions to their perspectives on what constitutes effective CET programs.

Then, there were over 800 working age Singaporeans who completed the survey, and then in the third phase over 270 educators and administrators working in polytechnics engaged in 6 workshops and 3 webinars that were used to translate the findings from the interview and survey phases into workable options for improving the provision of CET in Singapore.

It is also important to acknowledge that much of the latter phases of the project was undertaken in extremely difficult circumstances given the 'circuit breakers' or lock downs in Singapore. This meant that the workshops in the final phases of the project had to be conducted online and at a distance. Yet, in many ways these workshops highlighted a heightened use of electronic technology and platforms by working age Singaporeans. This necessitated the supplementary survey that was administered after the lockdowns to capture whether working age adults' attitudes towards online educational provisions had changed because of the enhanced use of electronic means of communication during the periods of lockdown.

Contents

Part I CET Imperatives, Practices and Policies

**1 Supporting Learning Across Working Life: Premises
for Effective CET Provisions** 3
    Continuing Education and Training: A Growing Interest 4
    CET Premises, Purposes and Processes 6
        Privileging CET as Well as Schooling and Initial Tertiary Education   8
        Consequences of Societal Educational Imperatives 11
        Repositioning Continuing Education and Training 12
    Preview of Contributions 17
    References 19

**2 Practice and Policy Implications for CET:
A Systemic Approach** 23
    Towards a Continuing Education and Training Promoting
Employability and Workplace Viability 24
        Key Considerations for a CET System 26
        The Role and Leadership of CET Institutions 27
        Factors Shaping Effective CET Provisions 29
    A CET Provision for Sustaining Employability
and Workplace Viability 30
        Positioning Adults as Learners 31
        Towards a Model of a (National) CET System 32
    Key Indicators of an Effective CET System 35
    Privileging CET as an Educational Sector 41
    References 42

**3 Continuing Education and Training: The Quest
for Effective Provisions** 45
    Promoting Employability Across Working Life 46
        Singapore Case Study 48

Continuing Education and Training: The Quest
for Effectiveness 52
Constituting Effective CET: The Tripartite Contributions
of the Tertiary Education Sector, Workplaces and CET Students...... 54
    Enterprise Outcomes from Engagement in CET 56
    The Role of Adult Education and CET Educators 57
    CET and Working Age Adults............................... 59
    CET and Workplace Experiences 61
The Quest for Effective CET Provisions........................... 62
References.. 64

Part II Singaporean Case Study

**4 Investigating Effective CET Provisions
to Promote Employability: Method and Procedures**............... 73
Continuing Education and Training to Sustain Employability 74
Case Study Context... 75
Exploring Effective CET Provisions: A Singaporean Investigation 78
Phase 1: Graduates' and Employers' Perspectives
on Effective CET Provisions..................................... 80
Phase 2: Verifying and Elaborating Findings Through
a National Survey 82
Phase 3: Advancing CET Provisions 86
Ethics.. 87
Applicability, Contribution and Impact of the Research............. 87
Limitations 89
Investigating Effective CET Provisions 90
Appendices 93
    Appendix 4.1—Phase 1 Pre-Interview Survey 93
    Appendix 4.2—Phase 1 Interview Schedule................... 97
    Appendix 4.3—Vignettes for workshops and webinars 98
References.. 101

5 Motivations and Affordances for Engaging in CET 103
Participating in Continuing Education and Training 104
Motivations and Affordances for CET Participation
and Engagement 106
    Perspectives on Motivation to Participate and Engage in CET...... 107
    Potential Barriers 108
Procedures... 110
Findings... 110
    Motivations for CET Participation 111
    Achievement of Purposes for CET Participation 113
    Affordances for CET Engagement 114
Motivations and Affordances for CET Participation................. 120
References... 122

6 Towards an Effective, Accessible and Scalable CET Provision: A National Survey 125
Provisions of Continuing Education and Training
and Working Age Adults 126
Adults' Perspectives of CET: The National Survey 129
   Procedures 129
   Findings 131
An Effective, Accessible and Scalable CET Provision 151
References 154

Part III Stakeholder Perspectives

7 Effective CET Provisions: Perspectives from Graduates and Employers 159
Continuing Education and Training to Sustain Employability 160
CET Initiative: The Case from Singapore 162
Investigating Effective CET Provisions: Workers'
and Employers' Perspectives 163
   Skill Acquisition 164
   Effective CET Provisions 166
   Qualities of CET Educators 169
   Qualities of CET Students 172
Conclusions and Implications 174
References 177

8 Advancing CET Provisions: Perspectives of Educators and Practitioners 181
Continuing Education and Training: A Quest
for Effective Provisions 182
Educators' and Practitioners' Perspectives of CET:
A Case from Singapore 186
   Support for Students Before and After the Course 187
   Support from Employers 188
   Support from Administrators 189
   Coping with New Online Education Provisions 190
   Skills Required of Contemporary Adult Educators 191
Recommendations for Effective CET Provisions 193
Towards an Effective Provision of CET 196
References 197

9 Working Women and CET: Enablers and Barriers 199
Working Women, CET and Employability 200
Women and Participation in Continuing Education and Training 202

	Women Graduates' Perspectives of CET:	
	A Singaporean Investigation	205
	Motivations for CET Participation	206
	Barriers to and Enablers for Participating in CET Programs	208
	Experience of CET Courses/Programs	210
	Working Women's CET Experience and Outcomes	214
	References	216
10	**CET Experience of and Outcomes for 'Older' Working Age Adults**	**219**
	Older Workers, CET and Employability	220
	Older Workers, Their Needs and Bases for Engagement in CET	222
	Factors Shaping Older Workers' Learning for and in Work	223
	Older Workers' Agency and Intentionality	225
	Singaporean Case	227
	Findings from CET Project	228
	Demographic and Work Background	228
	Motivations for CET Participation	229
	Factors Inhibiting Participation	232
	Factors Sustaining Engagement and Completion	233
	Achievement of Purposes	233
	CET Teachers	234
	CET Provisions	236
	Older Working Age Adults' Experiences and Outcomes in Sum	238
	References	240
Index		**243**

About the Authors

Stephen Richard Billett is Professor of Adult and Vocational Education at Griffith University, Brisbane, Australia, and an Australian Research Council Future Fellow. He has worked in vocational education, educational administration, teacher education, professional development and policy development in the Australian vocational education system and as a teacher and researcher in higher education.

Anthony Leow is currently the Assistant Director at the Centre for Educational Development of Republic Polytechnic. He completed his PhD at the University of Queensland, researching on the interface between public health and education policies. His current research interests include adult learning, workplace learning, continuing education and training of adults and lifelong learning.

Anh Hai Le is a Research Fellow at Griffith University, Brisbane, Australia. Her research interest focuses on workplace learning and curriculum development in tertiary education, with a specific emphasis on the process of building knowledge through scholarly engagement with industry and tertiary institutions. Much of her recent research has focused on lifelong and adult education.

Part I
CET Imperatives, Practices and Policies

This first section provides an overview of the contemporary national, workplace and personal imperatives for continuing education and training (CET) that make it an important focus for informed investigation through which to guide and support both policy and practice in this field. In this way, it sets out the premises for how such an educational provision might be considered by national governments, fitted within tertiary education systems and supported by enterprises and communities. These premises then also advise about how CET provisions can be designed, enacted, and evaluated. All of this is informed by a focused review of the extant literature and the multi-parted and large-scale practical inquiry that comprises a national case study from Singapore that comprises and informs much of this monograph. It comprises three chapters: Chap. 1—*Supporting learning across working life: Premises for effective CET provisions*, which sets out the rationale for a focus on CET and outlines the review and practical inquiry that comprises the case study from Singapore; Chap. 2—*Practice and policy implications for CET: A systematic approach* that draws on the findings of the review and the phases of the practical enquiry to offer suggestions for policy and practice; and Chap. 3—*Continuing education and training: The quest for effective provisions* that advances a review of the extant literature and its contributions to the effective provision of CET.

Chapter 1
Supporting Learning Across Working Life: Premises for Effective CET Provisions

Abstract Nation states increasingly require effective, accessible, inclusive, scalable and broadly engaged provisions of continuing education and training (CET) to develop further the capacities of their working age populations. This is no more the case than when those countries' social and economic needs rely largely or wholly on the capacities of their working age populations. Consequently, understanding what constitutes accessible and effective CET provisions enables informed decision-making about effectively realizing these national initiatives through developing skilled, employable, and adaptive workforces. Yet, to illuminate and elaborate what comprises efficacy, it is necessary to capture, analyze, understand and reconcile perspectives and needs for CET provisions, including national bodies, those who employ working age adults, education institutions, CET educators and, most importantly, working age adults themselves. Capturing and reconciling these perspectives is essential for establishing comprehensive account of what constitutes an effective CET system. This includes the kinds of CET provisions best able to meet the needs of working-age adults and their workplaces, and how they are delivered and engaged with by these adults. This opening chapter discusses the premises for understanding learning across working life and how it can be supported, guided, and enacted through CET provisions. It also overviews a research program on CET undertaken in Singapore and summarizes its key findings, conclusions, and contributions. The Singapore investigation secured contributions from interviews with CET graduate informants and their employers, and survey respondents from a larger population of working-age Singaporeans. It foreshadows the identification and need for a systematic approach to developing and enacting effective CET provisions to promote and sustain individuals' employability across lengthening working lives that are then elaborated in subsequent chapters. Like any other nationally based case study, it has strengths and limitations. Importantly, it provides a comprehensive case and important perspective from a nation state largely reliant on its working-age population's capacities and one that has an aged and aging profile. Hence, CET is central to its social and economic well-being and, indeed it is a sovereignty. Whilst there are limitations with a case study based within one country, these perspectives render it particularly helpful to inform discussions and decisions in others.

© The Author(s), under exclusive license to Springer Nature Singapore Pte Ltd. 2024
S. R. Billett et al., *Continuing Education and Training*, Professional and Practice-based Learning 36, https://doi.org/10.1007/978-981-97-2930-2_1

Keywords Continuing education and training · Educational purposes · Educational processes · Employability · Scalability · Social goals · Economic goals · Public enterprises · Private enterprises · Working age adults · Older workers · National priorities · Policy imperatives

Continuing Education and Training: A Growing Interest

National states with both developed and developing modern economies require effective, accessible, inclusive, and broadly engaged provisions of continuing education and training (CET) to develop further the capacities of their working age populations. This requirement goes beyond the effectiveness and profitability of the private sector enterprises that deliver much of the economic contributions and employment. The further development of those skills equally applies equally to public enterprises and particularly those focused on important social goals such as health and aged care, education and development and maintenance of physical infrastructure and caring for the environment. An effective provision of CET is especially important for countries whose viability is dependent upon the skills and adaptiveness of the working-age population, such as Singapore. That skillfulness is essential because of the absence of natural resources to sustain their economic well-being and providing for the nation state's social and economic needs. Moreover, in an era in which work is premised increasingly on adaptive human expertise, and a growing need for greater national self-reliance and self-sufficiency, these capacities are becoming vital for all nation states to meet their social and economic goals, and to maintain their national sovereignty. That is, in an era of geopolitical tensions, to have the resources available to resist unwelcome and unwarranted interference from other countries to national well-being. An effective provision of CET is also necessary because of the wide acceptance that the initial occupational preparation that occurs in most countries for young people in the transition from school to work is insufficient to maintain individuals' employability across lengthening working lives. The changing requirements for occupational practices and dynamic and specific needs of individual workplaces necessitate working age adults to continue to learn across their working lives who are required, on the one hand, to maintain their employability, but also contribute to their workplaces viability through an ability to adapt, on the other (Organisation for Economic Co-operation and Development [OECD], 2021).

Together, these circumstances emphasize the importance of the currency of the working-age population's occupational skills. These adults' adaptability is also becoming central to national governmental considerations about educational effort and for the ability of both public and private sector enterprises that provide the goods and services needed in these nation states (Economic Strategies Committee, 2010a). Consequently, the focuses on working-age adults' employability have been extended to include not only the ability to secure employment, but also to sustain that employability as the competence required for occupational practice constantly evolves as do workplace performance requirements (Billett & Hodge, 2016). Globally, these imperatives are leading to a growing interest by supranational government agencies (e.g., OECD, 2021; UNESCO, 2022), national governments, professional and employer bodies and representatives of employees in how that employability can be realized in ways that are scalable for and accessible to entire working populations. Indeed, the national economic review in Singapore in 2010 had as its first priority to maintain and develop further the capacities of all members of its working-age population (Economic Strategies Committee, 2010a). This policy aim has been advanced through establishing institutions and programs to support the ongoing development of working age adults in ways that are systematic and strategic, and embracing it is a national strategic priority. This national concern and priority was articulated clearly in a recent statement by the Minister for Education, who stated that:

> … If we need to top up the knowledge and skills of our people as they take on new jobs every four to five years, that means upgrading 20 to 25% of our roughly 3 million local workforce each year: or about half a million adult workers every year! … the definition of success for our education system cannot be just how well we produce a cohort of 30 to 40 thousand students each year for the job market. It should be how well we do *that* plus retraining and upgrading about half a million adult learners each year. (Minister Chan Chun Sing, 10th February 2022) (Ministry of Education Singapore, 2022)

What is proposed in this challenge for the education system and CET provisions is to develop the capacities of the entire national workforce over a four- or five-year cycle. Consequently, not only is there a need for effective provisions of CET, but for those to be scalable to accommodate an entire national workforce. However, this country is far from being alone, as many others have implemented policies and practices to promote and realize effective CET provisions for working-age populations, albeit in different ways depending upon their needs and aspirations (Bostrom, 2017; Guo, 2014; Lauder, 2020; Schuetze & Slowey, 2013; Zimmermann, 2020).

Therefore, understanding what constitutes accessible, effective and scalable CET provisions enables informed decision-making and actions about how best to achieve these important national goals. That importance extends beyond the nation state that comprises the case presented here as achieving a skilled, employable, and adaptive workforce have become an important policy focus globally (OECD, 2021). To understand what comprises that efficacy, it is necessary to capture, analyze, and reconcile the perspectives of key stakeholders including national bodies, education institutions, those who employed in both public and private sector workplaces, CET educators and, perhaps, most importantly, the working-age adults who will elect whether or not to engage in these educational provisions, for what reasons and how they will come to engage. Capturing and reconciling these perspectives is essential for establishing what constitutes an effective, accessible and scalable CET system. This includes what kinds of CET provisions can best meet the needs of these adults and their workplaces and how they are delivered and engaged with by all kinds and occupational classifications of working-age adults with diverse levels of educational backgrounds, across categories of gender and age.

As a starting point, this opening chapter discusses the purposes of and premises for understanding learning across working life and how it can be supported, guided, and enacted through CET provisions. That is, it establishes the foundations for exploring alternative purposes and forms of educational provisions, encouraging a departure from conventional or orthodox approaches to CET such as the traditional face-to-face learning experiences in tertiary education institutions. Inevitably, given the quest for scalability, identifying settings where CET can be enacted for working-age adults necessarily brings into focus the role of learning experiences within and through these adults' workplaces. Following this, an overview of the research program undertaken in Singapore, and summary of key findings, conclusions, and contributions are advanced in preview, which are subsequently detailed in subsequent chapters. These comprise a synthesis of recent literature and the phases of a national investigation conducted in Singapore (*see* Chapters 3—*Continuing education and training: The quest for effective provisions* and 4—*Investigating effective CET provisions to promote employability: Method and procedures*). The investigation furnished contributions from interviews with CET graduate informants and employers, and survey respondents from a larger population of working-age adult Singaporeans, including supplementary surveys to capture the potential of online CET provisions that became a priority during the COVID-19 pandemic (Billett et al., 2022). Further, it foreshadows the identification and discussion of a systematic approach to developing and enacting effective CET provisions to promote and sustain individuals' employability across lengthening working life that are elaborated in Chap. 2—*Practice and policy implications for CET: A systematic approach* including, a focus on older workers (*see* Chap. 9—*CET journey: Experience of 'older' working age adults*). This national study provides a salient case study as it refers to a nation state that relies on the capacities of its working age population and one that has an aged and aging profile.

CET Premises, Purposes and Processes

A review of approaches and provisions focused on goals for, modes and approaches to CET globally provides the basis for an exploration and elaboration of the purposes for, conceptions of and provision of CET in the contemporary era. As foreshadowed, CET is becoming an increasing concern of supranational agencies, governments, communities, enterprises and working age adults seeking to sustain their employability. It is reasonable to suggest that the kinds and level of interests that have previously been directed towards schooling and tertiary education for young adults is now being extended to CET. Now, such is the growing need for continuing learning and development in the contemporary era, as necessitated by lengthening working lives (Ebbinghaus, 2012; OECD, 2015), constant changes in occupational and workplace requirements (Billett & Hodge, 2016) and needs for greater national economic self-reliance (Eder, 2023). Consequently, heightened interest and unprecedented considerations are being given to its purposes and forms. All of this emphasizes the central role of CET in seeking to secure employability. Importantly, securing that employability is more than providing effective initial occupational preparation and aligning it with entry into the workforce. Instead, increasingly, it is about sustaining individuals' employment across lengthening working lives. That is, to assist them in maintaining their ability to achieve occupational and workplace performance. This has at least four implications at the personal, workplace and community and national levels.

Firstly, maintaining working age adults' employability is important for them to remain employed, adapt to changing circumstances, seek and realize career and workplace advancements and more broadly adapt and enact their occupational capacities in different ways as circumstances and work requirements change. Secondly, for the workplaces or work settings in which they are employed, those capacities are important for maintaining their ability to produce goods and services effectively thereby maintaining the viability and potentially advancing the scope and adaptability of those work settings. Thirdly, for the communities who consume the goods and services provided by these workers and enterprises, the maintenance of those capacities is central to their quality and effectiveness. Fourthly, collectively, employability not only assist these working age adults avoid unemployment, thereby preventing them from becoming a financial liability for nation states, but also their capacities are central to being able to be self-sufficient in the provision of goods and services and be both import competing and able to export those capacities in an increasingly globalized economy and now, one fraught with geopolitical tensions.

Yet, it is necessary for this educational provision to be viewed in terms of its own purposes, and practices, rather for those associated with pre-employment education and training. That is, it need to be organized and enacted in distinct ways from that mainly designed for young people transitioning from school to working life. This includes how its goals and provisions can best meet the needs of working age adults who, unlike children engage compulsorily in schooling or, young adults now mandated to participate in tertiary education. Instead, working age adults must identify the need for participation in CET, have means by which that participation can occur alongside other commitments and whose processes are such that these goals are likely to be realized. It follows that such a reconsideration of this education provision needs to be informed by accounts of practice occurring and targeted empirical work. These two concerns are addressed in this volume. It provides such a review and is also informed by the findings and outcomes from a study in the nation state of Singapore, which has long had a more developed and systemic approach to CET than most other countries. As noted, this is because it realized, early on in its formation as a nation state, the importance of sustaining the employability of its workforce as its key economic and social asset. Unlike many other countries who can draw upon provisions of natural resources or even an ability to export food products, this nation state relies on the talents, capacities, and expertise of its working age population. Hence, the development and maintenance of the qualities of its workforce becomes a central and national consideration. Yet, as other nation states move away from a reliance upon natural resources and focused upon what is sometimes referred to as the 'knowledge economy' (Billett, 2006), these considerations become far more central to policy goals and educational processes of nation states with both developed and developing modern economies.

The findings from this national study reported and discussed here explore how factors associated with what motivates working age adults to participate in post-compulsory education, the kinds of provisions that these adults find accessible and effective, the experiences of women and older workers and how these can be addressed with an effective provision of CET. Then there are detailed considerations of models and modes of CET arising from changes in how electronic communication, demanding working lives. These emerging imperatives press for a need for CET models that are more inclusive of electronic access, varied modes of engagement and utilizing workplaces as sites for learning and experiences and augmenting education. In addition, the need for a systemic approach that integrates education institutions, educators, adults, workplaces, and communities emerges rather than one being driven by individual educational institutions and adult students alone. In these ways, the present provisions of CET are used to propose how they might be enacted effectively now and in the future.

So, in all, this book seeks to elaborate the project of CET, its purposes, practices and prospects for future models and approaches. As such, it aims to detail how this important educational sector can achieve its goals both now and in the future. Often seen as a supplementary or additional educational sector, as noted, CET is now gaining increased relevance and importance. This arises from the need for individuals to remain employable across lengthening working lives, enterprises needing to maintain their viability and nation states requiring skilled workforces to deliver the goods and services they require. Hence, the contributions in this volume seek to inform how CET is currently provided, might be enhanced and envisaged for the future. In this way, it aims to provide both clear premises for proceeding with this important educational sector in an era of growing concerns about the currency of workforce capacities and sustaining employability across lengthening working lives.

This discussion commences by emphasizing why CET needs to be privileged as a provision of education now and in the future.

Privileging CET as Well as Schooling and Initial Tertiary Education

With good reason, much of the focus of most nation's educational effort has been and is directed towards the schooling of children and their preparation for post-school life either directly into workplaces or through tertiary education. Often, tertiary education which builds upon and follows on from that schooling. Tertiary education comprises what is referred to as vocational education and training, albeit in different forms across nation states, as well as higher education, usually provided through institutions labelled as universities and/or polytechnics. Since the formation of modern nation states, there has progressively been introduction of compulsory schooling in most, if not all of them (Smith & Lovatt, 1990; Skilbeck, 1984). This schooling is seen as providing not only the foundational skills that prepare young people to contribute productively through their social and economic responsibilities, but also is directed towards the continuity of the state (Gonon, 2009; Quicke, 1999). In this way, the educational purposes are often to equip each generation with the kinds of knowledge that permits them to function as productive members of society and to be respectful of and contribute to that society (Quicke, 1999). Of course, different nation states place emphases on aspects of school education depending upon their social and cultural needs, societal and historical traditions, and religious and ethnic sentiments (Hanf, 2002). That is, educational system that seeks to transmit variously the cultural, societal, and theological tenets of the nation state, which, in turn, shapes the kinds of schooling provisions that are enacted (Gonon, 2009; Quicke, 1999). For instance, in Finland, a country in which expectations for engagement in paid work are held equally amongst men and women, there is a well-established provision of early childhood care and education to enable birthing women to return to the workforce confident that their children will be well cared through those provisions of care. In Singapore, all children are taught their 'mother language' as well as English to enable and sustain the multilingual country with distinct cultural representations in its population (i.e., Chinese, Indian and Malay heritage). All of this is enacted to assist the generational engagement with the state and to secure its continuity, and incremental changes.

As schooling in most countries is either directly controlled or regulated by a combination of nation state or key religious institutions, it is perhaps not surprising that school education is often focused on those imperatives (Marsh, 2004). Moreover, the emphases of and changes in the desired educational outcomes reflects those imperatives and, as they change, so will the intended processes and outcomes of schooling. Hence, concerns about levels of literacy or numeracy, compared with other nations, might lead to emphases on raising the level of these educational outcomes within the school age population. Likewise, certain societal concerns prompt the reevaluation of content, the emphasis on topics to be taught, the types of experiences to be provided, and the expectations placed on teachers. All of this is usually set within the context of children and their needs are to be carefully guided, both in terms of what they are exposed to, but also their preparation as coming generations of citizens. In some nation states there are emphases on cultural or religious tenets that are seen as integral elements of society. So, as states invest heavily in the education of children they are directed by these important imperatives. Sometimes, this occurs in conjunction with religious institutions who have either separate or complementary educational systems but, usually with a shared focus on the transmission of sets of foundational capacities and beliefs that seek to sustain and advance the nation state.

So, there are range of sensitivities associated with the education of children that are variously governmental, societal and, perhaps increasingly, also viewed in terms of relative standing with other nations (e.g., The OECD's The Program for

International Student Assessment [PISA]). The significant investment in schooling systems, the demands for teachers to be professionally prepared and licensed to do so emphasizes the importance and focus on compulsory education, and its privileging within these nation states. This includes, the amount, funding and focuses of much educational research to assist in understanding how schooling systems can generate the kinds of outcomes that their societies demand of them and provide funding for those outcomes to be achieved. Unequivocally, all this effort and those focuses on schooling of young children are important, worthwhile, and unquestioned.

Equally, many countries have invested heavily in and developed tertiary education systems that are focused on preparing young people for working life and the development of specific occupational skills. Although technical and vocational education are provided through schooling in some countries, in many countries with advanced industrial economies that educational provision is provided through distinct postschool or tertiary education provisions. For instance, many of these countries have a dedicated vocational education system which can include provisions of apprenticeships, and these are usually organized, funded, and administered by the state. Whilst vocational education systems differ in their structures and degree by which the educational provision is occupational specific (Billett, 2011), rather than general education, these are usually structured in quite different ways to schooling. Their focuses, purposes and content are often decided, mandated or contributed by industry bodies, professional associations, and/or employee representatives (i.e., unions). As concerns about national economic performance, the supply of skilled workers, avoidance of unemployment within young people and the need to provide specialized occupational preparation arise, systemically and well-funded tertiary education systems have been established by the state. For example, in Singapore, there are five polytechnic institutions and an Institute for Technical Education, each serving distinct purposes. New Zealand has a network of polytechnics, while in Australia, Technical and Further Education (TAFE) colleges are overseen by individual states, though they adhere to national mandated educational focuses, purposes, and practices. In Britain, there are Further Education colleges, and European countries have various types of vocational education institutions and structures.

Some, but not all, of these provisions include experiences in the workplace, thereby engaging industry and enterprises as partners in the provision of vocational education, which is something less likely to occur with schooling, for instance. Arising from state interest and investment, tertiary education is seen as being responsible for young people's initial occupational preparation and carries with it national expectations that it will achieve those outcomes. So, like schooling, tertiary education provisions, including universities, are often privileged in terms of governmental support, institutional interests that extends from government across to private and public sector enterprises and are regulated nationally, in some instances such as apprenticeships, are legislated educational provisions.

Consequences of Societal Educational Imperatives

It seems this kind of societal imperative and associated investment in the education of children through schooling and young adults through tertiary education has at least four major consequences.

Firstly, it has meant that the key emphases and resourcing of educational effort is directed towards young children and those who are becoming of working age. Consequently, much of the orthodoxies of approaches adopted for education is premised upon the care and responsibilities for children whose teachers have responsibilities that extend beyond teaching. This influences the structuring of education such as having different levels based upon student ages or progression beyond when they commence schooling. Moreover, educational institutions are designed and built around certain class sizes and provisions of compulsory education, which includes the monitoring and other forms of care for children. Perhaps in particular, the central role of the teacher comes to be predominated in a model of schooling as providing instruction, guidance, closely assessing and monitoring development and determining the pathway of experiences, rather than a focus on student learning, for instance. The duty of care of young vulnerable people is privileged in schooling.

Secondly, because of its ubiquity, compulsory nature and this privileging has led to a discourse associated with schools and schooling being central to how the project of education is discussed. That is, it has led to the 'schooling' provision being viewed as orthodox. For instance, curriculum is often seen as being associated with achieving the goals of the school (Tyler, 1949), mediated by the teachers to achieve the kinds of ends that their sponsors (i.e., state, religious institution) want realized. There are very few instances of schools that are independent of these influences and even they are often directed by a particular approach to schooling (Skilbeck, 1984). Consequently, issues and expectations about attendance, assessment, the role of teachers and the positioning of students et cetera have all arisen from such an orthodoxy. This is not to say that these premises go unchallenged, but they provide inevitable starting point from which discussions about educational provisions per se proceed.

Thirdly, because of the predominance of schooling, much educational theorization, research activities, professional associations, practical inquiries, and understandings have focused on these young learners and the educational arrangements that best permit them to achieve the kinds of outcomes that national states want of them to achieve. Consequently, although childhood and adolescent years only represent a small portion of most individuals' lives, the educational effort, research, theorizations, and professional engagements are overwhelmingly premised on and associated with this schooling, either in this compulsory or post-compulsory forms.

Fourthly, and curiously because of this investment in and emphasis on duty of care towards children that assumptions are sometimes made about adults not requiring such levels of care, guidance and engagement, and with perceptions that societal investment is not so required here because the educational needs of adults are not so great or intense. So, issues of providing guidance, support and assumptions about readiness to engage in studies are often not fully considered, if they are at all. This perception is often buoyed by some theorists of adult learning and development who emphasize adults' self-directedness (Knowles, 1975, 1980), to the exclusion of the fact that when adults are engaging with a new domain of knowledge, they might not be so self-directed (Billett, 1998; Tennant, 1986).

All of this leads to the importance of considering and repositioning CET on its own terms and based on the particular purposes and goals that it needs to achieve and the readiness, requirements and imperatives of working age adults.

Repositioning Continuing Education and Training

In contrast to schooling, it is noteworthy that most education provisions for adults have, by tradition, come from communities, rather than from the state or religious institutions. There is a long-standing tradition within the adult education that it arises from localized responses to the needs of adult members of communities. Often referred to as 'movements' (Nesbit, 2011), these have manifested themselves in adult education associations, working men's (sic) clubs, worker improvement movements etc., and sometimes initiated by individuals (e.g., Birkbeck, leading to Birbeck College) (Bennett, 1938).

So, in comparison, the focus of the broad educational project on arrangements for and valuing of adults' education beyond schooling and initial occupational preparation through tertiary education, has been less emphasized and privileged. The possible exception here is the continuing education of workers who are labelled 'professions', have been the focus of some state interest, investment and research. Yet, up until recently, there has been restricted interest in, understandings about and theorizations associated with ongoing learning and education across the adult lifespan. Yet, it is now timely to reconsider this emphasis and be more inclusive of the educational and learning processes related needs across the adult lifespan. This includes more broadly and comprehensively considering the servicing of working age adults' goals, needs and aspirations, and who now need, perhaps more than ever, to maintain their employability and contributes to securing national social and economic goals. Whilst it is possible to identify countries having strong social motives for seeking effective provisions of adult education, such as Japan (Le & Billett, 2022), even there is often a strong economic imperative, usually associated with employability.

This focus on employability is privileged in the considerations for CET as advanced here. That is, as noted earlier, there is a growing interest in how to meet the educational needs of working age adults beyond the phases of schooling and initial occupational preparation. This is an imperative that, as foreshadowed, is being promoted by supra-government agencies (OECD, 2006; OECD, 2019), national governments and communities (Economic Strategies Committee, 2010a; Guo, 2014; Schuetze & Slowey, 2013), as well as by adults themselves. In this way, the provision of adult education as focused on personal and cultural betterment and being promoted and organized in locally through adult education movements has now shifted to one occurring across many countries through tertiary education institutions. The key purposes are now often associated with, how to support learning to promote their employability of adults across their work lifespan.

So, it is now timely to consider and be informed about how working age adults' learning across the span of that working life can be best informed, guided and supported. But also, it is timely to reappraise the orthodoxies associated with much of educational provisions that were founded for the education of children and young adults and advance educational purposes, processes, and modes of engagement that commensurate with the needs of working age adults. As indicated, for school children and young adults engaged in schooling and tertiary education respectively, this is often the key commitment of their time, energy and attention, and as supported by their parents/caregivers. However, working age adults' engagement in CET is often mediated by the conflicting demands of work, family, and community commitments. So, beyond considerations of educating adults, accommodating the different kinds and diverse levels of readiness within the adult population, there is also the need to acknowledge that adults' participation in CET is but one of their commitments and demands upon their energies. All of this is to suggest that rather than viewing the education of working age adults as being less demanding, requiring lower levels of understanding, limited educational support, the opposite may be the case for many CET systems. However, this merely underlines the importance of understanding more fully what constitutes their effective provision.

Some of the imperatives to understand more fully what constitutes effective CET provisions are quite pragmatic. Firstly, and put plainly, with the constant changes in the requirements for paid employment and occupational practice, the kinds of understandings, procedures and dispositions that are developed in initial occupational preparation is insufficient for a lifetime of employment (Economic Strategies Committee, 2010b; World Economic Forum, 2021). Also, beyond refinements, advances and changes in occupational requirements and work practices performance, work related technologies, have arisen a whole range of other kinds of changes (Billett, 2006). These include significant shifts in the demands for specific occupations that render working age adults redundant or struggling to find employment.

Secondly, there are also the kinds of understandings and practices required to use the new digital technologies that emerge and quickly become necessary requirements for occupational practice (Harteis, 2018). These kinds of requirements are often different or distinct from earlier kinds of the knowledge required for work, thereby again, threatening the relevance and employability of existing workforces. Many of these new requirements are complex and demanding to learn and existing models of learning through work practice may or may not be sufficient (Billett et al., 2016). So, whilst much of that learning can occur in and through work, there can be no certainty that all the required learning can be realized through adults' work activities alone, even when supported and guided in work settings (Billett, 1995). Consequently, it is important to understand how CET provisions can, on their own, develop those capacities all, do so in conjunction with experiences in work settings.

Thirdly, is the lengthening working lives of employees in many countries (Noon et al., 2013). Earlier, it was predicted that working lives would become shorter, but countering such predictions is that in countries with both developed and developing economies working life has become much longer (OECD, 2015). Some of the consequences of this change are that the longer the work lifespan, the greater the need for continuing education to assist workers remain current and employable. That assistance is more than the provision of instruction and educational experiences likely extends to providing advice about potential occupational pathways, educational options and counselling associated with aligning individuals interests and capacities with both educational programs and targeted occupations (e.g., Billett, 2023; Billett & Le, 2024). Moreover, as many countries populations are ageing there is a need to consider the consequences of not all work being age tolerant, thereby requiring workers often classified as being 'older' to transfer to different occupations and find new forms of employment in their fifth or sixth decade.

Fourthly, in addition to developing new skills and occupational capacities, such transitions also impact upon the sense of self or subjectivity of adults as workers. So, issues of maintaining working age adults' sense of self or subjectivity come together with the acquisition of new occupational capacities. The impact of these kinds of changes and threats to adults' sense of self cannot be underestimated. The intentionality that adults exercise is central to their learning and willingness and ability to adapt to new circumstances and occupations. Consequently, the exercise of their interest, agency and intentionality will be central to whether they decide to participate in CET programs, and how they participate, and the degree by which they can adapt to and engage effectively in educational provisions and employment after those CET provisions.

Fifthly, there are also changes in who participates in working life. In many countries, for instance, over the last three decades with developed economies, female participation in workforces has grown enormously (Billett, 2006). This has brought about shifts in the working age population, and how their needs as workers can be accommodated within conflicting demands often associated with being caregivers for their children and others, such as ageing parents. But the changing composition of the workforce is not restricted to females as migration both voluntary and involuntary (e.g., refugee migrants) has seen changes in the composition of workforces (Field et al., 2013). Consequently, a provision of CET needs to accommodate the needs of female workers who might have principal care duties for their children and, increasingly, aged parents. Then, also is the need for those provisions to accommodate adult students whose native language may be different from that which is used for instruction, adding to issues of guidance and readiness to participate effectively.

Sixthly and finally, there is also changes in how that work is being conducted. For instance, rather than working individually, in many work settings and situations, teamwork has become essential, and this requires workers to learn to engage with others, cooperate and collaborate on a regular basis to achieve workplace goals (Haraldseid-Driftland et al., 2022; Noble & Billett, 2017). Hence, rather than being valued for developing their own personal occupational capacities are other factors about working with others, collaborating and realizing outcomes that require either interprofessional or intra professional working (Reeves et al., 2010). Whilst some of these arrangements are long-standing in health and social care sectors, they are now becoming far more widely adopted and even in those sectors becoming far more central to the conduct of occupational practice and meeting the needs of clients, patients and consumers. Some of this change arises from increasing occupational specialisms. But the commitment needed for collaboration with specialist knowledge and others are also associated with teams of workers engaging to perform complex work, albeit in aged care, manufacturing, the provision of services or production of media, much of which are associated with the so-called knowledge and social care economies that are emerging as key areas of employment and ways of meeting social and economic needs.

Thus, these kinds of changes prompt and often mandate the need for ongoing learning and education across working life. However, the kinds and circumstances of intentional efforts to support that learning through educational programs, workplace-based experiences or other kinds of educative encounters need to be considered in ways that are different from those provided for young people in schooling or tertiary education. This is because, as mentioned, most of CET will likely occur alongside other kinds of commitments and demands upon the time and energies of working age adults (Rose, 2017; Su et al., 2018). Perhaps most centrally, those adults must balance their time and commitments across work, family and community life alongside participation in continuing educational programs. Furthermore, and importantly, whereas young people are required to attend school and, circumstances mandate that their participation in tertiary education is rendered a necessity by employment requirements, this is not necessarily the case for working age adults. That is, amidst conflicting demands upon their time and energies, they will ultimately decide about whether to participate in CET and there are broad sets and kinds of readiness that they possess to participate in that education that are central to how these adults engaged in with those educational processes. For instance, will they be willing to work collaboratively with other students or because of personal interests or commitments want to work and learn more independently?

Consequently, more than considerations about the goals and purposes of CET it is also how those provisions are offered or afforded to working age adults. It is probably fair to say that orthodoxies associated with CET provisions have largely arisen through models and practices associated with the tertiary education of young people moving into being working aged (Billett et al., 2016). That is, largely institutional based, taught and teacher-led kinds of provisions. Yet, such orthodoxies may be quite inconsistent with adult students' needs, readiness and interests. The point here is that replicating educational models and processes intended for quite different purposes and audiences may, at best, be inadequate for the CET of entire national cohorts of working age adults. So, at this time, with the increased demand for CET, it becomes also important to consider what might constitutes future approaches to CET which not only build upon but extend those that are currently available. For instance, workplaces stand as being accessible and applicable sites for contributing to working age adults' CET (Billett, 2004; Blacker, 1995; Evans et al., 2002; Lave, 2009; Moore, 2004). Yet, much of the pedagogic practices adopted within orthodox CET may not be suited to workplaces as environments for CET to progress across entire cohorts of working age adults. Instead, pedagogic practices that are more aligned to work activities and interactions are those that are required.

So, when seeking to understand what is effective within the current orthodoxy of CET provisions, it is essential to consider what other models, practices and processes may be helpful in providing these provisions which are effective and scalable to meet the needs of entire working age populations and are highly accessible to adults who have conflicting demands made upon their time and energies. All of this suggests that understandings of the effectiveness of existing practice are important, but this needs to be augmented through considerations of options for the future, and considerations of how models of CET can be inclusive of older and younger workers, as well as those from culturally diverse backgrounds and genders.

Beyond these pragmatic concerns, there are also a range of conceptual and theoretical issues that warrant further and deeper understanding, and clarity. So, for instance, the degree by which combinations of readiness (i.e., what individuals know, can do and value) (Billett, 2015), are aligned with their interests and values which shape not only whether they will participate in CET provisions, but also engaged with and learn through them require greater elaboration. All this is central to what might constitute curriculum and pedagogic practices that are appropriate for and aligned with adult students' needs. Then, there are the issues associated with adults' sense of self as workers (i.e., their subjectivities) (Fenwick, 1998) and intentionalities (Malle et al., 2001) and how the combination of personal and occupational subjectivities influences and shapes how they engage with educational provisions, are active as learners and for what purposes. So, there is a range of theoretical and conceptual issues that need to be understood further to be clear about and inform the ways in which these adults' learning and development can be considered, supported, guided, and evaluated.

In part, it was these concerns and goals that informed, shaped and directed the enactment of a national study of continuing education training in the nation state of Singapore (Billett et al., 2021; Leow, Billett, & Le, 2023a) which forms the basis of the case study advanced here. As foreshadowed, Singapore stands as a good choice for this investigation and for drawing on findings for CET more generally. Firstly, it is a country that relies on its human resources and capital because it lacks primary industries such as agriculture, mining that many other countries rely on. Moreover, manufacturing is a relatively small part of its overall economic activity, so it reflects the concept of a knowledge-based and service economy that is becoming increasingly common in advanced industrial economies. Moreover, it has an ageing population required to maintain its employability to, societally, sustain the level of social and economic benefits that the island nation enjoys, and, personally, to maintain livelihood in a country which does not have extensive financial support for the aged.

In overview, the investigation comprised four phases. Firstly, it commenced with a review of the available literature, and then, secondly, by comprehensive interviews with a strong sample of (n = 180) recent graduates from CET programs (Leow et al.,

2022) and employers (n = 40) who are supportive of CET for their employees (Leow et al., 2023b) to provide current, grounded and informed insights. Thirdly, a survey was administered to the Singaporean population to capture more broadly sentiments, ideas, and understandings of working age adults in Singapore. That survey was shaped by the findings of the interviews with graduates, but also with findings and propositions from the literature. The processes of this investigation were disrupted by COVID-19 pandemic and the consequential lockdowns which affected both educational and work arrangements in Singapore. However, fortuitously, these events also provided opportunity to capture the ways in which working age adults have adopted the use of new electronic technologies to communicate and engage during those lockdowns and it was possible to identify implications for CET from new and emerging practices by these adults (Billett et al., 2022). Fourthly, a series of workshops were held (albeit online) with administrators and educators from post-compulsory education institutions in Singapore (i.e., polytechnics) to allow these practitioners to engage and respond to the findings from the interviews and surveys. The aim of these workshops was to generate and hone practical strategies to bring about more effective provisions of CET within the island nation state.

It is this national study that provides much of the impetus, data, findings and conclusions that are advanced through the chapters of this volume. In many ways, this multi-parted investigation, provides grounded and empirically based considerations of what constitutes effective CET, albeit exercised in one nation state. However, what is advanced through these data is also informed by literature, other studies conducted by the authors and considerations how CET might be enacted not only in the country which hosted this study, but elsewhere. Indeed, the overall goal here is to use a detailed case study of what occurred in one country to identify findings, contributions and suggestions that might inform provisions of CET far more broadly and widely than those identified in one country at a particular moment in time. It is the contributions in the following chapters that seek to realize that goal.

Preview of Contributions

In preview, Chap. 2—*Practice and policy implications for CET: A systemic approach*—seeks to illuminate and advance how CET provisions might be enacted through a systematic approach to promote employability. It addresses three key issues central to identifying what constitutes of effective CET provisions. These are: (i) the need to align all elements of CET provisions ultimately with their intended educational outcomes for working adults, and by corollary, national social and economic goals; (ii) avoiding individual elements of the CET system being viewed in isolation or reductively; and (iii) the need for any change in the CET system to be inherently both.

Chapter 3—*Continuing education and training: The quest for effective provisions*—reviews the literature that focuses on the imperatives for adults to learn across working life, both for personal (i.e., employability) and institutional (e.g., government, workplaces) purposes. It highlights the importance of partnerships among tertiary education sector, workplaces, and working-age adults to develop effective CET provisions. In particular, the contribution of workplace learning is generative of important learning outcomes. It considers approaches for organizing, ordering, supporting, and guiding this intentional learning through CET provisions. It also discusses the Singapore CET landscape to contextualize the phenomenon under investigation in this research project.

Chapter 4—*Investigating effective CET provisions to promote employability: Method and procedures*—describes and justifies the method and procedures used for this investigation. In particular, it sets out the context, framing, procedures, and broad outcomes of a three-phase research project that sought to identify what constitutes effective CET provisions for working age adults. The practical inquiry was enacted through interviews with CET graduates and their employers in Phase 1, followed by a survey in Phase 2 administered to Singaporean working age adults in a range of employment and industry sectors to validate and advance the interview findings. In Phase 3, the consolidated findings from the first two phases were presented to CET educators and administrators who engaged in co-construction of the implications and generation of guidelines for curriculum and pedagogic practices.

Chapter 5—*Motivations and affordances for engaging in CET*—reports and discusses the project's findings about what motivates working age adults' participation in CET and the kinds of affordances for supporting their engagement in CET. The findings indicated that the recent CET graduates were motivated personally and professionally to take CET courses/programs. Yet, there was a mix of personal and institutional factors that support as well as inhibit their participation and engagement in CET. These findings inform how a provision of CET needs to be positioned to make attractive and accessible for working age adults.

Chapter 6—*Towards an effective, accessible and scalable CET provisions: A national survey*—reports and discusses findings from the national survey, Phase 2 of the research project. It illuminates and elaborates responses from 860 working age Singaporeans who may or may not have participated in a CET program. It was found that many of them claimed on-the-job training was the most effective way to acquire skills, thereby questioning an assumption that this could best be achieved through CET provisions offered through tertiary education institutions. Nevertheless, there was seen to be great value in these kinds of provisions to promote further the development of Singaporeans' capacities for both personal and professional purposes, and usually a combination of both.

Chapter 7—*Effective CET provisions: Perspectives from graduates and employers*—discusses the perspectives of a selection of diverse kinds of working age adults who have recently completed CET programs, and also small sample of employers about how their employability can be sustained through adults' participation and engagement in CET programs and the ways in which these might need to change to more adequately realize these important personal and societal goals. Findings indicated that there are similarities and differences in their views about how to effectively acquire and develop further occupational capacities and specific competencies required for workplace performance, what constitutes effective CET provisions, and qualities of effective educators and students. In some ways, these can be seen as complementary views about the efficacy of CET provisions.

Chapter 8—*Advancing CET provisions: Perspectives of educators and practitioners*—reports and discusses the third phase of the project. In this phase, the consolidated findings from the first two phases were presented to CET educators and administrators who engaged in co-construction of the implications and generation of guidelines for curriculum and pedagogic practices in tertiary education institutions. Overall, it was indicated that there is a need for collaboration and engagement with different partners and between different levels of CET. This collaborative approach not only enhances the practical relevance of the education provided but also opens avenues for networking, skill application, and real-world problem-solving, and subsequent opportunities for employment. Importantly, a systemic approach to such collaboration and engagement is essential for enacting effective CET provisions.

Chapter 9—*Working women and CET: Enablers and barriers*—illuminates and appraises the experience of working women through interviews with female CET graduates. Overall, it was found that the working women, just like their male counterparts, were driven by both personal and professional reasons to participate in CET courses/programs. These female informants reported that work and family commitments were key barriers to their full engagement. Understanding of these female gradates' perspectives and experiences is pivotal to respond to the quest of what constitutes effective CET provisions for working women.

Chapter 10—*CET experience of and outcomes for 'older' working age adults*—illuminates and appraises the experience of mature age or older working age adults through interviews with CET graduates aged 50 and above. It was found that these graduates' participation in CET was driven by both personal and professional reasons, the mix of which were shaped by individual needs and goals. Noteworthily, the majority reported being motivated by occupational or work role changes, which is central to their sense of self as working age adults and is also important in their transitions across working life and the ability to remain employed.

References

Bennett, C. A. (1938). The ancestry of vocational education. In E. A. Lee (Ed.), *Objectives and problems of vocational education* (2nd ed., pp. 1–19). McGraw-Hill.

Billett, S. (1995). Workplace learning: its potential and limitations. *Education+Training, 37*(5), 20–27.

Billett, S. (1998). Ontogeny and participation in communities of practice: A socio-cognitive view of adult development. *Studies in the Education of Adults, 30*(1), 21–34.

Billett, S. (2004). Workplace participatory practices: Conceptualising workplaces as learning environments. *Journal of Workplace Learning, 16*(6), 312–324. https://doi.org/10.1108/13665620410550295

Billett, S. (2006). *Work, change, and workers*. Springer.

Billett, S. (2011). *Vocational education: Purposes, traditions and prospects*. Springer Science & Business Media.
Billett, S. (2015). Readiness and learning in healthcare education. *Clinical Teacher, 12*, 1–6.
Billett, S. (2023). Learning across working life: educative experiences. In S. Billett, H. Salling-Olesen, & L. Filliettaz (Eds.), *Sustaining employability through worklife learning: Practices and policies*. Springer Nature.
Billett, S., & Hodge, S. (2016). Conceptualizing learning across working life, provisions of support and purposes. In S. Billett, D. Dymock, & S. Choy (Eds.), *Supporting learning across working life: Models, processes and practices* (Vol. 16, pp. 3–25). Springer Clam.
Billett, S., & Le, A. H. (2024). Engaging young people in occupations served by vocational education: Case study from healthcare. *International Journal for Research in Vocational Education and Training, 11*(2), 200–222.
Billett, S., Dymock, D., & Choy, S. (2016). *Supporting learning across working life*. Springer.
Billett, S., Leow A., Chua, S., & Le, A. H. (2021). *Aligning the polytechnic provision of CET with skills future: Meeting learners and employers' needs*. Final report, Grant No. GA17-05.
Billett, S., Leow, A., Chua, S., & Le, A. H. (2022). Changing attitudes about online continuing education and training in the Covid-19 era: A Singapore case study. *Journal of Adult and Continuing Education., 29*, 106–123. https://doi.org/10.1177/14779714221084346
Blacker, F. (1995). Knowledge, knowledge work and organizations: An overview and interpretation. *Organization Studies, 16*(6), 1021–1046. https://doi.org/10.1177/017084069501600605
Bostrom, A.-K. (2017). Lifelong learning in policy and practice: The case of Sweden. *Australian Journal of Adult Learning, 57*(3), 334–350.
Ebbinghaus, B. (2012). Europe's transformations towards a renewed pension system. *The politics of the new welfare state*, 182.
Economic Strategies Committee. (2010a). *Key Recommendations*. Singapore Government.
Economic Strategies Committee. (2010b). *Fostering inclusive growth*. Singapore Government.
Eder, J. (2023). Self-reliance and autonomous development. In F. Obeng-Odoom (Ed.), *Handbook on Alternative Global Development* (pp. 250–272). Edward Elgar Publishing.
Evans, K., Hodkinson, P., & Unwin, L. (Eds.). (2002). *Working to learn: Transforming learning in the workplace*. Kogan Page.
Fenwick, T. (1998). Women's development of self in the workplace. *International Journal of Lifelong Learning, 17*(3), 199–217.
Field, J., Burke, R., & Cooper, C. (2013). *Migration and workforce ageing. The Sage Handbook of Age, work and society*. Sage.
Gonon, P. (2009). *The quest for modern vocational education: Georg Kerschensteiner between Dewey, Weber and Simmel* (Vol. 9). Peter Lang.
Guo, S. (2014). Developing effective professional development programs: A case study. *New Library World, 115*(11/12), 542–557.
Hanf, G. (2002). *Introduction. Towards a history of vocational education and training (VET) in Europe in a comparative perspective*.
Haraldseid-Driftland, C., Billett, S., Guise, V., Schibevaag, L., Alsvik, J. G., Fagerdal, B., et al. (2022). The role of collaborative learning in resilience in healthcare—A thematic qualitative meta-synthesis of resilience narratives. *BMC Health Services Research, 22*(1), 1–12.
Harteis, C. (2018). The impact of digitalization in the workplace: An educational view. In *Machines, change, work: An educational view on the digitalization of work* (pp. 1–10). Springer.
Knowles, M. (1975). *Self-directed learning*. Association Press.
Knowles, M. (1980). *The modern practice of adult education*. Association Press.
Lauder, H. (2020). The roles of higher education, further education and lifelong learning in the future economy. In *In* (Vol. 33, pp. 460–467). Taylor & Francis.
Lave, J. (2009). The practice of learning. In K. Illeris (Ed.), *Contemporary theories of learning: Learning theorists ... in their own words* (pp. 200–208). Routledge.
Le, A. H., & Billett, S. (2022). Lifelong learning and adult education in Japan. *Australian Journal of Adult Learning, 62*(1), 31–55.

References

Leow, A., Billett, S., Le, A. H., & Chua, S. (2022). Graduates' perspectives on effective continuing education and training: Participation, access and engagement. *International Journal of Lifelong Education, 41*(2), 212–228. https://doi.org/10.1080/02601370.2022.2044398

Leow, A., Billett, S., & Le, A. H. (2023a). Towards a continuing education and training eco system: A case study of Singapore. *International Journal of Training Research., 21*, 226–242. https://doi.org/10.1080/14480220.2023.2203944

Leow, A., Chua, S., Billett, S., & Le, A. H. (2023b). Employers' perspectives of effective continuing education and training in Singapore. *Higher Education, Skills and Work-Based Learning, 13*, 217–232. https://doi.org/10.1108/HESWBL-05-2022-0115

Malle, B. F., Moses, L. J., & Baldwin, D. A. (2001). Introduction: The significance of intentionality. In B. F. Malle, L. J. Moses, & D. A. Baldwin (Eds.), *Intentions and intentionality: Foundations of social cognition* (pp. 1–26). The MIT Press.

Marsh, C. J. (2004). *Key concepts for understanding curriculum*. Routledge Falmer.

Ministry of Education Singapore. (2022). *Speech by Minister Chan Chun Sing, at Straits Times Education Forum, at the Singapore Management University*. Retrieve from https://www.moe.gov.sg/news/speeches/20220210-speech-by-minister-chan-chun-sing-at-straits-times-education-forum-at-the-singapore-management-university#:~:text=If%20we%20need%20to%20top,million%20adult%20workers%20every%20year

Moore, D. T. (2004). Curriculum at work: An educational perspective on workplace as a learning environment. *Journal of Workplace Learning, 16*(6), 325–340. https://doi.org/10.1108/13665620410550303

Nesbit, T. (2011). Canadian adult education: Still a movement. *Canadian Journal of University Continuing Education, 37*, 1–13.

Noble, C., & Billett, S. (2017). Learning to prescribe through co-working: Junior doctors, pharmacists and consultants. *Medical Education, 51*(4), 442–451.

Noon, M., Blyton, P., & Morrell, K. (2013). *The realities of work: Experiencing work and employment in contemporary society*. Palgrave Macmillan.

Organisation for Economic Co-operation and Development. (2019). *Getting skills right: Future-ready adult learning systems*. OECD. Retrieved from https://www.oecd-ilibrary.org/education/getting-skills-right-future-ready-adult-learning-systems_9789264311756-en

Organisation for Economic Co-operation and Development (OECD). (2006). *Live longer, work longer: A synthesis report*. OECD.

Organisation for Economic Co-operation and Development (OECD). (2015). *Pensions at a glance. OECD and G20 indicators*. OECD.

Organisation for Economic Co-operation and Development (OECD). (2021). *OECD skills outlook 2021*. OECD.

Quicke, J. (1999). *A curriculum for life: Schools for a democratic learning society*. Open University Press.

Reeves, S., Goldman, J., Burton, A., & Sawatzky-Girling, B. (2010). Synthesis of systematic review evidence of interprofessional education. *Journal of Allied Health, 39*(3), 198–203.

Rose, J. (2017). 'Never enough hours in the day': Employed mothers' perceptions of time pressure. *Australian Journal of Social Issues, 52*(2), 116–130. https://doi.org/10.1002/ajs4.2

Schuetze, H. G., & Slowey, M. (2013). Traditions and new directions in higher education: A comparative perspective on non-traditional students and lifelong learners. In *Higher Education and Lifelong Learning* (pp. 3–24). Routledge.

Skilbeck, M. (1984). *School-based curriculum development*. Harper and Row Publishers.

Smith, D., & Lovatt, T. (1990). *Curriculum: Action on reflection*. Social Science Press.

Su, Y., Feng, L., & Hsu, C. H. (2018). What influences teachers' commitment to a lifelong professional development program? Reflections on teachers' perceptions. *International Journal of Lifelong Education, 37*(2), 184–198. https://doi.org/10.1080/02601370.2017.1397786

Tennant, M. (1986). An evaluation of Knowles' theory of adult learning. *International Journal of Lifelong Education, 5*(2), 113–122.

Tyler, R. W. (1949). *Basic principles of curriculum and instruction*. University of Chicago Press.
UNESCO. (2022). *Transforming technical and vocational education and training for successful and just transitions: UNESCO strategy 2022–2029*. Retrieved from https://unevoc.unesco.org/home/UNEVOC+Publications/lang=en/akt=detail/qs=6644
World Economic Forum. (2021). *Upskilling for shared prosperity*. Retrieved from http://www3.weforum.org/docs/WEF_Upskilling_for_Shared_Prosperity_2021.pdf
Zimmermann, T. (2020). Social influence or rational choice? Two models and their contribution to explaining class differentials in student educational aspirations. *European Sociological Review, 36*(1), 65–81.

Chapter 2
Practice and Policy Implications for CET: A Systemic Approach

Abstract To achieve the kind of goals demanded of an effective continuing education and training (CET) system requires a systematic approach that is inclusive of the efforts of government, workplaces, communities and working age adults. That is, on their own the efforts of individuals, education institutions or workplaces will be inadequate to generate a system that supports the ongoing development of working age adults. This includes sustaining the viability of the enterprises in which they work and collectively the nation states in which they reside. That is, an interdependence amongst the agency, effort and contributions of individuals, workplaces, educational institutions and communities is required. This chapter reports and discusses key findings from the review of literature and national case study that collectively offer contributions to and advances about how the provision of CET might proceed. They suggest that this provision needs to encompass and accommodate a range of stakeholders, perspectives and needs. This includes those of working age adults, employers, educators and administrators in CET, and governmental imperatives, to enhance and maximize the effectiveness of CET provisions and the various subsystems within which these provisions are enacted. Thus, seeking to identify and elaborate a systematic provision of CET is a constructive way to draw together these findings of the review and the practical investigation. This approach permits each element of a CET system to be addressed, not just as individual elements, but systematically, as a set of interdependent elements. Such a systematic approach is also helpful for eliminating and elaborating the complexity of CET provisions—as a system whose purposes and outcomes are shaped by its settings, rules, roles, and actors. So, this chapter seeks to illuminate and advance how CET provisions might be enacted through a systematic approach to promote employability. It addresses three key issues central to identifying what constitutes effective CET provisions. These are: i) the need to align elements of CET provisions ultimately with their intended educational outcomes for working adults, and by corollary, national social and economic goals; ii) avoiding individual elements of the CET system being viewed in isolation or reductively; and iii) the need for any change in the CET system to be inherently both collaborative and engaging partners comprising adults, workplaces, education institutions and communities.

Keywords Employability · Continuing education system · National sustainability · Working age adults · Education system · Interdependence · Partnerships · Occupational currency · CET educators · Enterprise viability · Global competition · Geopolitical tensions · Collaboration · Adaptiveness · Innovative

Towards a Continuing Education and Training Promoting Employability and Workplace Viability

Working age adults in all kinds and classifications of work now need to continually engage in occupationally oriented and workplace applicable learning across their working lives to secure and sustain their employability (Organisation of Economic Cooperation and Development [OECD], 2013). That employability is salient for individuals in: (i) securing and retaining their employment, (ii) obtaining advancement and (iii) being able to move to other forms of work (Billett, 2011; Billett & Hodges, 2016). These three purposes are also often central to these adults' needs, subjectivities and the fulfillment of societally expected roles of providing for themselves and their families (Hodkinson & Bloomer, 2002; Le et al., 2023). Enacting those roles is important for adults of all ages and this is the case across different countries and cultures, which along with its important contributions to workplaces' viability and continuity explains a widespread and growing interest in continuing education and training (CET) that supports that employability (OECD, 2000). Yet, it likely plays out in distinct ways across countries and communities. For instance, skillfulness in occupational capacities are heralded strongly in countries such as Germany with its 'beruf' concept (i.e., focus on and importance of skills) (Deissinger, 2022), whereas the ability to remain employed and contributing to society is particularly valued in Confucian heritage countries, such as in Singapore (Billett, 2011; Economic Strategies Committee, 2010a), and other countries where social welfare provisions are limited and can be culturally stigmatizing. Yet, as noted, beyond personal imperatives of being and remaining employed, the skill currency that underpins that employability is also central to maintaining workplaces' viability, and to secure national economic and social goals (Department of Education Science and Training, 2002; Department of Innovation Universities and Skills, 2008; Economic Strategies Committee, 2010a), when addressing four imperatives.

Firstly, at the enterprise level, workers being occupationally current, able to resolve problems and to adapt occupational knowledge to new circumstances, emerging technologies, needs of their clients, patients or others are now necessary qualities for employability. That is, being able to respond to new requirements for the goods and/or services they provide, and the work practices and technologies utilized to provide them are central to the viability of both public and private enterprises (Billett, 2023). In an era in which continual change in the requirements for occupational practice and workplace performance has become orthodox; personal employability is inevitably aligned to the viability and advancement of both public and private sector enterprises in which they are employed. Although not wholly contingent upon the workforce's ability to adapt to such changing circumstances these enterprises' viability and continuity will become increasingly precarious without that ability. Collectively, therefore, the capacities that promote the employability of workforces are important to the well-being of nation states and regions within them.

Secondly, the requirement for working age adults' currency of occupational and workplace capacities, including the ability to be innovative is increasing needed in what is sometimes referred to as knowledge work (Billett, 2006) and also service provisions that are growing sources of employment and economic activity (Stiglitz, 2002). This requirement is particularly strong for those nations or regions whose economic and social viability is premised upon their human resources. In nation-states like Singapore that has little in the way of natural resources such as mines, hydrocarbons, forests, agricultural spaces, the capacities of the workforce are central to its economic and social viability (Economic Strategies Committee, 2010b). Amongst others, that viability has consequences for the kinds and extent of social welfare and healthcare provisions that can be provided for its citizens. So, this currency of knowledge is not just about enterprise profitability, but about the quality of social care provisions for citizens.

Thirdly, in an era of growing global competition and mobility of goods and services, all nation states are facing similar challenges regardless of whether their economies are classified as developed or developing (OECD, 2021). Nation-states must achieve the balance between the ability to export goods and services while also being capable of competing with imports. This dual capacity assists ensuring that domestically produced goods and services remain competitive within internal markets. Nations with developed economies often struggle to compete with imports produced elsewhere and of a scale and with lower costs than can be produced domestically, hence other avenues of economic activities are required, inevitably demanding skillful and adaptive workers. The consequences for a lack of such a competitive workforce are growing levels of enterprise closures, contraction in industry sectors and raising levels of unemployment.

Fourthly, with increasing geopolitical tensions has arisen the need for nation states to become more self-reliant and self-sufficient in the provision of goods and services, particularly those of strategic kind. This has been laid bare in recent times with pandemic and recent conflicts. So, whilst globalization of economic activity continues, there is a great risk of an over reliance on goods and services produced by other nation states whose interests, orientations and intentions are inconsistent with other nation states. Yet, the ability to be more self-sufficient and self-reliant is very much premised upon the skillfulness of the workforce and its adaptability. Mitigating the risk of being held hostage to limits in the access to the goods and services produced outside of nation states is now positioning the skillfulness and adaptability of national workforces as being central to their maintaining their sovereignty. That is to bulwark against and confront existential challenges to nationhood through a reliance of goods produced elsewhere.

It follows that for these four reasons, issues of working age adults' employability and the viability of both public and private sector enterprises, nation states are now needing well-structured, accessible and effective provisions of CET. Consequently, addressing these important concerns is the focus of the review and practical investigation reported and discussed across this volume. That is, what constitutes an effective, scalable and accessible CET provision that can meet these challenges. As previewed in Chap. 1—*Supporting learning across working life* and elaborated in Chap. 4—*Investigating effective CET provisions to promote employability*, the approach taken here was to review the extant literature. Then, to engage with working age adults whose employability is central to the issues mentioned above and whose capacities will be central to responding to the viability of the enterprises that employ them and their contributions to the nation state. Consequently, it is working age adults who, in the first instance, had participated in CET provisions that were the key focus in the data gathering and analysis. This was to understand what motivates their participation in CET, for what purposes and report on their experiences with CET and how it might be enhanced to make it more accessible, effective and engaging for an entire national working age population. That scalability is essential as workers of all kinds and classifications are subject to changes in occupational and workplace requirements and shifting bases for employability. Consequently, the data gathering, and analysis reported across this volume, whose conclusions are presented and discussed here aim to inform what kinds of provision of educative experiences in education institutions, electronically mediated, other kinds of engagements in both community and workplace settings are required to achieve these important personal, educational, economic and social goals.

Key Considerations for a CET System

From the findings reported across this volume, the following are some key overall considerations arising as outcomes from this investigation, which suggests that from this Singaporean case, a provision of CET is required to comprise the following elements:

- Impartial advice is helpful to inform working age adults about the most appropriate educational pathways and courses available across the tertiary education institutions and to gauge their readiness to participate in their preferred course and then make decisions about post-course employment pathways and options.
- Educational experiences should be aligned to achieve employability outcomes that are enacted in ways appropriate for working age adults, including being easily accessible through online provisions and/or face-to-face engagements that are sensitive to the needs of adults balancing family, work, and CET commitments.
- CET educators require competency and currency in the occupational field in which they teach, whilst also being adaptable and proficient adult educators.

- Establishing and sustaining productive partnerships between workplaces and CET providers is essential for meeting both working age students and workplaces' needs through informing the content and quality of CET provisions and extending CET provisions into workplaces and work practices.
- Working age adults need to identify clear purposes, appraise their readiness to participate in CET, be focused on their engagement in the course and with peers, and exercise both independence and interdependence as lifelong learners, to achieve those purposes.

The Role and Leadership of CET Institutions

To enact these kinds of measures and secure the outcomes referred to here are premised on establishing, developing and sustaining an effective and scalable system of CET provisions, that will need to be led by CET institutions. That is, the demands and requirements of the system are such that it cannot be left to happen by chance, but through intentional institutional leadership. This is because given what was argued above about their need, the establishment, enactment, and further development of such a system now stands as a priority for both nation states with developed and developing economies, which will require institutional leadership. Such systems will need to be scalable—(i.e., able to be extended and expanded to all kinds and classifications of workers within these nation states)—because there seems to be few, if any, exceptions in the need for workers to further develop their occupational capacities and workplace competences in the current era. Yet, being effective is more than responsiveness to current needs, it also entails being able to be sustained over time, by being adaptive and innovative. The circumstances of and needs for such systems differ across nation states depending upon their institutional arrangements, including relations between tertiary education institutes and workplaces. Yet, likely they will be premised upon collaboration, rather than competition amongst tertiary education institutions in workplaces. This is most likely achieved through: (i) mature partnerships that CET provisions can meet the diverse needs and assist in realizing the aspirations of working age adults, (ii) workplaces that employ their occupational capacities and (iii) educational institutions whose aim is to advance the capacities of working age adults. It is through such collaborative arrangements at the local level that CET systems are most likely to meet the needs of their communities and contribute collectively to the nation states' economic and social well-being. It is this localized engagement that can be provided through CET institutions.

Moreover, given that the adults who participate in these educational provisions do so from their own volition and interest (i.e., non-compulsorily), it is necessary to be aware of, respond effectively and engage with them as partners and co-constructors of these provisions. This engagement includes offering impartial advice about the kinds of program outcomes, how these are aligned with adults' employability goals, albeit through sustaining their current job, seeking promotion or advancement, and engaging in work practices in new situations and in responding to novel occupational and workplace challenges. All of this can only be enacted at the local level. Consequently, understanding and addressing the interests of the working age students and those who employ them is essential for enhancing the effectiveness of a national CET system that is premised on mature engagements with workplaces and effortful participation by working age adults. Indeed, perhaps, only through such collaborative working can these key elements of a tertiary education-led CET system realize the kinds of governmental, workplace, and individual goals for continuing learning across lengthening working lives, which are becoming increasingly common across countries with both developing and developed economies.

It follows that to achieve these kinds of goals requires a systematic and collaborative approach to CET that is inclusive of government, workplaces, communities and working age adults' contributions. On their own, individual efforts of working age adults, education institutions or workplaces will be inadequate to generate a CET provision capable and scalable for supporting the ongoing development of working age adult populations. Instead, there is a need for collaboration to sustain viability of public and private sector enterprises and, collectively, the nation states which they reside. Proposing a tertiary education-led CET system is driven by the recognition that its success hinges on the presence of administrative, social, and educational infrastructure at the local level. This is necessary to understand localized needs, respond to them, but also contribute to extending the capacities of educational institutions and workplaces to maximize opportunities, identify strategic pathways and elevate the contributions of the communities. This will be dependent upon having appropriate educational, social and administrative infrastructure at the local level.

These suggestions and those provided below are conclusions from the national investigation of CET in Singapore that has identified considerations for how the provision of CET might proceed. Aspects of this investigation are reported separately across chapters in this volume as foreshadowed in Chap. 1—*Supporting learning across working life*. As detailed in Chap. 4—*Investigating effective CET provisions to promote employability*—this investigation engaged with a range of informants and respondents through interviews and surveys, respectively, who provided appraisals of the existing provisions of CET and speculated on future needs and modes of engaging with others. This includes considerations of working age adults who have participated in CET programs and those who have not done so. Analysis of perspectives based upon gender and those of older workers, which is of relevance to the nation state of Singapore, with globally its third most aged population (Billett, 2010), are also included given the need for a highly inclusive approach to understanding the needs of the entire working age population. Hence, in advancing what this provision needs to accommodate, a range of perspectives including those of working age adults, employers, educators and administrators in CET, and governmental imperatives have been collated and verified as directed to enhance and maximize the effectiveness of CET provisions and the various subsystems within which these provisions are enacted.

Factors Shaping Effective CET Provisions

The following sections illuminate and advance how CET provisions might be enacted through a systematic approach to promote the employability of working age adults and the viability of the public and private sector in which they are employed. They address three key issues identified as being central to effective and scalable CET provisions: (i) the need to connect all CET provisions ultimately to their intended educational outcomes on working adults, and by corollary to the social and economic future of a nation state reliant upon its human resources (i.e., Singapore); (ii) the individual elements of the CET system being viewed in isolation or reductively; and (iii) the need for any change in the CET system to be collaborative and engaging partners comprising adults, workplaces, education institutions and communities.

In sum, five key factors shape considerations of these CET provisions.

- Firstly, there are at least three kinds of personal goals associated with employability (i.e., securing employment, sustaining it and securing advancement) that are central to working age adults needing to participate in continuing education and training. Given the evolving occupational demands and the competencies necessary for workplace performance, prioritizing employability is no longer a choice; it is essential for all types and classifications of workers.
- Secondly, there are also purposes associated with the viability of the workplaces in which they are employed and collectively contributing to a skilled workforce able to provide the goods and services required within nation states. These include workers' learning and ability to be adaptive and innovate in and through their work.
- Thirdly, this has led to the need for CET provisions that can provide guidance and advice about programs that adults should be participating in, and modes of engaging with those adults that are sensitive to the other demands being made upon their time and resources.
- Fourthly, that the range of experiences through which learning across working life is realized, can be supported and enhanced extends beyond CET programs per se and include the activities and interactions accessed in work settings and support and guidance that comes from within these workers' communities.
- Fifthly, given the requirement to understand and respond to adult students' needs and aspirations by tertiary education institutions, engaging with local enterprises and communities, it is likely that educational, administrative and social infrastructure will be necessary at the local level to realize effective CET provisions.

Building upon the findings from the review and practical investigations, the contributions set out in the chapters are collated and synthesized here to propose what might constitute a CET provision for sustaining employability and realizing workplace viability.

A CET Provision for Sustaining Employability and Workplace Viability

As proposed above, the personal and institutional purposes of CET, how it is enacted and engaged with by working age adults are the circumstances in which individual subjectivities converge on the range of experiences (i.e., activities and interactions) provided for them, and how they experience and learn through and from them. Thus, it is important to understand both what is provided for working age adults as opportunities for learning, on the one hand, and how they come to engage with them on the other. This is referred to as the duality between what is afforded individuals and how they come to engage with them (Billett, 2001). As found through the analysis of the data, these experiences include those in their workplaces, the educational programs in which they participate, including those provided by peers as well as teachers, and support they receive from within their families, familiars and communities (Leow et al., 2022). Hence, rather than the educative experiences comprising only what is provided through the CET programs, it is important to capture the contributions of other activities and interactions. For instance, peers and their contributions stand out as being important for success in CET programs, and family and familiars are important in initiating and supporting the engagement in CET provisions. Of course, these circumstances, contributions and their worth are valued differently by across a cohort of working age adults of both genders, the diversity of ages and with distinct kinds of work responsibilities and family and community commitments.

Consequently, the challenge is to identify how an education provision intended to be: (i) broadly inclusive, (ii) meeting the diverse needs of those for whom they are being designed and (iii) enacted in ways that are scalable to make them accessible for all kinds and classifications of workers in both physical and educational terms; and (iv) offering experiences that achieve the kinds of outcomes that these individuals want. It follows that provisions of CET need to develop students' and graduates' employability, but in ways and with outcomes that sustain and support these working age adults' sense of self (Stiglitz, 2002). Curiously, some earlier perspectives on adult learning and development were premised upon clinical psychological models associated with a primary focus on maintaining adults' potentially fragile individuals' sense of self (Rogers, 1969). In some ways, this sentiment was aligned by Goffman's propositions about the importance of adults' projection of self in daily life (Goffman, 1990). That is, the centrality of intentionality of personal narratives exercised and projected by individuals to sustain their sense of self or subjectivity as working age adults. This led to earlier accounts of adult education premised upon Rogerian clinical psychological models and concerned about facilitation of learning—making things easy—to maintain and manage adults' sense of self during periods of transitions (Rogers, 2001). Also aligned with such views were the concept of andragogy (Knowles, 1975) claiming that adults are used to being self-directed in many aspects of their lives that this should be how adult educational provisions be organised and enacted.

However, it was found to be the case that in the areas of new learning, particularly the time of key transitions in work or personal life, these where the circumstances in which adults' ability to be self-directed was clearly challenged (Tennant, 1986). That is, they did not have the readiness—the understandings, capacities and dispositions associated with the bodies of knowledge that need to be learnt (Billett, 2015a). Hence, emerging considerations are of how adults can be respected as responsible, self-directed and intentional learners, yet who may suffer from a lack of readiness to participate in learning bodies of new knowledge unaided. This is where considerations of how best that new knowledge can be mediated through the actions of educators, co-workers, peers and perhaps increasingly text and electronic forms can assist to enhance the level of these students' self-directedness.

Positioning Adults as Learners

There has been movement away from those considerations of adults as inherently being self-directed learners. Instead, the orientation is to embrace more comprehensive considerations of adults' orientation to learning and development, including their prior knowledge, earlier or premediate experiences, and more broad-based accounts of development (Valsiner, 2000). Yet, here, whilst not as fragile or precarious as perhaps was suggested in those earlier accounts, the importance of addressing adults' sense of self or subjectivity as learners and constructors of knowledge is perhaps never greater than considerations of their learning for, in, and through working life (Abrahamsson, 2006; Somerville, 2006)). Alignments between adults' subjectivities and their occupations, work roles, and satisfaction derived from working life are often indivisible as indicated in the data from the investigation reported and discussed here. In this way, the findings reflect the importance of the sociocultural perspective that draws upon and acknowledges the contributions of the relation between the suggestions of the social world and how individuals engage with those suggestions and learn through them (Billett, 2006).

Consistent with these concerns is that adults may lack information about the kinds of education provisions in which they might participate in and the readiness to do so effectively. Hence, the need for counselling and guidance, more than therapeutic interventions (i.e., Rogers, 1969, 2001) emerged from this investigation. That counselling and guidance is to assist working age adults in making informed choices about the kinds of programs they want to participate in and the alignments with their worklife goals, promoting their readiness to engage effectively, thereby supporting successful outcomes (Billett, 2015b) and being provided with the kinds of educational experiences which will achieve those employability goals. However, just as counselling might be required prior to participation in these programs, to advise about the appropriateness of programs and their alignment with these adults' aspirations, so might it be advanced at their conclusion to assist these graduates realize employability outcomes that motivated them to engage in CET programs in the first place. At the conclusion of these courses, it was found that often adults need advice about how to convert what they have learnt through their CET program into new pathways and employment and engagement in new industry sectors. The focus here is to assist graduates secure their employability goals, including transiting from current occupations to new ones.

Since the ability to participate in CET is mediated by individual and situational factors, which may expand or restrict one's choices (Sen, 1999), it is essential that the voices of CET students need to be heard, along with those from education and employers, and their contributions captured and carefully considered. The great risk is that without fully understanding the perspectives of these key stakeholders, provisions of CET may not be best aligned with their aspirations, immediate goals but also how they want to access, engage and progress with their education. An associated risk is that without accommodating these concerns, CET provisions will only serve to reinforce and perpetuate existing shortcomings in terms of access, engagement, attainment, and sustainability. This would be an unfortunate consequence, given the persistent challenges fueled by events like the COVID-19 pandemic, the growing reliance on digital technologies, and the imperative for nation-states to enhance self-sufficiency in providing essential goods and services for their communities. These factors collectively highlight the crucial and urgent need for CET more than ever.

Towards a Model of a (National) CET System

The findings from the practical investigation suggest that the pursuit of an effective CET system in enhancing continued employability necessitates a new paradigm grounded in CET being a social enterprise and shared responsibility, while upholding the principles of learner-centred education, albeit led by tertiary educational institutions. The interdependence and collective expertise of the tertiary educators and other CET providers, with the support of the state, can be harnessed both to support working adults' individual CET pursuits and to advance workplace productivity. When multiple CET pathways are available by which CET can be engaged and re-engaged over the working lifespan of adult workers, individuals are better able to benefit from a responsive and adaptive system that accommodates individuals' needs and circumstances, while contributing to a shared sense of responsibility, purpose, and identity among its stakeholders.

As noted, there is a need for a systematic approach for this educational provision is one that can guide, support, and enact a national model of CET comprising tertiary education institutions working collaboratively and in partnership with workplaces and working age adults. In establishing the need for and bases of this CET system, the following findings are provided to inform how best it can assist working age adults' employability and meet workplace needs. In all, sets of interdependent factors were identified that shape effective CET provisions. Collectively, these factors are referred to and presented here as contributions from government, CET institutions, educators, workplaces and, importantly, working age adults and their family members who provide guidance, advice, and support to them. Salient findings are that effective CET provisions are founded on a responsive and accessible system of advice and guidance, educational provisions, engagement, and support. Although referenced separately here, these elements of an effective CET system are interdependent and interconnected to optimize the efficacy of the key stakeholders within that CET system.

Advice and Guidance provision of guidance and advice by government, CET providers, CET educators, and workplaces for working age adults to align their needs, interests, and capacities with CET courses to achieve their employability goals that translate into successful engagement and direct post-course employability.

Educational Provisions provision of accessible (face-to-face and/or online) and responsive CET provisions, whose content and experiences are aligned with students' employability goals and enacted by adult educators with appropriate pedagogic skills and familiarity with the occupational practices and industry sectors in which what is being taught is to be applied.

Engagement working age adults need to purposefully and effortfully participate in CET provisions by engaging with course content, its modes of delivery, its teaching, and with peers. Wherever possible, this engagement needs to extend beyond the CET classroom to their workplaces, thereby making those settings integral elements of effective CET provisions. This includes CET providers and educators reaching out and engaging with both small and large enterprises to support their employees' learning.

Support in balancing commitments, working age adults require personal, financial, and educational support in different ways albeit from family, workplace, government, and educators to effectively engage in and complete their courses and translate them into employability outcomes.

There are aspects of these elements that require enacting before, during, and after actual engagement in CET provisions by working age adults, as presented in Table 2.1. In this table, in the left-hand column are elements of the system and in the right-hand column are periods of provision. Proposed in this table is that elements of this system are engaged with at different times of individual progression in their CET journey.

As is common to many education provisions prior to selecting the course of study, advice and guidance might be provided to assist that these adults make informed decisions about the specific programs in which they are enrolling, the mode of engagement in those programs, the kinds of commitments demanded of them and the outcomes that are intended through their completion.

More broadly, the findings from the interviews and survey suggest that an effective provision that promotes employability is shaped by a system that comprises contributions by government, CET providers, CET educators, Singaporean workplaces, and working-age Singaporeans depicted in Fig. 2.1. It is proposed through

Table 2.1 Elements of the system engaged with before, during, and after CET provisions

System element	Period of provision
Advice and guidance	Before, During, After
Educational provision	During
Support	Before, During
Engagement	Before, During, After

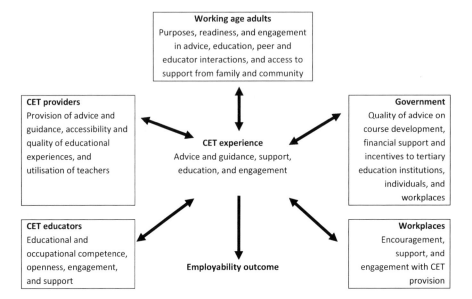

Fig. 2.1 A CET system for promoting employability among working age adults

this figure that the CET provision needs to be organized and enabled by a system comprising contributions by: (i) *government*—as providers of advice on course development, financial support and incentives and incentives to individuals and workplaces, (ii) *CET providers*—offering provisions of advice and guidance, and providing accessible and effective educational experiences experienced and qualified CET educators, (iii) *workplaces*—providing guidance and support and interacting with CET institutions, (iv) *CET educators*—having the occupational and educational capacities to provide effective learning experiences for students; iv) *working age adults*—who have person-particular purposes, readiness and abilities to engage with the educational process, peers and other forms of engagement from family, workplaces and community. What is being suggested is that collectively these elements of this CET system provide the guidance, advice, and support referred to above, as set out in Fig. 2.1.

Together, these elements are derived from the review and the empirical work and stand as a model for an effective and employability-oriented CET system that is intended to be driven locally by CET institutions. Central here is the responsiveness within the system as a principal quality; that is, the responsiveness of government in providing targeted advice, support, and assisting collaborations across better education institutions and with workplaces and ensuring the quality of programs. This action will assist CET providers in responding to the needs of working age adults and employers, and their responsiveness to the changing economic and social environments in which they work. Hence, the emphasis on localized engagements and responses. Additionally, CET educators need to be responsive in addressing the needs of their students; consequently, workplaces need to be responsive in supporting and sustaining learning outcomes that are important for both workplaces and workers. Added here is working age adults' responsiveness in being proactive, selective, focused, and engaged to achieve their purposes for participating in CET through optimizing the contributions provided by government, CET institutions, educators, and workplaces. Consequently, it is helpful to have some measures as key indicators that can be used to direct planning and enactment considerations.

Key Indicators of an Effective CET System

The review and practical investigations emphasized the importance of CET and provided a much-needed focus on the importance of an effective and interdependence amongst CET students, employers, and institutions that provide CET provisions to realize the potential of initiatives aimed at promoting the ongoing skill development and employability of the working age population. This project is significant and innovative as it connects with emerging policy and practice trends about students' co-construction of knowledge through their participation in both CET courses and the workplace. This connectedness to networks beyond the "school", together with a learner-centred orientation of school, is inevitable and will serve to dissipate the notion of the school as the dominant conduit for learning (Billett, 2004; Young, 1998). From a synthesis of the findings from the study and as advanced across the chapters of this volume, the following is a set of seven key indicators of an effective CET system as presented in Table 2.2. In this table, the key indicators are listed in the left column, key findings aligned with each of them are presented in the central column and the chapters from which they are drawn in the right column.

These seven indicators are now briefly elaborated.

1. Provision of advice, guidance, and support for working age adults

Working-age adults are resource and 'time jealous' (Billett, 2015a), and Singaporean adults seem not to be an exception here. They need to be informed about their investment in CET provisions and to be guided on the most appropriate course. That guidance needs to consider their personal and professional goals and their readiness to participate in their preferred course. That guidance might best be provided independently from an institutional imperative associated with securing adequate numbers of enrolment. That is, it should provide some separation between the economic imperative of the CET institution and appropriate guidance for working-age adults to expand their time and resources most effectively. As with other kinds of students,

Table 2.2 Key indicators of an effective CET system from a synthesis of the research findings

Key indicators of an effective CET system	Key findings	Reference to chapters
1. Provision of advice, guidance, and support for working age adults	Pre-course counselling for enrolment advice and post-course guidance associated with employment Understanding and being responsive working age adults' needs, challenges, sense of self and readiness Flexibility in course arrangements and considerations of adult students' needs in curriculum planning	5–10
2. Accessibility of CET provisions	Ease of accessibility including physical accessibility Combination of online and face-to-face interactions Integration of CET and workplace learning experiences	5–7, 9–10

3. Engaging and relevant educational experiences	Effective CET provisions are seen to:
	    Have qualities of Flexibility, Engaging, Authenticity, Convenience, and Leniency
	    Give students contextualized knowledge and skills which are immediately applicable to their jobs; and
	    Offer them current industry-specific knowledge
		5–7, 9–10

4. Maintaining currency of CET educators' occupational and pedagogic competence	Effective CET educators are perceived to:
	    demonstrate the level of currency with the occupational areas about which they are teaching,
	    Have an array of curriculum and pedagogic capacities to be able to respond to students' needs,
	    Engage with adult students in ways which is respectful and inclusive of their experiences and potential contributions, and
	    Be flexible and engage their approaches to the organization and enactment of educational experiences and assessment of student performance.
		6–7, 9–10

5. Building and sustaining productive relationships with enterprises	Support from employers and management enhances CET students' motivation and commitment to CET. Engaging with different kinds of partners and in diverse ways is central to a responsive and effective CET system. Workplaces can promote learning through engagement in new tasks, innovations, and structured experiences and direct mentoring.	6–8

(continued)

Table 2.2 (continued)

Key indicators of an effective CET system	Key findings	Reference to chapters
6. Recognition and certification of skills	Professional motivations for CET participation Enhancing employability: securing employment, shifting to new employment, or advancement within existing employment Progressing to the next education level	5–7, 9–10

7. Generating proactive, independent, and interdependent working-age adults	Effective CET students are believed to:
	    Be intrinsically motivated to learn for their personal and professional development,
	    Have lifelong learning dispositions (i.e., open to learning, see learning as an ongoing process),
	    Have perseverance and self-motivation to work through the course,
	    Possess good time management skills, and
	    Be proactive during educational processes to seek for the knowledge one needs.
		6–7, 9–10

support may be necessary for working-age CET students as they balance family, work, and study commitments. Hence, the provision of CET needs to extend to appropriate mechanisms of support to assist the successful completion of CET courses and securing desired outcomes. For working-age CET students who are seeking to change occupations or find employment, that support needs to extend to work experiences, job placements, or networking opportunities with potential employers. Hence, the qualities of independent advice and guidance before enrolment, and then support during and at the end of the CET program, are key indicators of successful CET provisions.

2. Accessibility of CET provisions

Given the time preciousness of working-age adults, the accessibility of CET provisions will be paramount in terms of participation, engagement, and achieving course completion and outcomes. Hence, accessibility, either through face-to-face contact or through electronically mediated means, will be a key basis for effective CET provisions. Accessibility, in terms of face-to-face engagements, is aligned with locations being easily accessed, fitting in with working days, and having food, drinks, and a comfortable physical environment. The timing, duration, and frequency of face-to-face meetings need to consider the kinds of educational experiences best provided through face-to-face encounters and the other commitments on the time of working-age adults. That is, face-to-face meetings need to be educationally necessary, in accessible locations, and accommodating of the needs of working-age adults.

Online educational provisions have the potential to provide accessible educational experiences for working age adults, but that accessibility needs to be realized through ease of access, user friendliness, and interactive qualities, as these are needed to address working-age adults needs, which include sociality (i.e., being able to interact with others).

3. Engaging and relevant educational experiences

Beyond accessibility, the quality of educational experiences provided through either face-to-face or electronically mediated engagements will be essential to provide effective CET provisions. Engaging students can be achieved through effective and well-designed presentations, but these need to be augmented by interactions and tasks that position the students as active participants in the educational provision. Specifically, opportunities for students to interact with the lecturer and their peers, both during the timetabled activities and outside of them, meet a range of these adult students' needs. Those needs include different kinds and levels of clarification, advice, and direct instruction based upon students' readiness, and interactions with peers for guidance and support to draw upon diverse experiences, concerns, and networks.

These experiences also need to be relevant in terms of the intended educational purposes; that is, being directed towards achieving the kinds of understandings, procedures, and dispositions that are intended to be developed. Decisions about the kinds, duration, and frequency of experiences, for instance providing opportunities to engage in workplaces, with peers, professional networks, and/or prospective employers, may need to sit alongside those associated with the projection of content. Making relevant that content to promote engagement and learning, therefore, can be achieved through a range of means that goes beyond presentational qualities to include other kinds of experiences that might be structured within or as additional experiences to those that are timetabled.

Considerations here need to extend to the ways in which workplaces or work experiences of different kinds can be provided and integrated into the CET provision; that is, for those who are currently working on seeking to extend their occupational knowledge, for opportunities within their work to be linked to educational provisions, and for those seeking employment to be given the provision and integration of work experiences.

4. Maintaining currency of CET educators' occupational and pedagogic competence

A perennial issue is the currency of CET educators' occupational and pedagogic competence. The former is related to current occupational competence and understandings and abilities associated with its enactment in contemporary work. The latter is associated with educational practices founded upon current understandings about student learning and development and with responding to imperatives such as shifting to online educational provisions when the need arises.

The former can be addressed through a range of means. These include maintaining currency through mature, reciprocal, and respectful engagements with students as current practitioners, engagement in industry forums, workplace visits or short-term industry attachments, or joint employment arrangements and project work, to name a few. If a reciprocal and respectful educational environment can be developed and sustained, interactions with working-age students can do much to inform educators about current practices and requirements. For some CET educators this may be sufficient, depending upon what they are teaching and to whom. However, other options such as workplace visits and short-term attachments can also be helpful to maintain that currency as well as to build relations among the educators, their institutions, and workplaces. The joint organization and participation in industry forums or those with professional bodies can also be helpful for maintaining general currency and relevancy about the specific occupation or industry. Then, there are more long-term placements or secondments to maintain currency, as well as options such as joint or part-time appointments. Underpinning these processes will be mature, reciprocal, and respectful relationships amongst educators, employers, co-workers, and educational institutions.

These educators' pedagogical competence can be achieved through ongoing professional development and systematic processes to support changes within educational provisions, such as online education or work-integrated learning experiences for students. It has been shown that targeted support during the transition to online education (Billett et al., 2022) can be particularly beneficial, especially when enacted through a supportive process, and the same is likely to be the case for other initiatives such as extending CET provisions into workplaces. Part-time teaching staff who have current occupational competence may need structured initial teacher education to support their capacities to be effective CET educators. Whilst many of these would have experienced earlier models of face-to-face teaching, not all those models would be currently applicable or beneficial; advances in approaches to educational practices and initiatives such as online education suggest the importance of professional preparation for these (part-time) educators.

5. Building and sustaining productive relationships with enterprises

Having mature and productive relationships between tertiary education institutions and local workplaces is an enduring quality of effective tertiary education provisions. CET offers no exception. Indeed, reciprocity and shared understandings about separate institutional imperatives and working collaboratively to achieve those outcomes through enduring relations are central to the development of not only the most prized occupations, but occupational capacities more generally. Those benefits are grounded educationally in the importance of the learning experiences that can be provided in both kinds of settings, and their integration. These extend to educators' understandings of the requirements for occupational competence and workplace requirements, and opportunities to sustain or advance their occupational currency. Collaboration rather than subservience leads to openness and mutual benefits, but these relationships need to be intentionally built and sustained. In the absence of professional bodies or chambers of commerce that facilitate these arrangements, it may well come down to either systemic initiatives from national, regional governments and/or individual tertiary education institutions.

6. Recognition and certification of skills

Having an open and fit-for-purpose scheme for the recognition and certification of skills is essential for effective CET. A key premise for the recognition and certification of working-age adults' learning is that much of it can arise prior to and outside of the experiences provided through CET. So, whilst it is understood that each program of study has its own assessment and certification requirements, there is a broader imperative associated with recognizing and optimizing these adults' learning and development. Hence, some countries, including Singapore, have adopted the concept of "skills passports" which are able to capture the recognition of learning from multiple sources. Moreover, given their limited resources and time preciousness, having means to provide working-age adults with the recognition for prior learning and credits within CET programs stand as important imperatives and these need to be considered alongside institutional imperatives associated with student numbers and funding. More so than for younger students, and to meet the goals of continuous worklife learning set out by the government, mechanisms for recognizing and certifying learning occurring throughout adults' working lives need to be incorporated into national processes for the recognition and certification of skills in a sustainable and resource efficient way.

7. Generating proactive, independent, and interdependent working-age adults

Educational provisions, whether in workplaces or through specialized institutions, are nothing more or less than invitations to change (i.e., learn). Ultimately, it is the effort, intentionality, and focus of working-age adults' learning-related efforts that will determine the quality of CET outcomes, their own development, achievement of goals, contributions to sustaining their employability and, collectively, contributions to the nation state. Their ability to do so depends upon their readiness, existing capacities, and the kinds of experiences they are afforded in education and work. In both activities, active, engaged, and effortful participation is most likely to yield the best outcomes. Part of the impetus to be proactive, independent, but also being interdependent is premised upon individuals' capacities and interests. These need to be engaged with and embraced in relevant ways within CET provisions to achieve intended goals through effortful participation. Wherever possible, educational experiences (i.e., activities and interactions) and assessment processes should be directed towards means that will engage working-age adults. Project work, open focuses directed towards their goals, principles that can relate to their existing or intended occupational practice, and other means of engagement need to be considered as part of the curriculum and pedagogic mix. Within these, there will be the need to promote engagement, personal responsibility, and proactivity if it is absent. Certainly, the mindset associated with active engagement and the responsibilities for learning and working interdependently with others (e.g., peers, educators, co-workers) need to be promoted to develop a personal sense of inquiry within working-age adults.

Privileging CET as an Educational Sector

In sum, it is important to privilege CET as a worthwhile and essential education sector with its particular purposes, practices and policies that sets apart from others. Certainly, working age adults need to continually engage in occupationally oriented and workplace applicable learning across their working lives to secure their employability, to contribute to their workplaces' viability, and to secure national economic and social goals. Identifying how best to guide and support this worklife learning is an important national project that has been exercised through the SkillsFuture Initiatives in Singapore and similar schemes elsewhere around the world (UNESCO, 2022). Initiatives like SkillsFuture seek to provide adults with learning opportunities to develop their fullest potential throughout life, regardless of their starting points. Drawing on the data of a 3-year research project investigating the perceptions of graduates of CET programs, employers, working age adults, and CET educators and administrators on what constitutes accessible and effective CET provisions, it was proposed that much of this learning can be realized through a CET system comprising contributions by government, CET providers, CET educators, workplaces, and working-age adults that collectively provide the guidance, advice, and support. In all, establishing and sustaining a CET system is now warranted and deserves to be privileged. Such a system requires collaboration rather than competition amongst tertiary education institutions as CET providers to meet the collective needs of working age adults. Habitually, understanding and addressing the interests of students and employers is essential for enhancing the effectiveness of a national CET system that is premised on mature engagements with workplaces and effortful participation by these adults. Perhaps, only through such collaborative working can these key elements of a CET system best lead, address, and realize governmental, workplace, and individual goals for continuing learning across lengthening working lives.

However, whilst the study findings here are premised upon what occurs in Singapore and for working age Singaporeans, the potential of these findings goes far further as they speak to issues that are currently being addressed in many countries, albeit with different kinds and combinations of education institutions and provisions of experiences. Yet, at their core are the key elements of how to bring together effectively governance provided by the state, in conjunction with industry and enterprises, the kinds and qualities of experiences provided to working age adults through educational systems, albeit supported by the quality of adult educators, and yet also the aspirations, needs and engagement by working age adults. Thus, the findings and conclusions here are far from being limited to the country in which this investigation occurred. What it points to is needing to understand the combination of national goals, institutions and educational provisions that afford CET provisions and how working age adults in those countries come to engage with them.

References

Abrahamsson, L. (2006). Exploring constructions of gendered identities at work. In S. Billett, T. Fenwick, & M. Somerville (Eds.), *Work, subjectivity and learning* (pp. 105–121). Springer.

Billett, S. (2001). Learning through work: workplace affordances and individual engagement. *Journal of Workplace Learning, 13*(5), 209–214.

Billett, S. (2004). Workplace participatory practices: Conceptualising workplaces as learning environments. *Journal of Workplace Learning, 16*(6), 312–324. https://doi.org/10.1108/13665620410550295

Billett, S. (2006). *Work, change and workers*. Springer.

Billett, S. (2010). *Promoting and supporting lifelong employability for Singapore's workers aged 45 and over*. Institute of Adult Learning.

Billett, S. (2011). Promoting lifelong employability for workforce aged over 45: Singaporean workers' perspectives. *International Journal of Continuing Education and Lifelong Learning, 3*(2), 57–73.

Billett, S. (2015a). Readiness and learning in healthcare education. *Clinical Teacher, 12*, 1–6.

Billett, S. (2015b). *Integrating practice-based experiences into higher education*. Springer.

Billett, S. (2023). Relevance of workplace learning in enterprise transformation: The Prospects for Singapore. *Singapore Labour Journal, 02*, 6–21. https://doi.org/10.1142/S2811031523000128

Billett, S., & Hodges, S. (2016). Conceptualizing lifelong learning across working life, provisions of support and services. In S. Billett, D. Dymock, & S. Choy (Eds.), *Supporting learning across working life: Models, processes and practices*. Springer.

Billett, S., Leow, A., Chua, S., & Le, A. H. (2022). Changing attitudes about online continuing education and training in the Covid-19 era: A Singapore case study. *Journal of Adult and Continuing Education., 29*, 106–123. https://doi.org/10.1177/14779714221084346

Deissinger, T. (2022). The standing of dual apprenticeships in Germany: Institutional stability and current challenges. In S. Billett, B. E. Stalder, V. Aarkrog, S. Choy, S. Hodge, & A. H. Le (Eds.), *The standing of vocational education and the occupations it serves: Current concerns and strategies for enhancing that standing* (pp. 83–101). Springer.

Department of Education Science and Training. (2002). *Employability skills for the future*. Department of Education Science and Training.

Department of Innovation Universities and Skills. (2008). *Higher education at work: High skills: High value*. Department of Innovation, Universities and Skills.

Economic Strategies Committee. (2010a). *Fostering inclusive growth*. Singapore government.

Economic Strategies Committee. (2010b). *Key Recommendations*. Singapore Government.

Goffman, E. (1990). *The presentation of self in everyday life*. Penguin Books.

Hodkinson, P., & Bloomer, M. (2002). Learning careers: Conceptualising lifelong work-based learning. In K. Evans, P. Hodkinson, & L. Unwin (Eds.), *Working to learn: Transforming learning in the workplace* (pp. 29–43). Kogan Page.

Knowles, M. (1975). *Self-directed learning*. Association Press.

Le, A. H., Choy, S., Smith, R., & Billett, S. (2023). Learning across working life: A case from Australia. In S. Billett, H. Salling Olesen, & L. Filliettaz (Eds.), *Sustaining employability through work-life learning: Practices and policies* (pp. 285–306). Springer Nature Singapore.

Leow, A., Billett, S., Le, A. H., & Chua, S. (2022). Graduates' perspectives on effective continuing education and training: Participation, access and engagement. *International Journal of Lifelong Education, 41*(2), 212–228. https://doi.org/10.1080/02601370.2022.2044398

Organisation for Economic Co-operation and Development (OECD). (2021). *OECD skills outlook 2021*. OECD.

Organisation for Economic Co-operational and Development (OECD). (2013). *OECD skills outlook 2013: First results from the survey of adult skills*. OECD.

Organisation of Economic Cooperation and Development (OECD). (2000). *Economics and finance of lifelong learning*. OECD.

References

Rogers, C. R. (1969). *Freedom to learn*. Charles E. Merrill Co.

Rogers, C. R. (2001). The interpersonal relationship in the facilitation of learning. *Supporting Lifelong Learning, 1*, 25.

Sen, A. (1999). *Development as freedom*. Oxford University Press.

Somerville, M. (2006). Subjected bodies, or embodied subjects: Subjectivity and learning safety at work. In S. Billett, T. Fenwick, & M. Somerville (Eds.), *Work, subjectivity and learning* (pp. 37–52). Springer.

Stiglitz, J. E. (2002). Employment, social justice and societal well-being. *International Labour Review, 141*(1–2), 9–29.

Tennant, M. (1986). An evaluation of Knowles' theory of adult learning. *International Journal of Lifelong Education, 5*(2), 113–122.

UNESCO. (2022). *Transforming Technical and Vocational Education and Training for successful and just transitions: UNESCO strategy 2022–2029*. Retrieved from https://unevoc.unesco.org/home/UNEVOC+Publications/lang=en/akt=detail/qs=6644

Valsiner, J. (2000). *Culture and human development*. Sage Publications.

Young, M. (1998). *The curriculum of the future: From a 'new sociology of education' to a critical theory of learning*. Falmer Press.

Chapter 3
Continuing Education and Training: The Quest for Effective Provisions

Abstract There are growing national and global policy focuses as well as local concerns about what is often referred to as 'lifelong learning', particularly as it pertains to adults' learning across working life. To understand and be responsive to those concerns in both policy and practice, it is helpful to articulate key precepts and premises. These are helpful to inform what constitutes effective provisions of continuing education and training (CET) and how, in their diverse forms, they can support individuals' learning across working lives. The effective promotion of, engagement in and support provided by CET is central to achieving important individual, workplace and national goals. These goals include sustaining individuals' employability as workplace and occupational requirements change, and supporting the viability of public and private sector enterprises that provide both employment for these adults but also, more importantly, the provision of goods and services that individuals and communities need. Collectively, these contribute to meeting national social and economic goals through the generation of the goods and services that nation states require to be globally competitive, import-competing and export-oriented. More than being about the profitability of these enterprises is the capacity to provide effective social provisions that nation states require (i.e., health, social welfare and education). It has been commonly acknowledged that individuals' initial occupational preparation is now insufficient to meet their needs for employability across lengthening working lives. The increasingly dynamic requirements for work and occupational practice mean that focused and sustained learning across working life is required by all kinds and classifications of workers, occupations, and industry sectors. This is the case for nation states albeit with developed and developing economies. Thus, the need for effective and scalable CET provisions to sustain workers' employability has never been greater. To provide the appropriate educative provisions for working age adults, it is important to identify the kinds of experiences, their accessibility and pertinence for them to sustain that employability. Based on a review of extant literature, this chapter sets out what is known and understood about the imperatives for adults to learn across working life, both personal and institutional and how that learning might be best supported, guided and realised, and in ways scalable to entire working populations. It considers approaches for organising, ordering, supporting, and guiding this intentional learning through CET provisions.

Keywords Working lives · Continuing education and training · Employability · Effectiveness · Enterprise viability · Provision of goods and services · Global competitiveness

Promoting Employability Across Working Life

Globally, there is a recognised need for working age adults to sustain their employability across lengthening working lives as occupational roles transform and workplace requirements change (Organisation for Economic Co-operation and Development [OECD], 2006; 2021). The learning required to sustain employability often necessitates engagement in forms of continuing education and training (CET) by all kinds and classifications of workers. Hence, identifying and enacting effective, accessible and scalable CET provisions is becoming a national priority (Centeno, 2011; Han, 2001; Osborne & Borkowska, 2017). This is because specific kinds of support and educational interventions are likely required to secure some, if not many, of the required learning outcomes. Already, for many occupations, it is widely acknowledged that ongoing professional development is a necessary requirement for workers to perform in their jobs effectively and safely (Friedman & Phillips, 2004; Herschell et al., 2010). This is because what constitutes occupational competence and workplace performance is constantly changing in response to new technologies, ways of working and evolving needs of the job market. It was noted, for instance, in a report from the UK Commission for Employment and Skills on the future of work, that focusing on techniques for innovation in education and training will be of great importance across all sectors with new technologies a concern in an era of continuous and fundamental change (UK Commission for Employment and Skills, 2014). From the study referenced in this volume, it was concluded that employees would need to rely increasingly on continuing education and lifelong learning initiatives to upgrade their skills (Leow et al., 2022). Supra governmental agencies also suggest that working adults are increasingly aware of the importance of and are interested in participating in CET (European Centre for the Development of Vocational Training, 2020). The latest UNESCO strategy to transform technical and vocational education and training (TVET) calls for a collective effort to 'enhance the relevance of TVET systems within a lifelong learning perspective' (UNESCO, 2022a, p. 7). So, these global agencies are articulating and emphasising an urgent need for effective CET provisions.

This chapter seeks to set out what the literature currently suggests ways for progressing this agenda with its global, national and situational imperatives. The review of literature reported and discussed here focused on the imperatives for adults to learn across working life, both for personal (i.e., employability) and institutional (e.g., government, workplaces) purposes. It considers approaches for organising, ordering, supporting, and guiding this intentional learning through CET provisions. It commences by outlining the situation in Singapore which is used in this volume as a national case study. Following this and pursuing the overall concern about what constitutes an effective CET system, subsequent sections address issues of the kinds of outcomes that enterprises wish to secure through CET, the role that adult educators play in these provisions, the need for engaging and accommodating working age adults and the prospects for utilising workplaces as sites for CET. These categories were identified within the review and have been informed by the focuses of the practical investigations which inform this volume. It commences with a general discussion of the global concern of CET then the tripartite relationship required for the adult education sector: CET institution, industry, and CET students.

The key points made in this chapter are as follows:

- There is a globally recognised need for working age adults to sustain their employability across working lives through ongoing learning;
- Pre-employment education and training merely commences the ongoing need for adults to develop further their occupational capacities across working lives;
- Worklife learning is aligned with working age adults' sense of self, their employability and transitions across working life;
- Adults' engagement in continuing education and lifelong learning initiatives are increasingly required to secure learning across working life;
- The competing commitments to engage in CET with other more compelling personal responsibilities of working age adults is a factor in the design and enactment of CET;
- Effective CET is critical to public and private sector enterprises' viability and currently competent and adaptive workforce;
- Effective CET provisions assisting working adults in (i) remaining their employability; (ii) contributing to their workplaces' continuity and development; and (iii) collectively addressing governmental economic goals;
- Work activities and interactions can make important and effective contributions to worklife learning;
- Effective CET provisions require collaborations among the tertiary education sector, workplaces and CET students;
- Beyond direct teaching are the essential contributions of educative experiences (i.e., facilitating access to experiences, advice and engagement);
- Educators needing to design, enact and evaluate students' experiences aligned with achieving their intended goals;
- Effective CET educators: (i) have applied knowledge and experience in their teaching fields; (ii) are pedagogically and educationally competent; (iii) can work with adults as knowledgeable partners, and (iv) display a positive attitude that earns respect;
- The perennial issue about sustaining CET educators' occupational currency is yet to be resolved;

- Beyond those of government and industry, addressing the need and imperatives of working age adults are central to effective provisions of CET; and
- The findings of this Singaporean case study are likely relevant to other countries with both developed and developing modern industrial economies.

Singapore Case Study

A collective and systemic approach to upskilling the Singaporean workforce has long been a part of this nation state's policy focus, which makes it an informative and instructive case study. Indeed, it has been lauded for its successful implementation of a training levy scheme (Dar et al., 2003), the quality and effectiveness of CET programs offered through polytechnics to help its working age population remain employable. Consistent with OECD's strategy to improve the future-readiness of adult learning systems (OECD, 2019), this imperative has been long acknowledged and also responded to in Singapore through governmental concern about employees being granted greater discretion to bring about change in their workplaces (Government of Singapore, 2018). That particular concern indicates that beyond workers' accessing opportunities to further develop their personal capacities, it will be in the work setting where the application of those capacities needs to extend to generating innovations in response to emerging needs and challenges (Billett et al., 2023). The current policy-based manifestation is through its aptly named SkillsFuture agenda that has its central concern about the ongoing development of the Singaporean workforce. So, with the SkillsFuture initiative (Government of Singapore, 2018), there is now a renewed emphasis on ongoing skills' development in Singapore (Sung et al., 2011), where participation in CET is increasingly becoming required to maintain the currency of occupational competence and employability as work practices and goals transform. A particular challenge for Singapore is how its post-secondary educational institutions (PSEIs) comprising the five polytechnics and the Institute of Technical Education can contribute to this national goal through effective CET provisions. These institutions primarily focus on pre-employment education and training (PET) for school leavers. Yet, an effective CET provision is likely to be distinct from much of the curriculum, instructional strategies and expertise currently being designed and enacted through the PET programs, that aim to meet the needs of school leavers who, in the main, have no experience of working life. In contrast, CET students will mostly be experienced and competent workers, who want and need to learn more about them (Leow et al., 2023). They are not novices nor occupationally or workplace naive, although likely have diverse levels of readiness to participate in CET provisions. They may also have greater access to current occupational and work practices than teachers in PSEIs. With demanding work lives and family and community commitments, how they can and should participate in and engage with CET programs will be distinct from what is intended and occurs in PET programs. The CET provision, however, is far from new to PSEIs. Many already offer specialist diplomas for working age adults that have different structures, requirements and more modes of access than the programs for school leavers. Nevertheless, the SkillsFuture agenda and need for employability-related CET across the Singaporean workforce suggest that gaps in the existing educational provisions and capacities of teachers in these institutions needs to be addressed. This was pointedly made in the recent statement by the Minister of Education (Ministry of Education, 2023):

> A key enabler is our Training & Adult Education sector, comprising our Institutes of Higher Learning (IHLs) and quality private training providers. Together, they cater to the heterogenous needs of adult learners, and provide capacity to train large swathes of our workforce yearly. To make skills training more accessible and timely, the sector is undergoing a digital learning transformation to better deploy the use of technology and online learning. Our aim is to raise the quality and industry relevance of training. To achieve this, we are investing in the professional development of adult educators and andragogy research to spur CET programme innovations … This must be a continuous process, where every Singapore will know what are the skillsets they have within their portfolio, and what other skill sets they might want to acquire if they are looking for career transition, or even if they're trying to stay competitive in the same job. (Minister Chan Chun Sing, 4th July 2023)

Together, these factors indicate an urgent need to identify how the continuing development of working age Singaporeans' occupational capacities and workplace requirements can be realised through effective, accessible, and scalable CET provisions. No longer is adults' CET being considered a nicety (i.e., only about cultural betterment and personal enrichment). Instead, it plays and is to play an increasingly central and critical role in upskilling and reskilling the Singaporean working age population. The island nation has achieved outstanding success with its educational systems to date. Yet, much of that has been in the schooling sector, higher education and through PET. The challenge now faced is for the CET system to be equally effective.

To elaborate this case, the section below outlines the policy and practice imperatives and actions undertaken to date in promoting CET, ongoing employability and the viability of public and private sector enterprises in Singapore.

Continuing Education and Training: Singaporean Context

Singapore is renowned for its success in developing a high performing education system as measured through international benchmarking exercises such as the Program for International Student Assessment (PISA) (OECD, 2022b) and the Program for the International Assessment of Adult Competencies (PIAAC) (OECD, 2022a). These successes are the product of sustained and steady commitment through financial and cultural investment in human capital and education systems within the island nation. The Singapore government has long been prescient in recognising the importance of developing the skills of working-age adults as evidenced with the establishment of the Skills Development Fund in 1979 (UNESCO, 2022b). It provided incentives to employers and training institutions to engage their workers in skills' upgrading. This initiative was supplemented by the establishment of the

Lifelong Endowment Fund Act in 2001 to financially support Singaporeans using CET to enhance their employability (Ministry of Manpower, 2001).

These earlier initiatives emphasise a key policy focus for Singapore. That is, given the lack of access to the range of natural resources upon which other countries rely, the skills of the workforce play a central role in its economic and social sustainability. Hence, there is the need for that workforce to be currently competent and ready to respond to the constant changes in global economic circumstances and to support the ongoing viability of Singapore's public and private sector enterprises. Its commitment to economic growth based on skills, productivity and innovation led it to launch the CET Masterplan in 2008, which was refreshed in 2014 and more recently in 2020, aiming to develop an integrated, high-quality system of education and training that responds to constantly evolving industry needs, as well as fosters a culture that supports lifelong learning. The new Masterplan has three key areas of focus: (i) building deep expertise in the Singapore workforce, with increased involvement by employers in building and valuing skills; (ii) enabling individuals to make informed learning and career choices through the improved delivery of education, training and career guidance; and (iii) developing a vibrant CET ecosystem with a wide range of high-quality learning opportunities (Ministry of Manpower, 2022). Each of these key focuses was reflected in the findings from the practical investigations reported in this volume.

As noted, the current emphasis on lifelong learning and CET is not new and this continuous focus on CET is currently most visible in the launch of SkillsFuture, the nation-wide initiative to promote Singaporean workers' ongoing employability. As part of this initiative, spending on CET increased from about $600 million per year in the previous 5 years to over $1 billion per year from 2015 to 2020 (Ministry of Finance, 2015). The SkillsFuture initiative aims to "… provide Singaporeans with the opportunities to develop to their fullest potential throughout life, regardless of their starting points" (Government of Singapore, 2018). Through this national initiative, courses and programs have been developed to cater to emerging skills' needs such as in data analytics, finance, and digital media (SkillsFuture Singapore, 2021a). To encourage employers to recruit, retain, and retrain local mid-career workers, the Government provides 20% salary support to employers who hire local jobseekers aged 40 and over and provide them with relevant training opportunities (SkillsFuture Singapore, 2021b). Also, the increasing competition for innovation is acknowledged in Singapore by governmental concern about employees being granted greater discretion to bring about change in their workplaces (Government of Singapore, 2016). Together, all these factors indicate an urgent need to identify how the continuing development of working-age Singaporeans' occupational capacities and workplace requirements can be realised through effective CET provisions (*see* Sung, 2011 for an overview of Singapore's CET system). Again, no longer is adult education only about cultural betterment: it is now positioned as playing a central and critical role in reskilling and upskilling workforces in Singapore and around the world.

The importance of learning across working life was highlighted in a report on Singapore's results in the survey of adult skills—a product of the OECD's PIAAC

(OECD, 2016). The survey provided a snapshot of adults' proficiency in three key information-processing skills—literacy, numeracy, and problem-solving. This survey was conducted in Singapore from 2014 to 2015 and 5468 adults aged 16–65 participated. The findings indicated that young adults aged 16–24 performed better than the OECD average in literacy and had the highest average score among participating countries in numeracy. By contrast, older adults, particularly those aged 55–65, attained some of the lowest scores in literacy and numeracy among all participating countries/economies. The findings highlighted that the gap between the most and least proficient adults in Singapore is wide. Indeed, Singapore stands out as the country in which variability in literacy is greatest, at 77 score points, compared to the OECD average of 62 score points. Whilst the report attributes the low proficiency among Singapore's older populations to the effects of age, educational attainment, and language barriers, it underscored the importance of CET for working-age Singaporeans.

Indeed, over the last decade, we have witnessed an exponential growth in senior Singaporean workers aged ≥65 still active in their post-retirement years i.e., 17.1% in 2010 vs 31.7% in 2021. As the legal retirement and re-employment age of Singaporeans are raised progressively to 65 and 70 respectively to support older Singaporeans who wish to continue working (Ministry of Manpower, 2021), there is added impetus to provide CET for working-age Singaporeans (especially the elderly workers) more so than ever. This issue is addressed explicitly within this volume in Chap. 10—*CET journey: Experience of 'older' working age adults*. Noteworthily, the majority of these older workers reported being motivated by occupational or work role changes, which is central to their sense of self as working age adults and is also important in their transitions across working life and the ability to remain employed.

Given the centrality of the occupational currency and workplace relevant capacities as goals for lifelong learning (Government of Singapore, 2016), it is pivotal that we understand more about how the development of adult students' work skills can be realised through CET provisions. Concurrently, as the adult education sector moves towards greater professionalisation (Institute of Adult Learning, 2017; SkillsFuture Singapore, 2023), it is important to understand what roles and how best the PSEIs and their educators can contribute to the effective provision of CET. This includes the development of CET educators' professional competencies.

As the participation in CET increases from 35% in 2015 to 48.5% in 2019 and from 465,000 individuals and 12,000 enterprises in 2018 to 500,000 individuals and 14,000 enterprises in 2019 (SkillsFuture Singapore, 2020), it becomes necessary to consider how to integrate workplace learning experiences as part of the CET provision for Singapore. With the impetus from the SkillsFuture policy initiatives, the partnering of educational institutions (i.e., polytechnics and ITE) with industry organisations, but more importantly workplaces, has direct consequences for: (i) how CET is viewed by students, employers and the community, (ii) what industry organisations perceive as the worth and potential of CET, (iii) what the learning needs and requirements of these CET students are and, consequently, (iv) how CET educators can be equipped with the necessary skills and knowledge to engage these

CET students. Hence, a holistic approach is needed to fully understand how best to advance CET provisions in Singapore.

However, although this case study refers to one country, the kinds of considerations, some of the same processes are likely to be relevant to countries around the world with both developed and developing modern industrial economies (OECD, 2019; UNESCO, 2022a). Consequently, the case study here while based upon one nation state has the potential to inform models and practices that might be adopted more broadly.

Continuing Education and Training: The Quest for Effectiveness

As noted, there is a growing global interest in providing effective CET provisions to meet the needs of working-age adults, the enterprises for which they work and to assist nation states realise their social and economic goals. Consequently, the effectiveness of such provisions is often considered in terms of how working adults can: (i) remain employable across lengthening working lives; (ii) contribute to their workplaces' continuity and development; and (iii) collectively address governmental goals of supporting a robust economic base and providing quality services (OECD, 1996, 2000, 2019). A key event explicitly driving the economic emphasis of CET provisions, globally, was the 1996 OECD Year of Lifelong Learning (OECD, 1996) that emphasised the needs for adult and further education to now focus on economic imperatives, including sustaining adults' employability. With constant changes to occupational and workplace requirements, and potential for accompanying unemployment and underemployment, CET is held to be central to supporting nation states' social and economic development (World Economic Forum, 2021). As noted, as the demand for and requirements of occupational competence and workplace practices constantly change and transform, initial occupational education often occurring in early adulthood is insufficient to sustain employability across lengthening working lives (Noon et al., 2013; Schuller & Watson, 2009). Securing that employability is more than initial occupational preparation. It is about the ability to: secure employment, maintain that employment as occupational requirements and workplace circumstances change and realise occupational advancement and/or learn new occupations (Billett, 2022). Consequently, CET is now being looked towards and held to play a central role in supporting and sustaining that employability through further developing working-age adults' existing occupational capacities and extending them into new roles and occupations. Globally, CET provisions are also held to contribute to national competitiveness through securing a current and highly skilled workforce (Kim, 2016), that is both import-competing and export-oriented and, able to adapt to changing requirements for the goods and services they produce and degenerative of novel approaches. In this way, individuals, workplaces, communities, and governments all have a collective and shared interest in what constitutes effective, accessible, and scalable CET provisions.

Hence, whilst is acknowledged that we all learn across our lives, provisions of lifelong education have goals associated with optimising that learning in ways that sustain employability. Importantly, rather than being an endpoint, young adults, upon graduation from their PET programs are just commencing a journey of needing to develop further their capacities across their working lives. This is why CET is so salient for individual, workplace and national sustainability. Beyond the transition into workplaces, they commence a journey comprising the further development and transformation of their occupational competence that will continue across their working lives (OECD, 2010). That is, secure the ability to be and remain employed as work practices and requirements change and be able to advance their careers premised upon the ongoing development of their occupational and personal competence. Yet, given the scale and frequency of changes to occupational competence and workplace requirements, for working-age adults, CET will likely be an essential feature of their adult life as they are required to be employable for longer (OECD, 1996, 2019) and more so than was required by earlier generations (Billett, 2006). Indeed, consistent with the concept of employability, CET has been defined as education and/or training in helping individuals to (i) improve or update their knowledge and/or skills, (ii) acquire new skills for a career move or retraining, and/or (iii) continue their personal or professional development (European Centre for the Development of Vocational Training, 2014). It includes the continuing professional development provided to professional workers to maintain and certify their occupational currency (Friedman & Phillips, 2004), initial occupational preparation of working-age adults transitioning from one occupation to another (Indabawa, 2004), but also other means by which those goals can be obtained. This includes advice and contributions from communities, but perhaps most importantly opportunities, support, guidance and intentional educational experiences provided by and through the enterprises where working age adults are employed. Indeed, the strong evidence suggests that everyday work activities provide a range of routine and nonroutine problem-solving activities that are generative of new knowledge and in combination both extend the kind of knowledge that workers prosses and reinforce and refine it through everyday activities (OECD, 2013). Therefore, a range of forms and processes of educative experiences exist that can be accessed and enable working-age adults to sustain and advance their employability.

However, as foreshadowed, more than these personal outcomes, effective CET is critical to public and private sector enterprises having workforces capable of adapting and responding to the changing requirements for the goods and/or services they produce (Harteis, 2018). So, the effective provisions of CET are important not only to ensure working age adults' employability, but are also necessary for enterprises to respond to changing requirements and needs of their clientele or customers (Leow et al., 2022). It has been reported, however, that there is a growing gap between what companies need and what recent graduates provide (Department for Education, 2018; Winterbotham et al., 2018). The rapid pace and evolving nature of workplace demands pose a challenge for tertiary education institutions. They currently struggle, and likely will continue to struggle, to equip their students with the necessary skills to meet the changing requirements and demands for occupational competence and workplace performance (McArthur et al., 2017). Consequently, whilst employers often identify the lack of current competence as a limiting factor in the success and viability of their enterprises (Bessen, 2014; Craig, 2019), it also highlights an area that great assistance, support and guidance might be able to be sourced. That is, the importance of workplace learning experiences in supporting that employability through optimising the learning potential arising from engagement in problem-solving activities (OECD, 2016), including intentional engagement in identifying and enacting workplace innovations (Billett et al., 2023). Most likely, for this goal to be realised, partnerships amongst CET providers, CET educators, and industry partners are required to provide for learning experiences that assist the development of capacities required by working age adults that are relevant and applicable in their work (Leow et al., 2022). This means that considerations of CET provisions need to extend beyond what PSEIs in Singapore have provided through face-to face provisions, or even electronically mediated educational provisions (E-education) to include workplace learning experiences.

Constituting Effective CET: The Tripartite Contributions of the Tertiary Education Sector, Workplaces and CET Students

Globally, governments, as rehearsed earlier, are increasingly interested in their working age populations remaining occupationally competent to secure employment, remain employed and contribute to rather than drawing on national social and economic provisions (e.g., unemployment benefits), and assist the viability of their employers in producing the goods and services that nation states require (Edwards, 2002; Kanwar et al., 2019). Yet, increasing globalisation and growing economic nationalism, coupled with the introduction of new technologies, have accelerated the need for currently competent workforces, and correspondingly reforms of CET and national upskilling initiatives in many countries, including Singapore (Economic Strategies Committee, 2010). These initiatives, in turn, acknowledge the important role that CET plays in workforce development. Therefore, what constitutes effective CET is a central concern for government and of pertinence to providers of CET programs. Certainly, there is a growing consensus that initial occupational preparation is insufficient for working age adults to maintain employability across lengthening working lives, as already noted. Consequently, the imperative for these adults to upskill and/or reskill to address constantly changing occupational and workplace requirements is growing. This imperative needs to be pursued across working lives, regardless of the occupation in which they are employed, which includes engaging in CET of different kinds to sustain their employability.

As noted, CET is a broad term referring to various forms of educational experiences that are provided beyond those associated compulsory education (i.e., schooling) and initial preparation for working life, which often includes identifying and engaging in developing occupational competence. It encompasses continuing professional development that comprises educational provisions for professionals to advance in their careers, to sustain occupational currency and to ensure and verify competence in their fields (Friedman & Phillips, 2004). CET also encompasses further or specialised vocational education or training in craft or trade skills for the semi-skilled worker (Indabawa, 2004). In all, it embraces all forms of training provisions in various formats enabling workers to learn the knowledge, skills, and competencies to maintain or change their job or career. Included here are short courses of no more than 6 months to meet short-term needs (Andersson & Wärvik, 2012), and longer courses such as diploma, undergraduate degree or master's courses to meet longer-term career needs. CET can also be inclusive of uncertified educational courses and programs that can be either structured or unstructured experiences (Rienzo, 2014; Taylor & Evans, 2009) that provide access to and assist in mediating the knowledge required for employability. Much of these latter kinds of learning occur in and through workplaces as individuals engage in their everyday work activities (Billett, 2001). They also arise through activities and interactions with familiars, co-workers and community in which individuals engage. These are referred to as broadly as educative experiences (Billett, 2023). They go beyond direct teaching and comprise facilitation of access to experiences, advice and engagement through that serve to support their learning and development. Importantly, these experiences are often engaged with outside of educational institutions and their programs. Instead, these are located in communities in which adults inhabit and engage, provided by familiars and family members, sourced in work settings and through engaging in both novel and repeated activities. Hence, it is also necessary to consider how the contributions of these other sources can be encouraged through partnerships of different kinds outside of educational institutions. So, there is a social system comprised of these elements that stand to provide these experiences and enrich them.

However, it is the educational processes and outcomes provided by the system that needs to be understood more fully and enhanced (Prensky, 2012) in ways that make them more effective and scalable across entire working populations. Effecting this transformation requires the development of curriculum and pedagogic arrangements that are effective in understanding, organising and providing experiences that meet the needs of working age adults. CET students who are mature and older aged may have specific preferences for the kinds of educational experiences that best supports their learning. This might include not being positioned as students, or being directed to and taught in orthodox classroom-based settings. Instead, some of these adults report preferring their experience and expertise to be recognised within the educational program and having the opportunity to learn from others in more reciprocal ways that is often afforded by classroom instructions (Billett, 2011). Consistently, working age adults also report preferring to sustain and develop their capacities through everyday work tasks and activities, such as being able to shadow other employees and learn from them through observing, listening to, and working closely with them, while being guided and monitored as they learn on the job (Billett, 2011). Thus, contributions to the continuing development of working adults through their workplaces need to be considered more fully because they offer highly accessible bases for opportunities to advance their knowledge and also provide a way of reconstituting CET provisions and how they can be optimised and made scalable for all kinds and classifications of working age adults.

With the broad recognition of the need for CET programs to keep their workforce competitive and economies growing (Centeno, 2011; Han, 2001; Osborne & Borkowska, 2017) has led to an associated public policy focus. That focus includes seeking to assist employers' and employees' decisions to further develop their employability, including provisions of subsidies and increasing job mobility from low-skilled to higher-skilled jobs (Lee & Morris, 2016; Sung et al., 2011). As such, it is important to understand how potential relations and collaborations among the tertiary education sector (particularly adult education and CET educators), workplaces and CET students can lead to effective CET provisions, albeit in hybrid educational institutions, work settings or via other means. So, the following sub sections commence with outlining the benefits for private and public sector enterprises from their engagement in CET in terms of those enterprises' viability and advancement. Then, the roles of adult education and CET educators, and working-age adults are discussed, followed by how the contribution of workplace experiences can be optimised as an approach to CET.

Enterprise Outcomes from Engagement in CET

Beyond individuals' employability being advanced through CET outcome, there are also essential contributions arising for public and private sector enterprises' viability and advancements from having a workforce that is currently competent and adaptive. These impacts can include increased productivity, innovation, profitability, and reduced turnover, improved employee engagement (e.g., Ocen et al., 2017; Sitzmann & Ely, 2011), and enhanced capacity for initiating and enacting innovations (Billett et al., 2023). Employees able to access CET opportunities report being more satisfied with their jobs, such as studies of nurses (Mlambo et al., 2021) and among hotel employees (Petrović & Živković, 2017), thus generating positive impact on employee retention rates and customer satisfaction with provided services. Enterprises investing in employee training are claimed to have 218% higher income per employee than companies that do not (Association for Talent Development, 2019). More widely, working age adults participating in CET report higher job satisfaction, increased productivity, and better career opportunities (Cedefop & European Centre for the Development of Vocational Training, 2020). In addition, individuals who engage in CET report higher wages and better employment outcomes (OECD, 2019).

Moreover, it has been shown that investments in CET are held to provide a return in the form of assisting enterprises develop skilled workforces able to adapt to changing work environments thus enhancing organisational competitiveness

(Friedman & Phillips, 2004). Indeed, CET has been shown to improve the capacities of professionals, maintaining their competence and capability of meeting the needs of their respective industries. For instance, CET participation had a significant effect on knowledge and skills development among healthcare professionals (Samuel et al., 2021) and the development of emotional intelligence among teachers (Pastore et al., 2019).

Yet, it would be mistaken to believe that CET provisions, alone, can achieve these kinds of outcomes for individuals and the enterprises in which they work and potentially can develop further their capacities and viability. There are specific ways that provisions of CET need to be organised and enacted to achieve these kinds of outcomes and these need to be enacted by educators who are both sensitive to the needs of adult students and competent in supporting their learning.

The Role of Adult Education and CET Educators

Having educators who are able to design, enact and evaluate experiences for students that are aligned with achieving the intended goals are essential for effective educational provisions. This includes being open to the range of possible experiences that can secure those outcomes. Given the dynamic nature of those goals, the currency and competency of adult educators is central to the CET provision. Earlier research demonstrated that continuing professional development of educators to maintain current and effective work skills can be driven by requirements of professional standards and continuing registration procedures (Friedman & Phillips, 2004). However, this impetus has been largely confined to that of medical professionals (e.g., Griscti & Jacono, 2006; Herschell et al., 2010; Ochieng & Ward, 2018; World Health Organization, 2013), while less is known about the CET educators in the tertiary and adult education sector (Chen et al., 2020) or how the work and the goals they need to achieve can be realised. Within the adult education sector, the provision of CET has to consider the characteristics of working age adults who will decide whether or not to participate and in what ways and organise the purposes and processes of CET accordingly. This includes being cognisant of these adults' goals for participating in CET educational goals (e.g., personal and professional enrichment) and processes for securing those goals. That is, those that can fit in and around these adults' other commitments, such as work and family life. This imperative is most salient for adult education per se as their readiness, needs and aspirations may not be the same as those for young people engaging in initial occupational preparation and transitioning to working life.

More specifically, qualities of effective CET educators are categorised into three domains: prior experience in the fields of teaching and pedagogy-related skills. Firstly, working age adults reportedly prefer their educators to have applied knowledge and experience in the fields in which they teach (Billett et al., 2016; Leow & Billett, 2022; Phillips et al., 2017). Secondly, educators' approach plays an important role in determining the effectiveness of an educator. Adult students have reported preferred educators who displayed a positive attitude, respected their students as adults who can contribute to their and others' learning, are understanding, fair, flexible, and enthusiastic, and can engage reciprocally with their students (Leow et al., 2023; Phillips et al., 2017). They also report preferring educators who were patient and non-judgmental, and who gave genuine praise and encouragement (Armstrong, 2007). In contrast, students in CET programs stated the most problematic qualities were educators not understanding or respecting of student needs, such as by being dismissive of students' experience, prior knowledge, and real-world constraints on their time, and arrogances, condescension, and rigidity (Billett et al., 2016; Leow & Billett, 2022; Phillips et al., 2017). This means that these working age adults expected their educators to be engaged with them as equals and reciprocally. These adults also indicated that their best educators were 'real' or authentic in their enthusiasm and passion about what they were teaching, related to the students as peers and adults, shared their own personal experiences with students to enhance learning, and had a sense of humour and were able to raise students' confidence (Armstrong, 2007; Leow & Billett, 2022).

Thirdly, the appropriateness of their pedagogies and teaching skills also characterises effective CET educators. Desirably, it is proposed that CET educators would commence their teaching career after prior experiences gained from another field and learned how to teach through hands-on practice (Chan, 2010). Some may have completed professional preparation as educators, but others may not. But, overall, working age adults value educators who are pedagogically strong. For example, valued are those able to design tasks at the right level of challenge to accommodate but also challenge students' readiness (Armstrong, 2007), provide timely and constructive developmental feedback (Armstrong, 2007; Martin et al., 2018), and manage group interactions through effective communication amongst students, moderating group discussions, and managing an environment that is open and respectful of others as well as their own contributions (Thomas & Thorpe, 2019). This involves fostering both group cohesion and inclusivity, while addressing individual challenges and ensuring fair participation in group activities, like turn-taking (Armstrong, 2007). They also reportedly valued educators who communicated well and were organised and prepared for their classes (Phillips et al., 2017). However, and potentially important for CET educators is that they also need to be competent and knowledgeable in their field of teaching and have had experience in the application of what they are teaching in work settings. That capacity is evidenced in their ability to use narratives, stories and examples from their practice, and be able to respond to questions based upon their experiences (Leow & Billett, 2022).

Of course, this raises a perennial issue about the occupational currency of the CET educators and how this can be sustained when they are employed in educational institutions, particularly how their currency exhausts over time when working as an educator. These qualities required of CET educators need to be taken into considerations in developing effective CET provisions.

CET and Working Age Adults

As foreshadowed, young adults, upon graduation from their PET programs and transition into the working life are just commencing a journey in the ongoing development of their occupational competence that will be required to secure their employability across working life (OECD, 2010). That is, needing to secure the ability to be and remain employed as work practices and requirements change, and being able to advance their careers premised upon the ongoing development of their occupational and personal competence. These are imperatives that working-age adults need to address across working lives regardless of their occupation, as all forms of work are subject to change. Hence, it is important to understand the qualities of educational experiences and their alignment with work life learning requirements that working age adults find engaging. Effecting this goal likely requires the organisation of and access to educational experiences that engage these adults and afford them effective pedagogies that addressed their readiness and assist meet their learning needs. Provisions of CET, therefore, need to be based not only imperatives of government, industry sectors, but also those of working-age adults who have the discretion to decide whether they will participate and how they will engage.

Consequently, as with any other educational provision, it is important to identify how CET provisions can meet the needs of those to whom it is directed (i.e., students). With compulsory education or immediate post-school tertiary education, students are compelled to participate to secure the knowledge and certification required to engage in specific occupations and enter the world of work. However, as noted, provisions of CET are usually premised upon working-age adults' electing to participate in them. They are not compulsory, nor are most adults pressed into attending them. Also, unlike many tertiary education students, who tend to be younger and have fewer commitments, working-age adults often have more work and family responsibilities and need to balance their time and effort across these commitments (Rose, 2017; Su et al., 2018). These commitments consume much of their time, leaving less time, energy, and effortfulness for engaging in CET. The term 'time jealousy' has been applied it to higher and tertiary education students, suggesting that more than being time poor, such as the commitments that they have to make decisions about how they distribute their time and effort (Billett, 2015a, b). This same concept can be used for working-age adults and how they need to be viewed in terms of educational needs. Hence, developing CET provisions that are responsive to working-age adults' needs has become a priority in many countries, as these provisions are seen as being a key source of supporting employability.

Personal commitments of time, energy and finance to engage in CET, as noted, compete with work, family, and community responsibilities that are often more compelling for working-age adults than younger students. This may even be more the case for those from the lower income groups and senior working adults, who have lesser inclinations or ability to participate in CET (Boeren et al., 2020). Consequently, unlike younger individuals who recently have been "schooled" in the processes of education, participation in CET is contingent on the working-age adults' interest and commitments. Therefore, issues of accessibility associated with ease of engagement and flexibility in participation are often key considerations for these adults (Billett et al., 2020). Engagement in CET can present real challenges for working-age adults in terms of their readiness, that is, having the capacities to engage in and effectively learn from the educational experience. One of the often-mentioned capacities is for working-age adults to effectively engage in learning is their ability to self-regulate or self-direct their learning (Herschell et al., 2010; Steffens, 2015). That is, individuals need to take control and responsibility of their learning, directing what and how something is learnt (Merriam & Bierema, 2014), which is associated with their readiness (Billett, 2015a, b). That ability is often viewed as being related to individuals' awareness and understanding of their own thought processes (i.e., metacognition) (Robson, 2012). That is, individuals are aware of and able to apply strategies helping them achieve their learning goals, including monitoring their progress, diagnosing learning problems and attempting to come up with solutions. Also included is the ability to acquire information or skills independently by interacting with training materials (Herschell et al., 2010), which often comes down to their literacy, the broader sense. The ideal is that these adults can advance their learning independently, set and achieve their learning goals, implement effective learning strategies, monitor and assess their goal progress, establish a productive learning environment and seek assistance when needed (Steffens, 2015).

However, whilst these are ideal and, in some way, desirable, they may not be principles in fact to advance CET provisions. For instance, the concept of andragogy as advanced by Knowles (1975, 1980), and widely adopted by some commentators, has long since been abandoned. This is partialy because it was premised upon the idea that adults were inherently able and needed to be self-directed in their learning and in ways that is distinct from children. Yet, when considered, this premise is easily challenged (Tennant, 1986). Whilst adults may be self-directed in fields within which they are competent, this is not necessarily the case when they lack understandings, capacities to achieve goals and dispositions associated with tasks that sit outside of their existing knowledge. Hence, self-direction may well be an outcome of participating in CET provision, but it may not be a starting point or a premise to organise such an educational program. Yet, whilst the expectations and capacities of adults are in some ways distinct from younger people in terms of their more extensive experience and ability to exercise personal discretion, fulfilling them may require structured and guided learning experiences, that are not so different from those provided for younger people. In fact, it might require more assistance, when seeking to learn new knowledge that sits outside of their previous experiences and competence (e.g., technology, language).

In all, individuals' learning and development is based upon how they construe and construct knowledge from what they experience (Billett, 2009). This is both premised on and salient to the further development of their occupational capacities. Central here is their readiness to engage in those learning activities and optimise the opportunities afforded to them. That readiness comprises having the kinds of understandings, procedures and dispositions (i.e., what they know, can do and value) that permit them to engage productively in activities from which they seek to learn. That readiness extends to their interest in the learning, and how they identify themselves as adult students. This is particularly important because learning new knowledge, and in particular challenging and extending what individuals know, can do and value is demanding and effortful. Such processes are only likely to be engaged with when individuals have the interest to do so. A key source of working age adults' interest and intentional learning is the need to be competent in their working life. This is because their sense of self and well-being is often associated with conduct of their work and recognition of and satisfaction with what they do within working life (Noon et al., 2013). Workers often report learning extensively and widely through their work, highlighting the importance of engaging in learning in workplaces (Chan, 2013; Le et al., 2023; Tyler et al., 2014) and they also indicate this as a preferred mode of professional development (Billett et al., 2016). Consequently, rather than restricting considerations of the circumstances in which CET can be enacted and worthwhile worklife learning occurring in educational programs and institutions, their activities and interactions in workplaces also need to be considered as important bases for that learning.

CET and Workplace Experiences

The contributions and value of the learning arising through work activities and interactions has been well acknowledged (*see* Billett, 2004; Blacker, 1995; Lave, 2009; Moore, 2004). Indeed, it is reasonable to propose that most of the learning that arises across working life has its sources in everyday work activities and interactions. Much of that learning does not require educational interventions, except when there is a need for knowledge to be accessed and engaged with that cannot occur within work settings. Yet, despite this acknowledgement and the almost universal acceptance of learning arising through work, this is often not viewed or counted as CET as is often classified as being informal rather than formalised educative experiences. That is, because it does not take the form or have the appearances of the kinds of educational experiences that are legitimised by being hosted and enacted through educational institutions that they are rendered as being of much lesser worth and acknowledgement. So, there is both a need for that kind of learning to be acknowledged, respected and incorporated within mainstream views about CET and having procedures that can optimise and formalise both the processes and outcomes of those experiences.

Similarly, Evans et al. (2002) further proposed "… the workplace is a crucially important site for learning and for access to learning" (p. 1). Despite the recognition of the need for workplace learning and the potential of workplaces as sites of learning, serious questions are raised about the extent to which this potential can be optimised in practice unless workplaces appreciate their potential and provide the kinds of support, guidance and opportunities that can realise their potential as a learning environment.

Drawing on the work of Lave and Wenger (1991), Billett (2004) proposed the re-conceptualisation of workplace as learning environments in which learning and participation in work are viewed as being inseparable. In era of constant change and transformation of work activities and professional competence it is desirable for workplaces to be seen as learning practices (i.e., learning as being an inherent expectation and outcome of work activities and being nurtured through workplace practices) (Billett & Newton, 2012). Although informed by different theoretical orientations, Griffiths and Guile (2003) concluded similarly and proposed the importance for the creation of strong partnerships between workplaces and educational institutions to foster positive learning environments in which knowledge is co-constructed, leading to a greater alignment between learning and what is needed in the workplace. This knowledge is however mediated and shaped by individual's intention and degree of engagement while situated within their life histories and learning experiences (Billett, 2001, 2004, 2021).

The Quest for Effective CET Provisions

In this review, the aim has been to capture and elaborate understandings about the imperatives for adults to learn across working life, both personal and institutional and how that learning might be facilitated. It highlights the importance of partnerships among tertiary education sector, workplaces, and working-age adults to develop effective CET provisions, including the contributions that adult educators can make to providing and enriching educative experiences. In particular, the contributions of workplace activities and interaction are held to be generative of important learning outcomes through and across working life. Indeed, nation states need effective, accessible, inclusive, and broadly engaged provisions of CET to develop further the capacities of its working age population. Understanding what constitutes accessible and effective CET provisions enables informed decision-making about effectively supporting the initiatives of achieving a skilled, employable, and adaptive workforce. To understand what comprises that efficacy, it is necessary to capture, analyse, and reconcile the perspectives of stakeholders including national bodies, education institutions, CET educators and, most importantly, working-age adults. Reconciliation of these perspectives is essential for establishing what constitutes an effective CET system, including what kinds of CET provisions can best meet the needs of these adults and their workplaces and how they are delivered and engaged with by working age adults.

In sum, key points advanced in this chapter are as follows.

- There is a globally recognised need for working age adults to sustain their employability across lengthening working lives through ongoing learning as occupational roles transform and workplace requirements change.

- Rather than being an endpoint, young adults, upon graduation from their PET programs are just commencing a journey of needing to develop further the capacities across their working lives.
- Working age adults frequently reported being motivated in that learning by occupational or work role changes, which is central to their sense of self as working age adults and is also important in their transitions across working life and the ability to remain employed.
- These adults need to rely increasingly on continuing education and lifelong learning initiatives to secure that learning.
- Working age adults' personal commitments of time, energy and finance to engage in CET, as noted, compete with work, family, and community responsibilities that are often more compelling for working age adults than younger students.
- More than personal outcomes, effective CET is critical to public and private sector enterprises having workforces capable of adapting and responding to the changing requirements for the goods and/or services they produce, thereby assisting public and private sector enterprises' viability and advancement and having a national workforce that is currently competent and adaptive.
- The effectiveness of CET provisions is often considered in terms of how working adults can: (i) remain employable across lengthening working lives; (ii) contribute to their workplaces' continuity and development; and (iii) collectively address governmental goals of supporting a robust economic base and providing quality services.
- It is important to understand how potential relations and collaborations among the tertiary education sector (particularly adult education and CET educators), workplaces and CET students can lead to effective CET provisions, albeit in hybrid educational institutions, work settings or via other means.
- The contributions and value of the learning arising through work activities and interactions has been well acknowledged. These are highly accessible, pertinent and effective learning environments for working age adults.
- A wider range of contributions referred to as broadly as educative experiences, that go beyond direct teaching and comprise facilitation of access to experiences, advice and engagement through that serve to support their learning and development make essential contributions.
- Having educators who are able to design, enact and evaluate experiences for students that are aligned with achieving the intended goals are essential for effective educational provisions.
- Working age adults report: (i) preferring educators to have applied knowledge and experience in the fields in which they teach; (ii) are pedagogically and educationally competent; (iii) whose approach is aligned to working with adults as knowledgeable partners, and iv) have reported preferred educators who displayed a positive attitude that earns respect.
- The perennial issue about the occupational currency of the CET educators and how this can be sustained has yet to be adequately addressed.

- Provisions of CET need to be based not only imperatives of government, industry sectors, but also those of working age adults who have the discretion to decide whether they will participate and how they will engage.
- Although this case study refers to one country, the kinds of considerations, some of the same processes are likely to be relevant to countries around the world with both developed and developing modern industrial economies.

So, this chapter provides background understanding of the phenomenon to be investigated in a CET research project based in Singapore. In overview, the project examined: (i) what constitutes effective provisions of CET and their delivery by those who have recently engaged in CET and can make judgements about their efficacy, (ii) how employers and a sample of working age Singaporeans inform about the purposes for participating in and what constitutes quality of CET provisions and its teaching in meeting these learning needs, (iii) the professional competencies required of adult educators, and (iv) how working age adults need to engage in learning-related activities to secure their employability and advance their workplaces' viability (*see* Chap. 4—*Investigating effective CET provisions to promote employability: Method and procedures* for detailed method and procedures).

References

Andersson, E., & Wärvik, G. B. (2012). Swedish adult education in transition? Implications of the work first principle. *Journal of Adult and Continuing Education, 18*(1), 90–103.

Armstrong, L. (2007). The significance of interpersonal skills and tutor behaviour in determining quality of teaching and learning in adult education. *Journal of Adult and Continuing Education, 13*(2), 231–248. https://doi.org/10.7227/JACE.13.2.9

Association for Talent Development. (2019). *2019 State of the Industry Report*. Retrieved from https://www.td.org/research-reports/2019-state-of-the-industry

Bessen, J. (2014, August 25). Employers aren't just whining–the "skills gap" is real. *Harvard Business Review*.

Billett, S. (2001). *Learning in the workplace: Strategies for effective practice*. Allen and Unwin.

Billett, S. (2004). Workplace participatory practices: Conceptualising workplaces as learning environments. *Journal of Workplace Learning, 16*(6), 312–324. https://doi.org/10.1108/13665620410550295

Billett, S. (2006). *Work, change, and workers*. Springer.

Billett, S. (2009). Personal epistemologies, work and learning. *Educational Research Review, 4*(3), 210–219.

Billett, S. (2011). *Vocational education: Purposes, traditions and prospects*. Springer Science & Business Media.

Billett, S. (2015a). *Integrating practice-based experiences into higher education*. Springer.

Billett, S. (2015b). Readiness and learning in healthcare education. *Clinical Teacher, 12*, 1–6.

Billett, S. (2021). The co-occurrence of work, learning, and innovation: Advancing workers' learning and work practices. In M. Malloch, L. Cairns, B. O'Connor, & K. Evans (Eds.), *SAGE handbook of learning and work* (pp. 34–48). Sage.

Billett, S. (2022). Promoting graduate employability: Key goals, and curriculum and pedagogic practices for higher education. In B. Ng Ling (Ed.), *Graduate employability and workplace-based learning development: Insights from sociocultural perspectives*. Springer.

References

Billett, S. (2023). Learning across working life: Educative experiences. In S. Billett, H. Salling-Olesen, & L. Filliettaz (Eds.), *Sustaining employability through worklife learning: Practices and policies*. Springer Nature. https://doi.org/10.1007/978-3-030-67930-9_23-7

Billett, S., & Newton, J. (2012). Learning practice: Conceptualising professional lifelong learning for the healthcare sector. In N. Frost, M. Zukas, H. Bradbury, & S. Kilminster (Eds.), *Beyond reflective practice: New approaches to professional lifelong learning* (pp. 52–65). Routledge.

Billett, S., Dymock, D., & Choy, S (2016) (Eds). *Supporting learning across working life: Models, processes and practices*. Springer. ISBN 978-3-319-29017-1.

Billett, S., Leow, A., Poh, S., Chia, M., Low, C., Khoo, G.-A., Zaman, S., & Tan, Y. K. (2020). *Research bulletin 1: Perspectives on effective and accessible CET provisions and effective CET teachers*. https://drive.google.com/file/d/1_PvycuDBJErgYEL_BNnUl7XW7MtMkRTP/view?usp=sharing

Billett, S., Tan, J., Chan, C., Chong, W. H., & Keat, J. S. C. (2023). Employee-driven innovations: Zones of initiation, enactment and learning. In W. O. Lee, P. Brown, A. L. Goodwin, & A. Green (Eds.), *International handbook on education development in Asia-Pacific* (pp. 1–19). Springer. https://doi.org/10.1007/978-981-16-2327-1_67-1

Blacker, F. (1995). Knowledge, knowledge work and organizations: An overview and interpretation. *Organization Studies, 16*(6), 1021–1046. https://doi.org/10.1177/017084069501600605

Boeren, E., Roumell, E. A., & Roessger, K. M. (2020). COVID-19 and the future of adult education: An editorial. *Adult Education Quarterly, 70*(3), 201–204. https://doi.org/10.1177/0741713620925029

Centeno, V. (2011). Lifelong learning: A policy concept with a long past but a short history. *International Journal of Lifelong Education, 30*(2), 133–150. https://doi.org/10.1080/02601370.2010.547616

Chan, B. T. Y. (2010). The changing roles of adult and continuing education practitioners in Hong Kong: Analysis from a historical perspective. *Journal of Adult and Continuing Education, 16*(1), 4–20. https://doi.org/10.7227/JACE.16.1.3

Chan, S. (2013). Learning through apprenticeship: Belonging to a workplace, becoming and being. *Vocations and Learning, 6*(3), 367–383.

Chen, Z., Ramos, C., Puah, L. D., & Chye, C. S. (2020). *Training and adult education landscape in Singapore: Characteristics, challenges and policies*. https://www.ial.edu.sg/content/dam/projects/tms/ial/Research-publications/Reports/TAE%20Landscape%20Report_Final.pdf

Craig, R. (2019). *America's skills gap: Why It's real, and why it matters*. Progressive Policy Institute.

Dar, A., Canagarajah, S., & Murphy, P. (2003). *Training levies: Rationale and evidence from evaluations*. World Bank.

Department for Education. (2018). *Employer skills survey 2017 research report*. Retrieved from https://assets.publishing.service.gov.uk/government/uploads/system/uploads/attachment_data/file/746493/ESS_2017_UK_Report_Controlled_v06.00.pdf

Economic Strategies Committee. (2010). *Report of the Economic Strategies Committee: High skilled people, innovative economy, distinctive global city*. Retrieved from https://www.mof.gov.sg/Portals/0/MOF%20For/Businesses/ESC%20Recommendations/ESC%20Full%20Report.pdf

Edwards, R. (2002). Mobilizing lifelong learning: Governmentality in educational practices. *Journal of Educational Policy, 17*(3), 353–365. https://doi.org/10.1080/02680930210127603

European Centre for the Development of Vocational Training. (2014). *Terminology of European education and training policy*. Publications Office of the European Union.

European Centre for the Development of Vocational Training. (2020). *Perceptions on adult learning and continuing vocational education and training in Europe, volume 1: Second opinion survey, member states*. Publications Office of the European Union.

Evans, K., Hodkinson, P., & Unwin, L. (Eds.). (2002). *Working to learn: Transforming learning in the workplace*. Kogan Page.

Friedman, A., & Phillips, M. (2004). Continuing professional development: Developing a vision. *Journal of Education and Work, 17*(3), 361–376. https://doi.org/10.1080/1363908042000267432

Government of Singapore. (2016). *Formation of the council for skills, innovation and productivity*. https://www.skillsfuture.gov.sg/newsroom/formation-of-the-council-for-skills-innovation-and-productivity

Government of Singapore. (2018). *SkillsFuture*. Retrieved from https://www.mom.gov.sg/employment-practices/skills-training-and-development/skillsfuture

Griffiths, T., & Guile, D. (2003). A connective model of learning: The implications for work process knowledge. *European Educational Research Journal, 2*(1), 56–73.

Griscti, O., & Jacono, J. (2006). Effectiveness of continuing education programs in nursing: Literature review. *Journal of Advanced Nursing, 55*(4), 449–456. https://doi.org/10.1111/j.1365-2648.2006.03940.x

Han, S. (2001). Creating systems for lifelong learning in asia. *Asia Pacific Education Review, 2*(2), 85–95. https://doi.org/10.1007/BF03026293

Harteis, C. (2018). Machines, change, work: An educational view on the digitalization of work. In C. Harteis (Ed.), *The impact of digitalization in the workplace: An educational view* (pp. 1–10). Springer.

Herschell, A. D., Kolko, D. J., Baumann, B. L., & Davis, A. C. (2010). The role of therapist training in the implementation of psychosocial treatments: A review and critique with recommendations. *Clinical Psychology Review, 30*(4), 448–466. https://doi.org/10.1016/j.cpr.2010.02.005

Indabawa, S. A. (2004). An appraisal of the adult and non-formal vocational education programs in Kano: Implications for northern Nigeria. *Journal of Adult and Continuing Education, 10*(1), 46–56. https://doi.org/10.7227/JACE.10.1.5

Institute of Adult Learning. (2017). *Adult education professionalisation*. Retrieved from https://www.ial.edu.sg/join-the-community/adult-educators-professionalisation-aep-scheme/benefits.html

Kanwar, A., Balasubramanian, K., & Carr, A. (2019). Changing the TVET paradigm: New models for lifelong learning. *International Journal of Training Research, 17*, 54–68.

Kim, J. (2016). Development of a global lifelong learning index for future education. *Asia Pacific Education Review, 17*(3), 439–463. https://doi.org/10.1007/s12564-016-9445-6

Knowles, M. (1975). *Self-directed learning*. Association Press.

Knowles, M. (1980). *The modern practice of adult education: From pedagogy to andragogy*. Cambridge Books.

Lave, J. (2009). The practice of learning. In K. Illeris (Ed.), *Contemporary theories of learning: Learning theorists … in their own words* (pp. 200–208). Routledge.

Lave, J., & Wenger, E. (1991). *Situated learning: Legitimate peripheral participation*. Cambridge University Press.

Le, A. H., Choy, S., Smith, R., & Billett, S. (2023). Learning across working life: A case from Australia. In S. Billett, H. Salling Olesen, & L. Filliettaz (Eds.), *Sustaining employability through work-life learning: Practices and policies* (pp. 285–306). Springer Nature. https://doi.org/10.1007/978-981-99-3959-6_13

Lee, M., & Morris, P. (2016). Lifelong learning, income inequality and social mobility in Singapore. *International Journal of Lifelong Education, 35*(3), 286–312. https://doi.org/10.1080/02601370.2016.1165747

Leow, A., & Billett, S. (2022). Sustaining the employability of working-age adults: A Singapore case study. In B. Ng (Ed.), *Graduate employability and workplace-based learning development: Insights from sociocultural perspectives* (pp. 45–66). Springer Nature Singapore.

Leow, A., Billett, S., Le, A. H., & Chua, S. (2022). Graduates' perspectives on effective continuing education and training: Participation, access and engagement. *International Journal of Lifelong Education., 41*, 212–228. https://doi.org/10.1080/02601370.2022.2044398

Leow, A., Billett, S., & Le, A. H. (2023). Towards a continuing education and training eco system: A case study of Singapore. *International Journal of Training Research, 1–17*, 226–242. https://doi.org/10.1080/14480220.2023.2203944

Martin, F., Wang, C., & Sadaf, A. (2018). Student perception of helpfulness of facilitation strategies that enhance instructor presence, connectedness, engagement and learning in online courses. *The Internet and Higher Education, 37*, 52–65. https://doi.org/10.1016/j.iheduc.2018.01.003

McArthur, E., Kubacki, K., Pang, B., & Alcaraz, C. (2017). The employers' view of "work-ready" graduates: A study of advertisements for marketing jobs in Australia. *Journal of Marketing Education, 39*(2), 82–93. https://doi.org/10.1177/0273475317712766

Merriam, S. B., & Bierema, L. L. (2014). *Adult learning: Linking theory and practice*. Jossey-Bass.

Ministry of Education. (2023). Shifting lifelong learning to a higher gear. *Opening Address by Minister Chan Chun Sing at the SkillsFuture Festival 2023, Lifelong Learning Institute*. Retrieved from https://www.moe.gov.sg/news/speeches/20230704-opening-address-by-minister-chan-chun-sing-at-the-skillsfuture-festival-2023-lifelong-learning-institute

Ministry of Finance. (2015). *Budget 2015: Building our future, strengthening social security*. Retrieved from https://www.singaporebudget.gov.sg/archives/budget_2015/fy2015_budget_statement.pdf

Ministry of Manpower. (2001). *Lifelong learning endowment fund bill*. Retrieved from https://www.nas.gov.sg/archivesonline/data/pdfdoc/2001011211.htm

Ministry of Manpower. (2021). *Retirement and re-employment (Amendment) Bill 2021 and CPF (Amendment) Bill 2021*. Retrieved from https://www.mom.gov.sg/newsroom/press-releases/2021/1101-retirement-and-re-employment-amendment-bill-2021-and-cpf-amendment-bill-2021

Ministry of Manpower. (2022). *Refreshed Continuing Education and Training (CET) Masterplan*. Retrieved from https://www.mom.gov.sg/employment-practices/skills-training-and-development/refreshed-cet-masterplan

Mlambo, M., Silén, C., & McGrath, C. (2021). Lifelong learning and nurses' continuing professional development, a metasynthesis of the literature. *BMC Nursing, 20*, 1–13.

Moore, D. T. (2004). Curriculum at work: An educational perspective on workplace as a learning environment. *Journal of Workplace Learning, 16*(6), 325–340. https://doi.org/10.1108/13665620410550303

Noon, M., Blyton, P., & Morrell, K. (2013). *The realities of work: Experiencing work and employment in contemporary society*. Palgrave Macmillan.

Ocen, E., Francis, K., & Angundaru, G. (2017). The role of training in building employee commitment: The mediating effect of job satisfaction. *European Journal of Training and Development, 41*(9), 742–757.

Ochieng, B., & Ward, K. (2018). Safeguarding of vulnerable adults training: Assessing the effect of continuing professional development. *Nursing Management, 25*(4), 30–35.

Organisation for Economic Co-operation and Development. (1996). *Lifelong learning for all: Meeting of the education Committee at Ministerial Level, 16–17 January 1996*. OECD Publishing. Retrieved from https://www.voced.edu.au/content/ngv:25305

Organisation for Economic Co-operation and Development. (2000). *Economics and finance of lifelong learning*. OECD Publishing.

Organisation for Economic Co-operation and Development. (2006). *Live longer, work longer*. OECD Publishing.

Organisation for Economic Co-operation and Development. (2010). Learning for jobs: Synthesis report of the OECD reviews of vocational education and training. OECD Publishing. Retrieved from Paris: http://www.oecd.org/education/skills-beyond-school/Learning%20for%20Jobs%20book.pdf

Organisation for Economic Co-operation and Development. (2016). *Skills matter: Further results from the survey of adult skills*. https://www.oecd.org/skills/piaac/Skills-Matter-Singapore.pdf

Organisation for Economic Co-operation and Development. (2019). Getting skills right: Future-ready adult learning systems. OECD Publishing. Retrieved from https://doi.org/10.1787/9789264311756-en.

Organisation for Economic Co-operation and Development. (2021). *OECD Skills Outlook 2021*. OECD Publishing.

Organisation for Economic Co-operation and Development. (2022a). *Education GPS (Singapore) adult skills (survey of adult skills, PIAAC, 2015)*. OECD Publishing. Retrieved from https://gpseducation.oecd.org/CountryProfile?primaryCountry=SGP&treshold=5&topic=AS

Organisation for Economic Co-operation and Development. (2022b). Education GPS (Singapore) Student Performance (PISA 2018). Retrieved from Osborne, M., & Borkowska, K. (2017). A European lens upon adult and lifelong learning in Asia. *Asia Pacific Education Review, 18*(2), 269–280. https://doi.org/10.1007/s12564-017-9479-4.

Organisation for Economic Co-operational and Development. (2013). *OECD skills outlook 2013: First results from the survey of adult skills*. OECD.

Osborne, M., & Borkowska, K. (2017). A European lens upon adult and lifelong learning in Asia. *Asia Pacific Education Review, 18*(2), 269–280. https://doi.org/10.1007/s12564-017-9479-4

Pastore, S., Manuti, A., & Scardigno, A. F. (2019). Formative assessment and teaching practice: The point of view of Italian teachers. *European Journal of Teacher Education, 42*(3), 359–374.

Petrović, P., & Živković, D. (2017). Continuing education of hotel employees and their shared vision of the organization. *Hotel and Tourism Management, 5*(1), 85–93.

Phillips, L. A., Baltzer, C., Filoon, L., & Whitley, C. (2017). Adult student preferences: Instructor characteristics conducive to successful teaching. *Journal of Adult and Continuing Education, 23*(1), 49–60. https://doi.org/10.1177/1477971416683488

Prensky, M. (2012). *From digital natives to digital wisdom: Hopeful essays for 21st century learning*. Corwin.

Rienzo, P. D. (2014). Recognition and validation of non formal and informal learning: Lifelong learning and university in the Italian context. *Journal of Adult and Continuing Education, 20*(1), 39–52.

Robson, S. (2012). *Developing thinking and understanding in young children: An introduction for students*. Routledge.

Rose, J. (2017). 'Never enough hours in the day': Employed mothers' perceptions of time pressure. *Australian Journal of Social Issues, 52*(2), 116–130. https://doi.org/10.1002/ajs4.2

Samuel, A., Cervero, R. M., Durning, S. J., & Maggio, L. A. (2021). Effect of continuing professional development on health professionals' performance and patient outcomes: A scoping review of knowledge syntheses. *Academic Medicine, 96*(6), 913–923.

Schuller, T., & Watson, D. (2009). *Learning through life: Inquiry into the future for lifelong learning*. National Institute of Adult Continuing Education.

Sitzmann, T., & Ely, K. (2011). A meta-analysis of self-regulated learning in work-related training and educational attainment: What we know and where we need to go. *Psychological Bulletin, 137*(3), 421–442.

SkillsFuture Singapore. (2020). *500,000 individuals and 14,000 enterprises benefitted from SkillsFuture programmes in 2019*. Retrieved from https://www.skillsfuture.gov.sg/newsroom/500-000-individuals-and-14-000-enterprises-benefitted-from-skillsfuture-programmes-in-2019

SkillsFuture Singapore. (2021a). *My skillsfuture*. Retrieved from https://www.myskillsfuture.gov.sg/

SkillsFuture Singapore. (2021b). *SkillsFuture credit*. Retrieved from https://www.skillsfuture.gov.sg/credit

SkillsFuture Singapore. (2023). *Skills framework for training and adult education*. https://www.skillsfuture.gov.sg/initiatives/training-providers/skills-framework/tae.

Steffens, K. (2015). Competences, learning theories and MOOCs: Recent developments in lifelong learning. *European Journal of Education, 50*(1), 41–59. https://doi.org/10.1111/ejed.12102

Su, Y., Feng, L., & Hsu, C. H. (2018). What influences teachers' commitment to a lifelong professional development program? Reflections on teachers' perceptions. *International Journal of Lifelong Education, 37*(2), 184–198. https://doi.org/10.1080/02601370.2017.1397786

References

Sung, J. (2011). *The Singapore Continuing Education and Training System*. Retrieved from https://www.researchgate.net/publication/258831168_The_Singapore_Continuing_Education_and_Training_CET_system

Sung, J., Loke, F., Ramos, C., & Ng, M. (2011). *You and your work: Skills utilisation in Singapore*. https://www.ial.edu.sg/getmedia/fdc73e72-88ec-40f1-8f84-31227d35f8cf/You-and-Your-Work-Skills-Utilisation.pdf

Taylor, M., & Evans, K. (2009). Formal and informal training for workers with low literacy: Building an international dialogue. *Journal of Adult and Continuing Education, 15*(1), 37–54.

Tennant, M. (1986). An evaluation of Knowles' theory of adult learning. *International Journal of Lifelong Education, 5*(2), 113–122.

Thomas, G., & Thorpe, S. (2019). Enhancing the facilitation of online groups in higher education: A review of the literature on face-to-face and online group-facilitation. *Interactive Learning Environments, 27*(1), 62–71. https://doi.org/10.1080/10494820.2018.1451897

Tyler, M., Choy, S., Smith, R., & Dymock, D. (2014). Learning in response to workplace change. In C. Harteis, A. Rausch, & J. Seifried (Eds.), *Discourses of professional learning: On the boundary between learning and work*. Springer.

UK Commission for Employment and Skills. (2014). *The future of work: Jobs and skills in 2030*. https://www.gov.uk/government/publications/jobs-and-skills-in-2030

UNESCO. (2022a). *Transforming Technical and Vocational Education and Training for successful and just transitions: UNESCO strategy 2022–2029*. Retrieved from https://unevoc.unesco.org/home/UNEVOC+Publications/lang=en/akt=detail/qs=6644

UNESCO. (2022b). *Singapore Skills Development Fund*. Retrieved from https://unevoc.unesco.org/countryprofiles/docs/UNESCO_Funding-of-Training_Singapore.pdf

Winterbotham, M., Vivian, D., Kik, G., Hewitt, J. H., Tweddle, M., Downing, C., et al. (2018). *Employer skills survey 2017: Research report*. Department for Education.

World Economic Forum. (2021). *Upskilling for shared prosperity*. Retrieved from http://www3.weforum.org/docs/WEF_Upskilling_for_Shared_Prosperity_2021.pdf

World Health Organization. (2013). *Transforming and scaling up health professionals' education and training: World Health Organization guidelines 2013*. Retrieved from http://apps.who.int/iris/bitstream/10665/93635/1/9789241506502_eng.pdf

Part II
Singaporean Case Study

This section comprises three chapters that describe and justify the method procedures used in the national case study from Singapore, and present and discuss general findings from the interviews of recent CET graduates and employers about the motivations of working age Singaporeans to participate in CET programs and their perspectives on how they were guarded and supported in making decisions about participating and also the quality of the education experiences and also the quality of the experiences provided by the educators in the tertiary education institutes in which the undertook the programs. Also, data from a national survey that was undertaken to go beyond the cohort of graduates and employers who were interviewed for the project. That survey provided a large database of working at Singaporeans which the interview findings can be considered and validated. The elements of this section, therefore, comprise Chap. 4—*Investigating effective CET provisions to promote employability: Method and procedures*, which provides a detailed overview of the practical inquiry; Chap. 5—*Motivations and affordances for engaging CET*, and Chap. 6—*Effective CET provisions: A national survey*. Together, these chapters provide the overview of and initial findings from the practical inquiry that informed the case study.

Chapter 4
Investigating Effective CET Provisions to Promote Employability: Method and Procedures

Abstract This chapter describes and justifies the method and procedures used for investigating what constitutes effective continuing education and training (CET) provisions in Singapore. These were used to develop a comprehensive case study of current practices of CET and how they might be enhanced. With one of the highest aging populations globally and its primary assets lying in its human resources, Singapore presents a case that is pertinent not only to its own context but also imparts valuable lessons that may be applicable to other regions. Certainly, Singapore's key national economic policy emphasises the importance of its working-age adults' engagement in CET to sustain their employability and across lengthening working lives, and in ways that contribute to their workplaces' continuity and development. Together, these personal and enterprise imperatives play a crucial role in achieving governmental objectives of bolstering a strong economic foundation and maintaining the capacity to deliver the necessary goods and services for the nation state, a scenario likely mirrored elsewhere. Moreover, other concerns are now being echoed about importance of CET as nation states seek to become more self-sufficient and self-reliant in an era of geopolitical challenges.

Consequently, it is increasingly important for nation states to understand what constitutes effective CET provisions and how they might be designed and enacted to achieve these outcomes. Yet, that effectiveness is premised on more than achieving the goals of educational institutions or governmental edicts. Central to the efficacy of CET is its ability to attract participation by, engagement in and achievement of outcomes for working-age adults, and the enterprises in which they are employed. Therefore, instead of viewing CET solely through the lens of individual employability, it is crucial to recognize its role in sustaining enterprise viability and contributing to the fulfillment of social and economic goals within nation-states.

It follows then that to investigate how these processes and outcomes might be understood, this chapter sets out the context, framing, procedures, and broad outcomes of a three-phase research project of CET undertaken in Singapore. In essence, the investigation sought to identify what constitutes effective CET provisions for working age adults. The practical inquiry was enacted through interviews with CET graduates and their employers in Phase 1, followed by a survey in Phase 2 administered to Singaporean working age adults in a range of employment and industry sectors to validate and advance the interview findings. In Phase 3, the consolidated findings from the first two phases were presented to CET educators and administrators who engaged in co-construction of the implications and generation of guidelines for curriculum and pedagogic practices. It is these procedures that are described and elaborated here to inform and justify the approach adopted in this case study, but also to inform how these approaches might be adopted elsewhere.

Keywords Method · Procedures · Case study · Singapore · Singaporeans · Quantitative · Qualitative · Working age adults · Employers · Graduates · Governmental goals · Data analysis · Survey · Guidelines · Effective provisions · Informants · Respondents · Employment

Continuing Education and Training to Sustain Employability

Globally, there is a recognised need for workers to sustain their employability across lengthening working lives as occupational roles transform and workplace requirements change. So, as working life gets longer and the amplitude and frequency of changes to occupational requirements and workplace practices increases, it become imperative to understand how best to sustain that employability. Sustaining it comprises an educational challenge for advancing occupational competence amidst these changes, and in ways that might be distinct from initial occupational preparation (Noon & Blyton, 2007). Several factors, including evolving business needs, technological advancements, changing workplace structures, and a shifting workforce composition, are constantly reshaping and redefining the requirements for remaining employable (Billett, 2006). Equally, the emergence and proliferation of new technologies, particularly electronic ones, and global volatility is being accompanied by an expectation supported by global agencies such as OECD (1996) that is increasingly shifting the responsibility for skills development to individual workers, rather than their employers (UK Commission for Employment and Skills, 2014). However, determining what these skills requirements are and how best they can be learnt, is far from straightforward, and beyond individual efforts alone. Not the least here is because they are often manifested in specific workplaces requirements and practices and subject to constant change. So, these are the educational challenges faced by institutions and teachers providing continuing education and training (CET). These include person-specific needs and readiness, new kinds of knowledge to be learnt, the provision of experiences likely to realise those outcomes, and those being made accessible to working age adults with overlapping family, work, community and educational commitments.

Indeed, the need for effective CET provisions to sustain workers' employability has perhaps never been greater than now. The employability agenda has driven the continuing skill development of workforces to becoming national priorities, including demonstrating currency of competence on regulated professional development across a growing range of occupations. Yet, all of this requires formed and evidence-based actions in terms of policy goals, prescriptions and also practice related initiatives associated with what constitutes effective CET. This chapter describes and justifies the approach taken to secure the empirical basis of what constitutes this national case study, make specific references to the country context of that case study and also the kind of findings that are advanced from it. The chapter commences with a brief section outlining the country context, which is then followed by the detailing of the method and procedures used to gather and analyse data, and arrive at conclusions and recommendations.

In all, the key points in this chapter are as follows:

- There is a need to identify, consider any changes/transformations of educational experiences currently being provided to address the emerging goals for and needs of adults learning across their working lives.
- The efficacy of CET educators and CET provisions are contingent on their engagement with students and links to workplaces.
- Elements of the teaching-learning dyad need to be understood through appraising the experiences and perspectives of working age adults of CET participation.
- Participants were selected to provide grounded data. They comprised of CET graduates and their employers recruited for interviews, a larger sample of working age Singaporeans for a national survey.
- Data analysis was conducted to identify factors facilitating and/or inhibiting CET experiences and to how these can be redressed through CET provisions.
- The impact of an effective CET system on the motivations and engagement of CET students, educators and employers was necessarily investigated.
- Through that process, the expectations and aspirations of a CET system and its educational provisions were elaborated.

Case Study Context

The issues foreshadowed above have led to the realisation that specific kinds of support and educational interventions are required to sustain working age adults' employability across lengthening working lives. Singapore is no exception in this regard, as evidenced by the government's central focus on the ongoing development of the Singaporean workforce through the SkillsFuture agenda. A specific challenge for Singapore lies in determining how its post-secondary educational institutions (PSEIs), including Singapore's five polytechnics and the Institute of Technical Education (ITE), which have traditionally emphasized pre-employment education and training (PET) for young people transitioning from school to the workforce, can play a growing role in supporting the national agenda. This involves providing effective CET provisions while simultaneously engaging in occupations that align with their capacities and interests. The requirements of CET provision are distinct from much of the PSEIs current curriculum, instructional strategies and expertise.

CET students are mostly experienced and competent adult age workers, whose interest and needs are distinct from the younger PET students. They are not novices nor occupationally or workplace naive. They often have greater access to current occupational and work practices than teachers in PSEIs. Also, with their work lives and family commitments, how these adults need to engage with the PSEIs will also be distinct from those in PET programs. However, as in any other country, the CET provision is not wholly new to tertiary education, and many PSEIs are already offering specialist diplomas for working age adult students. Nevertheless, the SkillsFuture agenda and need for employability-related continuing education across the Singaporean workforce suggest that gaps in the scope of existing educational provisions and capacities of teachers in these institutions need to be addressed to realise personal, workplace and national goals.

It follows that there is a need to identify the kinds of educational experiences that are currently being provided and how these might be changed, improved or transformed to address these emerging imperatives. This includes appraising what is afforded CET students by PSEIs and within workplace settings to promote these kinds of adaptable employability outcomes. Such considerations extend to the kinds of curriculum and pedagogic practices that PSEIs need to adopt, how experiences in work settings might be integrated and enhanced and how these two sets of experiences might be integrated to assist CET students further develop their capacities and interests to promote and secure the occupational and workplace adaptability that will sustain their employability. Likely, these sets of experiences comprise how those in CET courses and workplace settings will need to be ordered and integrated in particular ways (i.e., curriculum) that assist students to develop the requirements for occupations and their workplace variations. In addition, pedagogic practices within the CET courses that engender adaptable occupational capacities will need to be identified and enacted. So, central here also is the further development of CET students' personal practices directed towards active engagement and innovation (i.e., adaptation for change). Therefore, a consideration of curriculum and pedagogic practices for PSEIs and their extension to CET students' workplaces, and the development of active and focused approaches to learning by working age adults is needed.

In a report released by the UK Commission for Employment and Skills on the future of work, it was noted that as international competition for innovation continues to increase, focusing on techniques for innovation in education and training will be of great importance across all sectors (UK Commission for Employment and Skills, 2014). It also suggested that employees would need to rely increasingly on further education and lifelong learning initiatives to continually upgrade their existing skills. This situation has long been acknowledged in Singapore.

In his 2015 budget statement, Deputy Prime Minister, Minister for Finance and Chairman of the SkillsFuture Council, Tharman Shanmugaratnam, who became the President of Singapore in 2023, laid out plans for Singaporeans to develop and sustain the skills critical for advancing our economy (Ministry of Finance, 2015). While the SkillsFuture Council has been succeeded by the Future Economy Council (Ministry of Trade and Industry, 2024), its core work remains unchanged. That is:

(i) developing an integrated system of education, training, and career progression for all Singaporeans; (ii) driving industry transformation by overseeing implementation of plans for key clusters through skills development, innovation, productivity and internationalisation strategies; and (iii) fostering a culture of innovation and lifelong learning in Singapore (Ministry of Manpower, 2014).

The importance of lifelong learning was highlighted in a recent report on Singapore's results in the survey of adult skills—a product of the Organisation for Economic Co-operation and Development (OECD) Program for the International Assessment of Adult Competencies. The survey, which has been administered in over 30 countries, provides a snapshot of adults' proficiency in three key information-processing skills: (i) literacy (i.e., the ability to understand and respond appropriately to written texts), (ii) numeracy (i.e., the ability to use numerical and mathematical concepts) and (iii) problem solving in technology-rich environments (i.e., the capacity to assess, interpret and analyse information found, transformed and communicated in digital environments). The findings highlighted that the wide gap between the most and least proficient skilled adults in Singapore. Indeed, Singapore stands out as the country in which variability in literacy is greatest, at 77 score points, compared to the OECD average of 62 score points. Whilst the report attributes the low proficiency among Singapore's older populations to the effects of age, low levels of educational attainment and language barriers, it underscored the importance of lifelong education.

Following from the advent of the SkillsFuture policy initiative and their accompanying emphases on the PSEIs as providers of CET, there is an increased interest in the transformation and professionalisation of those who organise programs in and enact CET (Institute of Adult Learning, 2017a; SkillsFuture Singapore, 2023). Specifically, there is an enhanced emphasis on creating opportunities for working age adults to upskill and reskill through CET, including learning through their work activities and in their workplaces. Perhaps more than other educational sectors and provisions, the efficacy of CET educators and providers, programs and approaches are contingent on their links to workplaces and their students who work in them. It follows that to better understand what is required to be learnt through CET programs and how best this knowledge can be learnt, it is necessary to identify and capture the requirements of both CET students and their employers, as their perspectives will be central to effective CET provisions and students' engagement in them.

As the emphasis on CET precipitated by the SkillsFuture initiatives is quite recent, there is limited data on the effectiveness of the educational provisions that can enhance Singaporean workers' ongoing learning and employability. Yet, given the salience of the acquisition and utilisation of deep skills (Committee on the Future Economy, 2017) and lifelong learning (Government of Singapore, 2016), it is pivotal that we understand more about how: (i) policy goals associated with the development of adult students' work skills should be formulated and (ii) curriculum and pedagogic practices identified and enacted that can lead to developing the required critical skill sets through CET provisions. Concurrently, as the adult education sector moves towards greater professionalisation (Institute of Adult Learning,

2017a, b), it is important to elaborate and validate what roles and how best PSEIs and their educators can play in these processes, including the development of CET educators' professional competencies.

Earlier investigations demonstrate the need for continuing professional development of educators to maintain current and effective work skills can be driven by requirements of professional standards and continuing registration procedures (Friedman & Phillips, 2004). However, this impetus has been largely confined to that of medical professionals (e.g., Brigley et al., 1997; Ferguson, 1994; Griscti & Jacono, 2006; Rouse, 2004; World Health Organization, 2013), while less is known about the CET educators in the Training and Adult Education (TAE) sector (e.g., Billett, 2001; Cranton, 1996; Smith et al., 2003), the diverse ways they work and the goals they need to achieve can be realised.

The research project[1] delves into and thoroughly examines facets of the teaching-learning dyad, involving both learners and those delivering educational experiences. This exploration specifically focuses on the experiences of working-age adults regarding their need for and reasons behind participating in CET. The study also explores the reported experiences they encountered and those they desire to encounter. Beyond exploring CET students' experiences, it also investigated employers of CET graduates and CET educators' perspective of these purposes and practices. Employers' perspectives were largely and unsurprisingly directed to their specific enterprise needs, which were not always aligned with those of the adult participants, who had wider personal purposes. The data gathering also sought to capture CET educators' perspectives regarding the facilitators and barriers to CET teaching and learning. This extended to how their professional development in the CET terrain can be realised, but with a particular emphasis on those working in PSEIs. By examining the CET experience from both perspectives of the teaching-learning dyad, the personal, professional and organisational dimensions of the CET experience can be illuminated and elaborated, albeit in just some of its many contexts and possibilities.

Exploring Effective CET Provisions: A Singaporean Investigation

The research project specifically examined: (i) the nature of change CET students in their personal and professional lives beyond graduation from their CET courses, (ii) how the CET providers can more effectively meet both adult students and employers' needs through the CET courses, (iii) the professional competencies required of adult educators, (iv) realising the continuing professional development

---

[1] The project was funded through the Workforce Development Applied Research Fund of SkillsFuture Singapore, but was conducted in a wholly independent way, albeit guided by an advisory committee that was initiated by the research team.

Exploring Effective CET Provisions: A Singaporean Investigation

opportunities for CET educators, and (v) how working Singaporean adults need to engage in learning-related activities to secure their employability.

The overarching question guiding the research project was:

> What are the kinds of capacities and institutional practices required for CET educators to provide accessible and effective CET provisions for Singapore's adult working population and how might these capacities be developed?

The informing sub-questions were:

> What are the learning needs and requirements of adults in Singapore to remain employable across lengthening working lives?
>
> What kinds of curriculum models, practices and pedagogic strategies will best meet the needs of these learners?
>
> How can the educational capacities required to meet these needs be developed within and across the PSEIs?
>
> How should adult Singaporeans come to engage in the task of securing their employability?

The project's practical inquiry comprised three phases of qualitative and quantitative procedures in the gathering and analysis of data. These procedures included (i) using pre-interview surveys and interviews with Singaporean worker-informants who have taken CET courses and employers who are supportive of CET in Phase 1, (ii) administering a survey developed from the findings of the first phase to Singaporean working age adults from a range of employment and industry sectors in Phase 2, and (iii) consolidating findings to draw out deductions, followed by a dialogue forum and discussions with CET educators and administrators. Through workshops with these practitioners arose the co-construction of the implications and generation of guidelines for curriculum and pedagogic practices in PSEIs, in Phase 3. Figure 4.1 summarises the procedures associated with each of these three phases. This figure indicates the approach, participants and procedures used in each of the three phases.

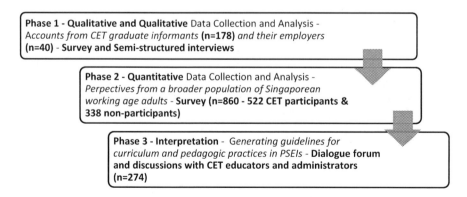

Fig. 4.1 Practical inquiries across the three phases

The research activities were conducted sequentially, including sampling, data collection, and data analysis across the three phases. In the following sections, the research procedures used in each of them are now described and discussed under these phases.

Phase 1: Graduates' and Employers' Perspectives on Effective CET Provisions

In Phase 1, all the graduate interviewees had recently participated in CET programs. They provided qualitative accounts from Singaporean working age adults about their experiences in and through their CET programs that have supported their learning in and for working life were secured and also the contributions of CET courses/programs. A qualitative approach was used to capture the factors contributing to that learning. Factors in individuals' personal histories prior to, during and after their CET experiences identified these factors. The Phase 1 data gathering included retrospective interviews with recent graduates from CET courses/programs from the 5 Singaporean polytechnics who informed about their learning experiences within and outside of the CET courses/programs, and their contributions to their on-going employability. These informants were drawn from a mix of long-standing and recent CET courses with different modes of education and certification (i.e., full qualification or modular). The actual data gathering comprised identifying and contacting potential informants, securing their consent to engage, having them complete a pre-interview survey (*see* Appendix 4.1) and then conducting an interview using a series of open questions (*see* Appendix 4.2). The schedule of the interview questions and the accompanying survey were developed from the research questions and were subsequently trialled and refined with a sample of working-age adults. At the interviews, the informants first completed the pre-interview survey about their backgrounds, interests, reasons for CET courses, and the degree by which they had achieved their goals by participating in them. They then participated in a semi-structured interview to elaborate on their survey responses and discuss their views about CET participation and experience of CET teachers, CET course provision and its future. The informants offered insights into what motivated them to enrol in CET courses/programs and what constituted effective provisions of CET from their perspectives. The data analysis focused on identifying facilitating and/or inhibiting factors in their CET experiences and to how these factors can be developed through CET provisions.

Criterion-based sampling was used to identify participants who were well positioned to provide detailed information on their experiences in and perspectives of CET. This included their suggestions for how these provisions might be best designed, enacted and experienced to support the ongoing employability of working-age Singaporeans. Thus, access to CET graduates with reasonable periods of working experience was required. That is, those who had graduated from CET courses/

programs within 4 years from the project's commencement and possessed at least 5 years' working experience. In this way, all the informants were highly qualified to comment on the quality of the educational experience afforded to them including how the courses/programs were taught. The selection process resulted in 178 graduate informants interviewed for the project had graduated from CET programmes within 4 years from the time of study.

Phase 1 also engaged a selection of employers (N = 40), seeking their views about CET, its worth and potential from their perspective, and their willingness to support their employees in CET. It was important to identify these insights, as how supportive employers are can influence their employees' access and success in CET. Employers also stand to benefit directly from any gains in knowledge and skills of their employees, although there will always be tension between the degree by which such programs should focus on enterprise specific outcomes and ones that are more generally applicable across enterprises and within the occupational sector.

The informants selected (i.e., graduates and employers) were those best positioned to provide grounded data about the requirements for sustaining employability and means by which these requirements can be learnt. These informants were confronting the issues that this project sought to illuminate and address. The background demographics of the informants are summarised in Table 4.1. This table presents data of the informants' gender, age, highest qualification, industry sector and enterprise size. These data are then presented through a series of characteristics and their numbers and percentages are provided in the right columns.

As presented in Table 4.1, the graduates comprised 63.6% male (n = 112) and 36.4% female (n = 64), who have a range of educational backgrounds. However, this sample is considered highly educated in the Singaporean context as they all report holding at least a post-secondary certificate, whether a diploma, degree, or postgraduate degree. Importantly, there is a significant difference in the level of participation in education across the ages of the national population with older citizens having far less tertiary education than their younger counterparts. Hence, the educational profile of these informants are quite well aligned with the profile of the current working age population (Singapore Department of Statistics, 2022). The informants are employed from across a range of industry sectors, but predominately from education, health, and professional services. About half of them worked for multinational companies (MNCs) with above 200 staff, with the rest working in small and medium enterprises (SMEs) ranging from less than 20 to 200 staff.

Of the 40 employers, 24 are male and 16 are female. The youngest is 21 and the oldest 62 years, with the mean age at 44. Most of them have either undergraduate or postgraduate degrees as their highest educational qualifications. These employers work in companies of different sizes, with 14 of them from MNCs and 26 of them from SMEs. These enterprises are in a range of industry sectors including manufacturing, built environment, modern services, essential domestic services, and lifestyle services. Of these 40 informants, more than half of them (n = 29) were responsible for their employees' professional development. Open-ended questions were used to ascertain responses about their responsibilities in helping their employees remain employable.

Table 4.1 Characteristics of graduate and employer informants

Background	Characteristics	Graduates (n = 178)		Employers (n = 40)	
		n	%	N	%
Gender	Female	64	36.4	24	60.0
	Male	112	63.6	16	40.0
Age	21–29	30	17.8	4	10.0
	30–39	42	24.9	10	25.0
	40–49	57	33.7	16	40.0
	50+	40	23.7	10	25.0
Highest qualification	O levels/NITEC[a] or higher	0	0.0	4	10.3
	Diploma	52	29.7	5	12.8
	Degree	70	40.0	15	38.5
	Postgraduate	53	30.3	15	38.5
Industry sector of current job	Manufacturing	12	6.8	4	10.0
	Built environment	20	11.3	5	12.5
	Trade & Connectivity	12	6.8	9	22.5
	Essential domestics services	66	37.3	9	22.5
	Professional services	35	19.8	10	25.0
	Lifestyle	16	9.0	3	7.5
	Others	16	9.0	4	10.0
Workplace size	< 20 staff	34	19.9	10	25.0
	20 to 100	31	18.1	14	35.0
	101 to 200	21	12.3	2	5.0
	>200 staff	85	49.7	14	35.0

[a]The National ITE Certificate (NITEC) is a vocational and technical education qualification awarded by ITE Singapore. The NITEC courses are designed to provide students with practical skills and knowledge in various technical and vocational fields. These courses aim to equip students with the necessary skills to enter the workforce directly after completion or to continue their education at a higher level

Phase 2: Verifying and Elaborating Findings Through a National Survey

The findings from Phase 1 interviews were used to develop, pilot and administer an online survey to verify and elaborate the findings from the first phase. This allowed further and deeper exploration of what constitutes effective CET provisions with a larger sample of working age Singaporeans and identify patterns using quantitative approaches. So, the aim of Phase 2 was to understand how CET is viewed by a larger sample of working age Singaporeans, including those who have not taken any form of CET. This data gathering was enacted using an online survey that included items on the expectations of CET and the learning needs and requirements of working age Singaporeans. Furthermore, data on respondents' views about subsidies and whether these made a difference to their willingness to participate in CET were also gathered. The survey comprised six sections gathering data and responses about: (i) demographic background, (ii) participation in CET, (iii) mode of attendance and delivery of CET course, (iv) CET teachers and students, (v) assessments, and (vi) future provision of CET. It provided both quantitative and qualitative data. The survey items consisted of a series of multiple-choice, Likert-scaled and open-ended questions. Five-point Likert scales were used to measure, for example, the effectiveness of graded assessment formats, the degree of achieving the purposes for participating in CET. Table 4.2 provides a summary of the items.

The items in the survey gathered demographic information in the first section about age, gender, highest qualifications, industry sector and current employment status. The next five sections invited responses to a set of items arising from interview data about (i) participation in CET including support facilitating that participation, and (ii) views/experiences with CET courses, including delivery, teaching and learning, assessments and future provision of CET.

In developing and refining the survey instrument, iterations of the survey were developed through discussions, including tentative findings and cycles of testing the instrument on colleagues. Only when there was consensus that the instrument was clear and accessible was the online survey administered. To attract respondents, those who provided their email addresses were entitled to participate in a lucky draw to win one of a hundred $100 shopping vouchers. In addition, to gain the participation of older Singaporeans, strategies such as taking electronic tablets or hard copies to the communities were also undertaken.

The survey was administered nationally. The goal was to capture the views of a representative sample of Singaporean workers, not only those who were graduates of CET programmes of PSEIs. The sample of respondents was obtained through circulating an invitation through electronic means in a number of databases of potential respondents, including the alumni list from two of the polytechnics, trade associations' contact lists, professional associations, personal and professional contacts and web announcements. Over 1000 responses were received, and 860 useable surveys were analysed. Table 4.3 summarises the characteristics of these respondents and is organised in a similar way to Table 4.1.

Complete survey respondents comprised 55% males (n = 466) and 45% females (n = 388). Respondents' age range was widely distributed from 21 years old to over 50 years old. As a cohort of informants, they report being more highly qualified than the average adult Singaporean population that is only educated up to secondary school education (Department of Statistics Singapore, 2021), although that is made aberrant within age population and mainly work as professionals, managers, executives, and technicians (PMET). Of these respondents, 60.7% (n = 522) reported having engaged in CET programmes, overwhelmingly through public providers (e.g., PSEIs; 85% of them), while 39.3% (n = 338) did not. Of those who indicated that they had participated in a CET course, the kind they had attended was not stated, hence it is presumed they included CET courses ranging from full-qualification programmes (i.e., long courses leading to a certification, diploma, or degree), to short courses, lunch time talks, or other once-off provisions.

Table 4.2 Summary of the survey structure and item examples

Survey section	Examples of questions	Type of question
Background including work and job training	Age, gender, highest educational level	Multiple choice
	Employment status, industry sector, workplace size	Multiple choice
	Effective ways to acquire skills for work	Ranking (up to 3)
Participation in CET	Degree of achieving purposes for participating in CET	Likert scaled
	Essential support to successfully complete a CET course	Multiple choice
	Support given by employer	Ranking (up to 3)
	Support expecting from employer	Ranking (up to 3)
	Expected challenges when participating in CET	Multiple choice
Mode of attendance and delivery of CET course	Preferred time for participation	Multiple choice
	Most convenient/effective mode of CET	Multiple choice
	Reasons for face-to-face/online/combination of both to be effective	Ranking (up to 3)
	Factors associated with effective learning materials	Ranking (up to 3)
	Important CET education experiences	Ranking (up to 3)
CET teachers and students	Characteristics of effective teachers/students	Ranking (up to 3)
Assessments	Effectiveness of graded assessment formats	Likert scaled
	Helpfulness of assessment criteria	Likert scaled
Future provision of CET	Effective workplace actions to support learning	Ranking (up to 3)
	Effective work-based actions by CET providers to support learning	Ranking (up to 3)

These respondents reported being employed in a range of workplaces with different work arrangements, with most of them having official office hours and many of them working in the public sector (44.3%) and observing normal office hours (72.2%). Most of them claimed to be employed full-time (75.3%) with over a tenth of these respondents reported being unemployed (10.8%). They reported working in a range of industry sectors, with 39.5% in the healthcare and education sectors and 30.9% in the professional services, information, communication and technology

Table 4.3 Characteristics of the survey respondents (n = 860)

Variable	Values	N	%
Gender	Female	388	45.4
	Male	466	54.6
Highest qualification	N levels	5	.6
	O levels	10	1.2
	A levels	7	.8
	NITEC	7	.8
	Higher NITEC[a]	3	.4
	Diploma	182	21.8
	Specialist diploma	24	2.9
	Advanced diploma	12	1.4
	Degree	332	39.8
	Postgraduate	253	30.3
Current employment	Employed full time	646	75.3
	Self-employed	62	7.2
	Employed part time	32	3.7
	Unemployed (seeking for work)	21	2.4
	Unemployed (not seeking for work)	93	10.8
	Retired	4	.5
Industry sector	Construction, Architecture, Engineering, Real Estate, Cleaning, Security	71	8.3
	Energy & Chemicals, Precision Engineering, Marine & Offshore, Aerospace, Electronics	54	6.3
	Food services, Retail, Hotels, Food manufacturing	60	7.1
	Healthcare, Education	336	39.5
	Logistics, Air/Sea/Land/Public Transport, Wholesale Trade	67	7.9
	Professional Services, Information, Communication and Technology and Media, Financial Services	263	30.9
Occupational category	Administration and support workers	208	29.4
	Agricultural and fishery workers	2	.3
	Associate professionals and technicians	76	10.7
	Cleaners, labourers, and related workers	3	.4
	Professionals	287	40.6
	Plant and machine operators and assemblers	7	1.0
	Legislators, senior officials and managers	81	11.5
	Service and sales workers	43	6.1

[a]The Higher National ITE Certificate is awarded by ITE Singapore. It is a vocational and technical education qualification designed for individuals who have completed the NITEC (National ITE Certificate) or its equivalent. The Higher NITEC qualification is typically a two-year full-time program that combines classroom instruction with practical training. It is aimed at preparing students for entry-level positions in their chosen field or providing a pathway for further education, such as pursuing a diploma or other advanced qualifications

and media and financial services sector. A small percentage of them work in other sectors like construction, logistics, and hotel sectors. An even smaller number come from the service and sales industries. Finally, about 40% classify themselves as professionals, about 30% are administrators and support workers, and about 20% are managers, senior officials, and technicians. So, whilst not wholly representative of the working age Singaporean population, the respondents were well distributed across gender and age and represented a range of industry sectors and occupations within them. In this way, the sample, whilst not perfect, provided a range of insights from the perspectives of many working age Singaporeans.

Descriptive analysis (i.e., frequency counts) was conducted with the survey data, identifying patterns of responses to be presented in tables and graphs. The results of this survey were reported and discussed in Chap. 6—*Towards an effective, accessible and scalable CET provisions: A national survey*—in this book.

Phase 3: Advancing CET Provisions

In Phase 3, CET educators and administrators engaged with these findings and, through collaborative processes co-constructed guidelines for curriculum and pedagogic practices in the post-secondary educational institutions and how Singaporeans needed to engage as learners across working lives. The aim of Phase 3 was to gain feedback on and identify ways of enacting the kinds of changes being advanced by informants in the first two phases from CET educators and administrators. To realise this goal, key findings from Phases 1 and 2 about what graduates from CET programmes and working age Singaporeans reported as effective CET provisions were presented to CET educators and administrators who engaged in group deliberations. This phase was undertaken to allow these practitioners to contribute their perspectives and understandings in response to these findings and to communicate what needs to occur for the translation of these findings into practice.

Six workshops and three webinars were conducted with 274 CET educators and administrators enlisted from three sources. It should be noted that this data gathering phase occurred during the Covid period when Singapore was in lockdown and all these events had to occur online. The process used was that firstly a key government agency associated with continuing education and training (i.e., Institute for Adult Learning) sent an electronic direct mailer (EDM) to members of their Adult Educators' Network. Second, a cohort of Singaporean postgraduate students and recent graduates in the field were sent the EDM, as were sent to all polytechnics in Singapore—Ngee Ann Polytechnic, Temasek Polytechnic, Republic Polytechnic, Singapore Polytechnic, and Nanyang Polytechnic. In total, 274 CET educators and administrators participated in these workshops and webinars.

Each online workshop commenced with a 20-min presentation on the findings of Phases 1 and 2. The participants, who had been given a worksheet with three focus questions, were divided into breakout groups in which they discussed their responses to those questions. Thereafter, the entire group reconvened to share and discuss their responses. For the webinars, the presentation of the findings of Phases 1 and 2 was prefaced with a talk on workplace learning. Subsequently, the participants shared their perspectives on the findings. The sessions were recorded through Zoom. Thereafter, the sessions were transcribed, and the transcripts were analysed thematically and organised into vignettes to illustrate the data that consisted of participants' individual and collective stories.

Ten vignettes were generated from the CET educators and administrators' discussions over the nine sessions (*see* Appendix 4.3). They are short stories that capture key aspects of the responses from the CET educators and administrators, including their struggles and successes in their roles. Some of these vignettes capture individual stories, whilst others are a composite of multiple stories. They provide qualitative accounts of key issues faced by CET educators and administrators today. The vignettes were categorised into five main themes/requests: (i) support for students before and after the course, (ii) support from employers, (iii) support from administrators, (iv) coping with the new online education provisions, and (v) skills adult educators need today. These vignettes provided glimpses into the complex work of Singaporean CET educators and some of the challenges they face. These educators, and those who are administering CET courses and programmes, must constantly adapt to changes in demand for courses and the qualities required of these enactments, government policies, and priorities, and in working collaboratively with students, employers, and administrators.

Ethics

Ethical approval was sought and obtained by the Institutional Review Boards of Griffith University (GU ref. no: 2018/850) and Republic Polytechnic (HSR-CED-F-2018-020). To ensure confidentiality and privacy, informed consent was secured, and explanation of the procedures and participants' rights was provided prior to commencing the interviews. Participants' permission was also sought to record the interviews. Further, to maintain participants' confidentiality and anonymity, names were removed throughout reports and publications when excerpts of interview data are presented.

Applicability, Contribution and Impact of the Research

The project's applicability was premised upon four factors. Firstly, the informants selected (i.e., graduates and employers) were those best positioned to provide grounded data about the requirements for sustaining employability and means by which these requirements can be learnt. These informants were confronting the issues that this project sought to illuminate and address. Secondly, the research sought to build upon the provision of and experiences within existing CET programs offered by the 5 polytechnics as a platform to offer practical and viable options for changing CET provisions and how they are supported by educators within PSEIs. Thirdly, engaging with educators from within PSEIs as co-constructors of educational responses meant that the applicability of what they proposed was likely to be high and relevant to those working within these institutions and this process also commenced generating commitments to propose practices. Fourthly, the research design sought to illuminate and validate within each phase of its progress.

This project was developed from presentations to, questions from and discussions with PSEI administrators and teachers about the challenges they need to confront for responding effectively to the national governmental agenda (i.e., SkillsFuture) and meeting the needs of CET students. In this way, the project was well aligned with the national thrust to promote sustainable employability within the Singaporean workforce. In doing so it complemented and augmented initiatives within the national agenda and by engaging with key stakeholders whose understandings and commitment are essential to realising successful outcome for this agenda. Consequently, the research project contributed directly to a research thrust associated with supporting and sustaining Singaporeans adults' learning across working life.

The impact of this project was vouchsafed by its processes, focused outcomes and guidelines that were developed by well-positioned informants (i.e., graduates and employers), through engaging broadly with all five polytechnics and advanced by those who must implement them (i.e., PSEIs teachers). Through it, these informants and those who implement the findings were engaged in an iterative development process. This led to guidelines that are relevant to learning and employability of CET students thereby promoting their impact in the institutions and staff who were involved in the project. Furthermore, since these guidelines were formulated by the individuals responsible for their implementation, and the Phase 3 processes involved engagement with teachers across all major Singaporean PSEIs, the conditions were favourable for achieving the desired impacts.

Moreover, by investigating the impact of an effective CET system on the motivations and engagement of CET students, educators and employers, this study illuminated the expectations and aspirations of what working age adults and their employers want of a CET system and its educational provisions. Further, as Singapore seeks to professionalise the TAE sector, the findings from this study also served to inform and had impact on this process of professionalisation.

An associated impact was the development of research expertise within the polytechnic sector. As part of the engagement with the five polytechnics, staff members were invited to join the research team, specifically with the goal of enhancing their research-related skills, which includes designing and conducting a research project and publishing findings. The aim was to provide professional development opportunities for these staff and build research capacity within these PSEIs.

In all, the study offered insights into how individuals, employers, PSEIs and policymakers understand and support effective CET provisions, including the professional development of CET educators that are central to key government imperative and processes (i.e., SkillsFuture agenda). Therefore, its take-up is likely to be strong. Further, the findings of this study also contributed to understanding the policy effects of that policy agenda in advocating for mindset shifts and culture change in public and private sectors as nations like Singapore seeks to focus on the development of skills and fostering a culture of lifelong learning and education.

Limitations

There are limitations within this investigation. First, the sample of CET graduates was restricted to Singapore-based participants who were purposively selected using a set of criteria (i.e., graduated from CET programmes and the subsequent case within 4 years from the project's commencement and possessed at least 5 years of working experience). The participants predominantly were working in education, health, and professional services sectors. Thus, the sample has insufficiently covered working age adults from the lower income groups, despite research indicating that it is often this group that have the least access to CET (Geertshuis, 2011) and have the most challenges with further education (Mannay & Morgan, 2013). The sample from Phase 1 engaged informants who had the capacity to take an additional diploma or were employers, while the sample from Phase 2 was disproportionately skewed towards those who had at least a diploma as their highest qualification. In contrast, adults working in lower paid manual jobs, such as cleaners, labourers, and machine and plant operators and assemblers, were under-represented. This is even though it has been estimated that about 10–12% of the resident households belong to this group, unable to meet their basic needs in the form of clothing, food, shelter, and other essential expenditures (Donaldson et al., 2013), and they are the ones who are most in need of the benefits that CET can provide. As shown by Lee and Morris (2016), this group of low-paid/low-skilled workers do not benefit much from the system of lifelong learning in Singapore meant to improve incomes and enhance socioeconomic mobility. This group of Singaporeans may not always have the capacity to "upskill" or find work as they have other challenges to deal with because of poverty. Because of their life circumstances, their perspectives of what makes effective CET may be significantly different from the middle- or higher-income groups. Moreover, it is this group that has been found to engage in the least amount of CET (Sung et al., 2011). It is encouraging that the findings in Phase 2 indicated that, generally, respondents recognised that this group of working age Singaporeans are most in need of subsidies and agree that they should be prioritised in receiving subsidies. In summary, it is advisable that future studies should make more deliberate effort to study how our current CET policies and provisions cater to the low-income and low-skilled group.

Second, the interview data comprised self-reports, making them prone to recall and response biases. Third, participants' list of motivations for participating CET, factors facilitating and inhibiting their attendance, and the qualities of effective CET teachers were not exhaustive and are not representative of CET students per se. Due to these limitations, the findings can only report what these informants advised. This research project was also limited by using a web-based survey that restricted the length and types of questions that could be asked, in addition to making assumptions about the technological confidence of participants.

Thirdly, and as already discussed, the data gathering, analysis and findings are drawn from comprehensive case comprising one country which, like all the others has a particular set of institutional, economic and social structures, as well as being a particular point in its development. It is a relatively young country. So, there can be no claims about generalisations from findings in this study directly to other nation states, or workers and CET systems within them. However, this case is germane given the strong focus in this nation state of advancing the ongoing skills currency and development of its adult workforce.

Investigating Effective CET Provisions

This research project that informs many of the chapters of this monograph aimed to explore the qualities of effective provisions of CET provided through PSEIs that are accessible, effective, and targeted to meet the needs of working age Singaporeans and their workplaces. This was achieved by capturing, analysing, and reconciling the perspectives of recent CET graduates, employers, and a broader sample of working-age Singaporeans. The goal was to identify the purposes for which Singaporeans participate in CET, the enabling factors for their participation, the desired quality of learning experiences, ways in which CET educators can enhance the learning experiences of CET students, and the optimal engagement strategies for adult learners. This included identifying facilitators and barriers to their participation and successful completion, and achievement of their purposes for engaging in their courses and programmes. The project adopted a 'mixed methods' approach comprising a combination of qualitative and quantitative procedures for the gathering and analysis of data. The practical inquiries were structured in three phases.

Overall, the findings from Phase 1 set out some basis for understanding the purposes for which working age adults engage in CET programs by gaining access to the perceptions of graduates and employers who have either directly or vicariously experienced these programs as elaborated in Chaps. 5 and 7 in this volume. This includes their identifying and ranking sets of factors about their participation and the quality of the CET programs (Chap. 5—*Motivations and affordances for engaging in CET*), including the means of accessing courses, engaging with teaching staff and peers, the desired qualities of CET educators, and how working age Singaporeans should come to participate in these educational provisions (Chap. 7—*Effective CET provisions: Perspectives from graduates and employers*). Noteworthy throughout is that there are complex sets of interdependent factors. Working age adults have both personal and professional purposes for participating in CET. Their ability to participate is founded upon the accessibility of the course provisions, locations and ease of access, support from within family to manage those commitments, and the valuing of participating in face-to-face provisions when it is needed and interacting with peers. Equally, complexity is found in the requirements of their teachers to be both occupationally competent and effective educators, and they themselves needing to be both independent but also interdependent learners.

Accessing a larger sample of working age Singaporeans in Phase 2 has enabled tentative findings from that original and smaller cohort to be assessed, elaborated, and extended as reported through their responses to the survey (*see* Chap. 6—*Towards an effective, accessible and scalable CET provisions: A national survey*). This led to a set of conclusions about the purposes for, practices of, and means of engaging in CET. Quite purposefully, the investigation first gathered this kind of data from those who were recipients of CET provisions. What they point to is the importance of a CET system that not only extends across the range of PSEIs but is supported by the Singapore government and the community, in particular families and workplaces and in the engagement and actions of individual Singaporeans. In this way, although centred on provisions offered through PSEIs, what emerges is an ecosystem that supports the provision of CET which extends far beyond what those institutions planned for, enact, and manage. However, it is these institutions, through their existing provisions and prospects for change, that much of this systematic provision of CET will need to be enacted (*see* Chap. 2—*Practice and policy implications for CET: A systemic approach*).

In the third and final phase of the project, teachers and administrators from educational institutions responded to the tentative findings from the first two phases of the project. This allowed the broad recommendations to arise. These included (i) provision of informed and impartial pre- and post-course student counselling, (ii) opportunities for collaborations prior to, during, and after CET programmes, (iii) expanding the professional profile of adult educators, and iv) regulation of the processes and outcomes of CET to ensure quality provisions (*see* Chap. 8—*Advancing CET provisions: Perspectives of educators and practitioners*).

In sum, the following points are advanced:

- There is a need to identify the kinds of educational experiences currently being provided and how these might be changed, improved or transformed to address the emerging imperative of adults learning needing to continually across their working lives.
- Perhaps more than other educational sectors and provisions, the efficacy of CET educators and providers, programs and approaches are contingent on their engagement with students and links to their workplaces.

- The practical investigations explored elements of the teaching-learning dyad through appraising the experiences of working age adults, including their need for and purposes for participation in CET, whether these were realised and the experiences they encountered and would like to encounter.
- The data analysis included identifying factors that facilitate and/or inhibit their CET experiences and to how these can be redressed through CET provisions.
- Graduate and employer informants were selected to provide grounded data about the requirements for sustaining employability and means by which these requirements can be learnt.
- An online survey verified and elaborated the first phase findings from, allowing a further and deeper exploration of what constitutes effective CET provisions with a larger sample of working age adults including identifying patterns generated by quantitative approaches.
- These interviewees and survey respondents reported being employed in a range of workplaces with different work arrangements.
- The project's validity and applicability are premised on: (i) the kinds of informants selected as being well positioned to provide grounded data; (ii) the research procedures built on the provision of and experiences within existing CET programs, including support of educators; (iii) engaging with educators as co-constructors of educational responses aimed to enhance the findings' applicability; and (iv) the research design illuminate and validated findings in each phase.
- By investigating the impact of an effective CET system on the motivations and engagement of CET students, educators and employers, the expectations and aspirations of what working age adults and their employers want of a CET system and its educational provisions are elaborated.

Importantly, key project findings collectively made important advances and contributions to how the provision of CET in Singapore might proceed. Thus, a systematic approach is a constructive way to draw together these findings to see each element as a part of a CET system which must be addressed, not just individually, but systematically, as each part is interdependent with the others. A systematic perspective can be helpful for elucidating the complexity of CET provisions—as a system whose purposes and outcomes are shaped by its settings, rules, roles, and actors *(see* Chap. 2—*Practice and policy implications for CET: A systemic approach).*

Appendices

Appendix 4.1—Phase 1 Pre-Interview Survey

Section A: About you

Full name:	
Email address:	Contact number:

(Only for administration of token gift)

1) Gender: ☐ Male ☐ Female

2) Age:

	20 – 24		25-29		30-35		35-39		40-44		45-49
	50-54		55-59		60-64		65-69		70 & above		

3) What is your highest education qualification and title? (E.g., Diploma of ….)

☐ N levels ☐ O levels ☐ A levels ☐ NITEC ☐ Higher NITEC ☐ Diploma

☐ Degree ☐ Postgraduate

Title of your highest education qualification (e.g., Diploma of ….):

_____

Section B: Your work and job training

4) We want to learn about your work in the last 5 years and how you have learnt for and through your work.

Current job title		Industry sector	
Duration of employment	Year(s) [e.g., 4 years 2 months]		
Previous job title		Industry sector	
Duration of employment	Year(s)		
Previous job title		Industry sector	
Duration of employment	Year(s)		

5) What is the size of your current organization? (Please tick one)

☐ < 20 staff ☐ 20 to 100 ☐ 101 to 200 ☐ >200 staff

6) What is the main mode of your work? (Please tick one)
☐ Office hours ☐ Shift work ☐ Weekends ☐ Self-employed ☐ Freelance ☐ Part-time

7) On average, how many hours do you

a. Travel to and from work per day?	
b. Work a weekday, including over-time?	
c. Work on a weekend?	

(continued)

8) Please indicate the three (3) most effective ways you acquired the skills for your current or most recent job?

How you acquired the skills for your current or most recent job	Most effective (Rank Top 3) (1st, 2nd, 3rd)
a. I was mentored by my supervisor	
b. I was supported by my buddy who was more experienced	
c. I attended team meetings/team discussions with my manager/in-house trainer, held in the workplace	
d. I attended in-house training programmes	
e. I attended external training held in the workplace	
f. I attended external training held outside the workplace	
g. I participated in online courses	
h. Other, (please name): _____	

Section C: Your CET course

9) Please provide the name of the CET programme (e.g., Advanced Diploma, Specialist Diploma, SkillsFuture Earn and Learn Programme (ELP), Part-time Diploma, short-course, online course) you have completed most recently and from which institution?

Title of program/course (e.g., Diploma of ….)	Educational institution

10) From whom did you receive financial support for your CET (Tick all that apply):

☐ Employer ☐ Self-sponsored ☐ Family sponsored ☐ Government Subsidies
☐ Others (Please name): _____

11) Do you finance any of your own continuing education and training?
☐ Yes   ☐ No

12) What was your motivation to enrol in that CET course? (Please indicate all that apply and also rank up to three most important reasons) (1st, 2nd, 3rd)

Reasons for enrolling	Tick all that applies	Top 3 Rankings (1st, 2nd, 3rd)
To get a job		
To develop or start my own business		
To try for a different career		
To get a better job		
To get a promotion		
To fulfil a job requirement (e.g., work certification)		
To acquire extra skills for my job		
To get into another course of study		
To get to the next level of education		
To get skills for community/voluntary work		

(continued)

To gain personal development		
Government subsidies (e.g., Skills Future Credit)		
Employer's Support (e.g., study leave)		
Other reason (please specify)		

13) To what degree did you achieve those 3 purposes?

Fully achieved	Partially Achieved	Not really achieved	Too early to tell	My goals were unrealistic

14) What barriers did you face in completing the CET course? (Tick all that applies)

Child-care	Family care	Venue	Travel time	Job	Use of Technology	Course fees	Course requirements	Travel cost	Other - name

15) Which of the following factors kept you going to successfully complete the course?

Family	Friends	Employer	Personal interest	Achieving my motivations/goals	Financial penalties	Subsidies	Other - name

Section D: Mode of delivery of CET course

16) Please indicate the mode of delivery used in the CET course (tick one).

	Face-to-face		Online learning		Combination of face-to-face and online		Others (please name):

17) The following questions assesses the overall effectiveness of the mode of delivery for your CET course.

	Very effective	Effective	Partially effective	Ineffective	NA
A. How effective is this mode of delivery?					
B. How effective was this mode in creating opportunities to interact with other students?					
C. How effective was this mode in providing opportunities to interact with lecturers?					

18) When was your CET course/ programme taken? (Tick all that apply):

Daytime classes	Evening classes	Weekends	Intensive (Full day training)	Self-paced	Other (please name)

19) How convenient was of the timing for you to attend the CET course?

Very convenient	Convenient	Inconvenient	Not at all convenient

(continued)

20) Which is the best way for you to participate in a CET course? (Tick one)
- ☐ Daytime classes   ☐ Evening classes   ☐ Weekends
- ☐ Intensive (Full day training) ☐ Self-paced   ☐ Others (please name): _____

21) How were the course arrangements helpful for your learning experience?

	Very helpful	Helpful	Partially helpful	Not helpful	NA
a. Learning materials					
b. Teaching strategies					
c. Facilitator's experience					
d. Attendance requirements					
e. Lecture Video Recordings					
f. Learning Management System					

Section E: CET course assessments

22) Please indicate the assessment formats used in your course and indicate their effectiveness in assessing your learning.

Assessment formats	Assess effectiveness		
	Effective	Not effective	NA
Short Tests/ Quizzes			
Examinations			
Practicums (work placement)			
Individual Assignments			
Group assignments			
Individual Project			
Group projects			
Practical			
Presentations			
Portfolios			
Other (please name)			

23) How helpful were the assessment criteria?

	Very helpful	Helpful	Partially helpful	Not helpful	NA
a. Topic					
b. Clear guidelines					
c. Fairness					

24) Was there any provision for recognition of prior learning (RPL), exemption or advanced standing?

Were you able to benefit from RPL?			
	YES		NO

Appendix 4.2—Phase 1 Interview Schedule

Individual factors

1. What was a key incident or motivating event that prompted you to enrol in the CET course?
2. What challenges did you encounter in juggling between study and work (and/or family/personal life) when you were taking the CET course/program? [work-life-study balance]
    (a) If there were challenges, what kept you going?
    (b) What were your coping strategies?
3. To what extent did the CET course assist you to realise the purposes (e.g., promotion, work opportunities) you set out to achieve in taking up the course and how?

CET Lecturers

4. How did the CET lecturers teach in ways that were different from your PET/ formal schooling experience (e.g., Secondary school, ITE, Polytechnic, University (undergraduate))?
    (a) If no: Do you think there should be a difference?/How could it be different?
    (b) If yes: Did you like the difference? If so, why?
(a) To what extent did the lecturer: (the boxes here are only visual prompts for interviewer)
5. If there is one piece of advice you could give the lecturers about improving working with adult students, what would it be?

	NA	Occasionally	Sometimes	Frequently
1) Treat you as an adult learner?				
2) Draw on your experience to facilitate learning?				
3) Facilitate peer learning or peer sharing?				
4) Enable self-directed learning?				
5) Use reflection as a form of learning?				
6) Use learning activities you found engaging?				

CET Course Provision Within Institute

6. How were the course arrangements helpful for your learning experience? (e.g., Learning materials, Teaching strategies, Facilitator's experience, Attendance requirements, Lecture Video Recordings, Learning Management System)
7. How helpful were the assessment criteria? (e.g., related to topic, context, clear guidelines and fairness)
8. How could the mode of delivery used in this course be made more convenient to busy working adults, who also have family responsibilities?
9. If there is one thing you could change about the programme, what would it be?

Future Provision of CET

10. There is increasing discussion about CET needing to occur "beyond the classroom". (Examples of "beyond the classroom": workplace, internet, community, augmented reality). What would the provision of CET beyond the classroom look like to you and be helpful for you?

Concluding Remarks

11. Would you recommend the CET course/programme you took, to any of your colleagues or friends? Why?
12. If there is one piece of advice you could give to the next batch of students, what would it be?
13. Do you have any other comments about the learning or training you undertook for your work?

Appendix 4.3—Vignettes for workshops and webinars

Vignette 1—Sharifa
Sharifa works in a polytechnic and her role is to recruit adults for CET programs. One of her key performance indicators is the number of students she recruits. Hence, she is driven to promote the CET courses to enrol more students and additional revenue for the polytechnic. However, there were times where she counselled students and realised that her polytechnic's courses were not suitable for them and a course from another polytechnic would suit students better. She reported feeling conflicted about whether she should advise the potential students about the other courses or try to fulfil her role of promoting her polytechnic's courses to students. She noted an independent counsellor who could advise students based on their needs would be a better arrangement for fairly advising potential CET students.

Appendices

Vignette 2—Mr. Lee

Mr. Lee decided to take a computing course after being retrenched as a banker. As part of the course, he was provided with networking opportunities to help students find employment. Every month, as part of the course, they visited different IT companies in Singapore and attended Zoom meetings where people from the industry share about the latest trends. During one of the company visits, one of the managers was impressed by Mr. Lee's finance knowledge and his many years of experience managing teams at the bank. The manager invited Mr. Lee to apply to work as an IT manager in his company after he completes his course. Mr. Lee was thankful that his education institute had arranged for various activities that allowed him to meet people who are in hiring positions that directly increase his chances of finding a job when he graduates.

Vignette 3—Kelvin

Kelvin taught a CET course to a group of attendees from a company. He was surprised that on the first day of the training, the manager came and emphasised to his staff about the importance of the training. On the last day of the course, the manager also handed out the certificates and congratulated each of his staff. Kelvin has never experienced any management so supportive of their staff training and noted that this endorsement was a strong factor in why the students remained motivated throughout the course. Since that experience, he always encouraged management to visibly support their staff training in one way or another.

Vignette 4—Peter

Peter is an engineering lecturer at a polytechnic. When he wanted to study a Masters degree, his polytechnic paid for the programme and gave him a reduced workload. They also supported him in other CET programs, often paying fully for them. Peter remained loyal to the polytechnic, working for over 15 years for them. He reported that his efforts were always recognised and appreciated by his management and there were ample opportunities to succeed and grow.

Vignette 5—Wei Ling

Wei Ling works as an adult educator for a training institute. Having been informed that she would be teaching a day course on marketing principles to a group of 20 students from a company, she inquired more about the students' profiles and abilities. However, the administration was unable to provide such information to her. At times, she reported feeling like a nuisance to be always asking administrative staff questions to which they seemed either unwilling or unable to respond. On the day of the training, Wei Ling was surprised that many students had little or no background in marketing and believed she was underprepared to teach them. She wished that there was more communication about the students' profiles prior to the commencement of the course.

Vignette 6—Siva

Siva was engaged by a training institution to teach computer programming to a group of trainees. The administration advised him that he had to pass the entire class because they had promised all students that they would not fail the course. Siva believed his authority as a teacher was challenged. How could he agree to pass everyone if he had not even met and taught his students? Furthermore, the administration mandated a particular software to be used to teach his class. Siva preferred another software that he believed to be more suitable. Lastly, the administration told him that, to pass, all students required a minimum of 80% attendance. This requirement also troubled Siva because, from his experience, it was unreasonable to ask working adults for so much commitment. Moreover, his course would be taught online and recorded, so students could watch lessons that they missed, rather than being physically present for all lectures. Because of these expectations, Siva reported being pressured and constrained and could not teach optimally.

Vignette 7—Sarah

Sarah has many years of mostly face-to-face teaching experience. When the Covid-19 pandemic struck, her institution mandated a switch to online teaching via Zoom. Being unfamiliar with online education, she was initially uncertain whether she could manage this switch. To help herself, she asked her colleagues for tips and attended free online training sessions on how to conduct online training. Over time, she gained confidence in online teaching and engaging her students online. Her institution also informed her that it is unlikely they would return to fully face-to-face training because of considerable cost savings from not having to rent training venues. Many students have provided feedback to her that they enjoyed online training as it was more convenient for them. She realises that online education may become the standard mode of CET and hopes that more subsidies can be provided for adult educators to upgrade their online teaching skills.

Vignette 8—Rachel

Rachel realised that many of her students are unfamiliar with online education. She was able to ease their discomfort with online learning by conducting an orientation about online education. During the orientation, she laid out some ground rules, such as that students should turn on the video function if their situation allows for it so that she can get a sense of their understanding and attention and so students can get to know one another. She also introduced them to the online platforms and tools that she frequently uses so that students know what to expect. She found that having such an orientation reduces the anxiety and confusion for her adult learners who are new to online education.

Vignette 9—Wei Song

Wei Song teaches investment skills. His courses are attended by students with a wide range of readiness, with some requiring handholding while others, he claimed, were even more experienced than he was. To cater to his advanced students, he uploads materials for future lessons ahead of time so that they can self-study at their own pace. He reports that student diversity means the demands on the teacher are very high for adult education. Though he needs to put in more effort in planning and organising the course to cater to learners of different abilities, he feels rewarded when he empowers his learners to be independent.

Vignette 10—Rita

Rita worked in events management for over 10 years before becoming a lecturer at a polytechnic. Over time, although her teaching skills increased and improved, she has increasingly lost touch with the industry. Recently, she was given a class of CET students. On the first day, she told her students about her work history and what she knows and does not know. Her teaching style is such that she engages the expertise of the students in class as a resource. So, even though she is not as currently knowledgeable as some of her students, students report enjoying and benefitting from Rita's facilitation of her lessons. Much of this is because they learn from one another and are guided to relevant resources to deepen their learning. The classroom atmosphere is warm and inclusive, and everyone is open to learning from each other as Rita guides them through the course.

References

Billett, S. (2001). *Learning in the workplace: Strategies for effective practice*. Allen and Unwin.
Billett, S. (2006). *Work, change, and workers*. Springer.
Brigley, S., Young, Y., Littlejohns, P., & McEwen, J. (1997). Continuing education for medical professionals: A reflective model. *Postgraduate Medical Journal, 73*(855), 23–26.
Committee on the Future Economy. (2017). *Report of the committee on the future economy, pioneers of next generation* (pp. 22–27). Government of Singapore.
Cranton, P. (1996). *Professional development as transformative learning: New perspectives for teachers of adults*. Jossey-Bass Publishers.
Department of Statistics Singapore. (2021). *Latest highlights*. Retrieved from https://www.singstat.gov.sg/
Donaldson, J. A., Loh, J., Mudaliar, S., Md Kadir, M., Wu, B., & Yeoh, L. K. (2013). Measuring poverty in Singapore: Frameworks for consideration. *Social Space*, 58–66.
Ferguson, A. (1994). Evaluating the purpose and benefits of continuing education in nursing and the implications for the provision of continuing education for cancer nurses. *Journal of Advanced Nursing, 19*(4), 640–646.
Friedman, A., & Phillips, M. (2004). Continuing professional development: Developing a vision. *Journal of Education and Work, 17*(3), 361–376. https://doi.org/10.1080/1363908042000267432
Geertshuis, S. (2011). Paying for community education. *Journal of Adult and Continuing Education, 17*(1), 63–80. https://doi.org/10.7227/JACE.17.1.6
Government of Singapore. (2016). *Formation of the council for skills, innovation and productivity*. Singapore. Retrieved from https://www.moe.gov.sg/news/press-releases/formation-of-the-council-for-skills%2D%2Dinnovation-and-productivity
Griscti, O., & Jacono, J. (2006). Effectiveness of continuing education programmes in nursing: Literature review. *Journal of Advanced Nursing, 55*(4), 449–456.
Institute of Adult Learning. (2017a). *Adult education professionalisation*. Singapore. Retrieved from https://www.ial.edu.sg/join-the-community/adult-educators%2D%2Dprofessionalisation-aep-scheme/benefits.html
Institute of Adult Learning. (2017b). *Training and adult education professional competency model (TAEPCM)*. https://www.ial.edu.sg/find-resources/skills-career-development-advisory/training-adult-education-professionaltaepcm.html
Lee, M., & Morris, P. (2016). Lifelong learning, income inequality and social mobility in Singapore. *International Journal of Lifelong Education, 35*(3), 286–312. https://doi.org/10.1080/02601370.2016.1165747

Mannay, D., & Morgan, M. (2013). Anatomies of inequality: Considering the emotional cost of aiming higher for marginalised, mature mothers re-entering education. *Journal of Adult and Continuing Education, 19*(1), 57–75. https://doi.org/10.7227/JACE.19.1.5

Ministry of Finance. (2015). *Building our future, strengthening social security*. Retrieved from https://www.mof.gov.sg/docs/default-source/default-document-library/singapore-budget/budget-archives/2015/fy2015_budget_statement.pdf

Ministry of Manpower. (2014). *SkillsFuture council begins work: Driving national effort to develop skills for the future*. Retrieved from https://www.mom.gov.sg/newsroom/press-releases/2014/skillsfuture-council-begins-work-driving-national-effort-to-develop-skills-for-the-future

Ministry of Trade and Industry. (2024). *The future economy council*. Retrieved from https://www.mti.gov.sg/FutureEconomy/TheFutureEconomyCouncil

Noon, M., & Blyton, P. (2007). *The realities of work* (3rd ed.). Palgrave Macmillan.

Organisation of Economic Cooperation and Development. (1996). *Lifelong learning for all*. OECD.

Rouse, M. J. (2004). Continuing professional development in pharmacy. *Journal of Pharmacy Technology, 20*(5), 303–306. https://doi.org/10.1177/875512250402000509

Singapore Department of Statistics. (2022). *Education, language spoken and literacy*. Retrieved from https://www.singstat.gov.sg/find-data/search-by-theme/population/education-language-spoken-and-literacy/latest-data

SkillsFuture Singapore. (2023). *Skills framework for training and adult education*. https://www.skillsfuture.gov.sg/initiatives/training-providers/skills-framework/tae

Smith, C., Hofer, J., Gillespie, M., Solomon, M., & Rowe, K. (2003). *How teachers change: A study of professional development in adult education*. Retrieved from http://files.eric.ed.gov/fulltext/ED508607.pdf

Sung, J., Loke, F., Ramos, C., & Ng, M. (2011). *You and your work: Skills utilisation in Singapore*. https://www.ial.edu.sg/content/dam/projects/tms/ial/Research-publications/Reports/You%20and%20Your%20Work%20Skills%20Utilisation.pdf

UK Commission for Employment and Skills. (2014). *The future of work: Jobs and skills in 2030*. https://www.gov.uk/government/publications/jobs-and-skills-in-2030

World Health Organization. (2013). *Transforming and scaling up health professionals' education and training: World Health Organization guidelines 2013*. Retrieved from http://apps.who.int/iris/bitstream/10665/93635/1/9789241506502_eng.pdf

Chapter 5
Motivations and Affordances for Engaging in CET

Abstract There are compelling imperatives from governmental and enterprise perspectives for working-age adults to participate in continuing education and training (CET). These are associated, respectively, with them remaining employable across lengthening working lives, having highly skilled national workforces able to sustain the viability and responsiveness of the private and public sector enterprises in which working age adults are employed. Consequently, whether and how adults elect to participate and engage in CET provisions is central to those imperatives being realised. Yet, that participation and engagement is shaped by a range of factors about which these adults make decisions. Unlike in compulsory education that is legislated or has mandated requirements for initial occupation preparation, working age adults' participation in CET (i.e., whether they enrol or not) is largely premised on their interest and imperatives. That participation is likely premised on: (i) the purposes that they want to achieve, (ii) how these provisions are aligned with their needs in terms of accessibility and relevance, and their (iii) readiness to engage. This complex of factors includes opportunities to engage and trade-offs in terms of financial, personal and time commitments. Thus, securing desired levels of participation in CET to support individual employability across working life and workplace viability is partially dependent upon working-ages adults' electing to participate and engage effectively in CET provisions. Drawing on data from the national study, this chapter reports and discusses the findings about what motivates working age adults' participation in CET and the kinds of affordances for supporting their engagement in CET, and the degree by which those motivations are realised. The findings indicated that the recent CET graduates were motivated personally and professionally to take CET courses, and that most of them partially or fully achieved their purposes. Importantly, they report valuing learning not only for instrumental purposes such as employability, but also learning for its own sake. Yet, there was a mix of personal and institutional factors supporting as well as inhibiting their participation and engagement in CET. These findings inform how a provision of CET needs to be positioned to make them attractive and accessible for working age adults.

© The Author(s), under exclusive license to Springer Nature Singapore Pte Ltd. 2024
S. R. Billett et al., *Continuing Education and Training*, Professional and Practice-based Learning 36, https://doi.org/10.1007/978-981-97-2930-2_5

Keywords Participation · Successful completion · Intrinsic motivation · Extrinsic motivation · Intentionality · Family · Workplaces · Adult educators · Work experience · Participation · Educational engagement

Participating in Continuing Education and Training

Accessing, updating, and remaining currently competent with the kinds of occupational and workplace knowledge that working age adults need for personal, social, and economic purposes has become a key priority for the adult population. For these adults, that currency has become an important and necessary resource in the twenty-first century, and that needed for remaining employable is no exception. In the current era, workers of all kinds and classifications are required to adapt to emerging developments in occupational practice, workplace requirements, technologies and ways of working, often necessitating accessing novel kinds and areas of understandings, know-how and dispositions (e.g., valuing). Consequently, critical characteristics expected of workers in this era include an ability to learn, adapt and be responsive to the changing work environment and requirements (e.g., Billett, 2020; Stephenson, 1999). Continuing education and training (CET), therefore, is no longer a nicety, but a necessity for much of the adult population, and particularly those who are of working age. In the dynamic, modern work environment, the rate and scope of change is seemingly increasing constantly to cope with the level of change, individuals must continually learn (Billett, 2006; Roscoe, 2002). As Roscoe (2002) states "… no professional completes their initial training equipped to practice competently for the rest of their life …" (p. 3). Such a realization underpins the fact that workers of all kinds and classifications must remain currently competent to maintain the relevance of their skills and employability (Lester, 1999; Noon et al., 2013;). So, regardless of whether it is through structured experiences in educational institutions or through work-related experiences, or some combination of both, there is a need for working age adults to remain currently competent in their occupational practice and for workplace performances. This is required to remain employable within working age adults' existing occupational field and circumstances of practice.

Additionally, the changing nature of occupations and careers requires workers to be alert to and prepare for change whilst responding to immediate needs and challenges (Browell, 2000). From both governmental and enterprise perspectives, CET serves as a key mechanism to assist workforces in remaining adaptable, competitive, and attuned to the ever-changing demands of the contemporary working life. For adults, this participation is not merely a matter of mandatory professional development; it likely needs to be a conscious and pivotal choice underpinning their ability to remain employable, secure advancement and broaden the applicability of their knowledge in a dynamic employment scenario throughout their careers (Noon et al., 2013). A commitment to intentional learning seems central to enhancing these workers' ability to remain current and respond to frequent changes in the structure and nature of work tasks and goals to ease the transition to new positions and

Participating in Continuing Education and Training

challenges (Billett, 2006, 2022). Thus, the need for effective CET provisions to sustain workers' employability has perhaps never been greater.

Consequently, in response to these challenges, identifying the kinds of educational practices and processes required to secure the ongoing employability of working age adults is now both a personal and institutional (e.g., workplace, government) imperatives. To provide the appropriate educational provisions for these workers, it is important to identify the kinds of experiences required to be provided for CET students by tertiary education providers, and within workplace settings to sustain that employability. Potentially, understanding what motivates working age adults' participation in CET and the kinds of affordances for supporting their engagement in CET is key to providing effective CET provisions, because, ultimately, it is they who decide whether to participate in these educational provisions and in what ways to engage. To this end and drawing on data from the Singaporean research project aiming to align CET provision with the national agenda (i.e., SkillsFuture) in meeting students' and employers' needs (*see* Chap. 4—*Investigating effective CET provisions to promote employability: Method and procedures*), this chapter offers findings, deductions and insights on how to proceed. Specifically, this chapter reports and discusses the project's findings in relation to CET graduates' motivations and affordances for engaging in CET that were provided through detailed interviews.

Its key points are:

- There is a greater need now than ever for effective CET provisions to sustain workers' employability.
- There are both professional and personal reasons for working age adults' participation in CET.
- Trade-offs for CET participation are premised on: (i) the purposes that adults want to achieve, (ii) how these provisions are aligned with their needs in terms of accessibility and relevance, and (iii) their readiness to engage.
- Adults, ultimately, take the initiative to make decisions about and accept the responsibility to engage in CET.
- Understanding what motivates working age adults' CET participation and what educational experience can sustain their interests is important for its efficacy.
- Purposes for CET participation were partially or fully achieved, in the main.
- Understanding factors leading to the achievement of CET participation purposes is important.
- There is a complex of personal and work factors that assist and enable successful CET completion.
- Engagement in a combination of online and face-to-face interactions is the most preferred way of supporting working age adults' learning in CET programs.
- Desired qualities of CET educators are a combination of competence in educational practices and relevant industry experiences.
- Educators' capacity to demonstrate their teaching material with relevant industry examples is valued.
- Workplaces' inadequate support jeopardises realising enterprises' and national CET goals and places an unfair expectation of and burden on CET institutions.

Motivations and Affordances for CET Participation and Engagement

While governments and enterprises can create policies and opportunities, it is ultimately the adults themselves who make decisions about and accept the responsibility to engage in CET. This decision is not only instrumental in shaping their career trajectories, but also plays a fundamental role in sustaining the viability of the enterprises in which they work and the communities and organisations they serve. Understanding factors that influence adults' decisions to participate in CET and how this requires a capturing and consideration of range of determinants as these are multifaceted and often unique to each individual. The factors shaping adults' participation in CET are multi-fold, although realizing personal and professional goals is central to their motivation. For the purposes of illuminating and elaborating these factors, data was gathered on the working age informants' backgrounds, attitudes about and purposes for participation and engaging in CET programs as well as barriers to that participation and engagement. The motives to 'get an education' can positively contribute to adults' participation in education, but motivations for doing so are multifaceted. Deckers (2018) defines motivation as, "to be moved into action" or "to be moved into cognition, feeling, and action" (p. xiii). Many informants state that they participate in training because they want to learn something new, though some attend because they must (e.g., Illeris, 2006; Leow et al., 2022).

From some psychological perspectives, motivation is seen the driving force behind our behaviours through which "goal-directed activity is initiated and sustained" (Mulenga & Liang, 2008, p. 291). Enhanced self-motivation is seen to lead to rich human development by promoting self-regulation and psychological well-being (Ahn & Janke, 2011; Ryan & Deci, 2000; Vallerand et al., 1995). Studies on motivation are mostly framed by the premise that human beings are inherently curious, logical and motivated to learn, and motivational problems are often associated with personality traits and situational and/or structural barriers (Ahl, 2006; Legault, 2016; Ryan & Deci, 2000). Carré's model of motivation for adult education (Carré, 2000, 2001) suggests a typology of such motives. These are delineated into two groupings: intrinsic and extrinsic. Intrinsic motives include (i) epistemic (i.e., learning as a source of satisfaction), (ii) socio-affective (i.e., to develop social contacts) and (iii) hedonic (i.e., pleasure taken from space and materials available in the educational setting). For working age adults, these kinds of motivations include sustaining their personal subjectivity (i.e., their sense of themselves) (Billett, 2008; Eteläpelto & Saarinen, 2006) and that being associated with a particular occupational practice (Chan, 2013). Extrinsic motives include those associated with: (i) economic benefits, (ii) prescribed (i.e., when the learning activity is provided for by someone else), (iii) derivative (i.e., participation to avoid unpleasant activities), (iv) professional-operational (i.e., to develop occupational competencies, knowledge or skills for work activities), (v) personal-operational (i.e., to develop competencies, knowledge or skills required for activities outside the job and working life), (vi) vocational (i.e., demand for skills or symbolic recognition needed to get, preserve or evolve in a job) and (vii) identity-based (i.e., appreciation of one's own subjectivity). The personal interest in being occupationally competent is perhaps not surprising given working age adults' needs to provide shelter, sustenance for themselves and their families, to remain employed, regarded as an effective practitioner and sustain their employability and contributes to their work, professional and social communities.

Perspectives on Motivation to Participate and Engage in CET

Theories in educational gerontology and psychology provide helpful frameworks to understand adults' motivations to participate in educational activities. According to Havighurst (1964), adults' educational activities can be classified into two types depending on the learner's needs: instrumental and expressive. The former is an investment of time and energy in the expectation of future gain (Havighurst, 1964; Adair & Mowsesian, 1993); and, thus, it tends to relate to pragmatic activities to improve health, finances, social support, and so on. In contrast, the goal of the latter lies in the act of learning itself, and it is associated with psychological needs such as identity, competence, joy and satisfaction, and relatedness (Adair & Mowsesian, 1993). In a similar vein, and as stated above, in the self-determination theory (Ryan & Deci, 2000), adults' educational acts can be analysed as arising from two types of motivation: extrinsic (i.e., motivations which rise from the intention to gain specific outcomes and consequences) and intrinsic (i.e., motivations stemming from personal interest and the satisfaction gained from the activity). Whereas extrinsically motivated individuals may engage in instrumental educational activity as a self-regulating strategy, intrinsically motivated people often cite the joy of learning, a desire for intellectual challenges, or a sense of achievement as reasons for their continued learning (Ahn & Janke, 2011; Legault, 2016; Ryan & Deci, 2000). Legault (2016) points out that, "intrinsic motivation is a natural human tendency – in other words, people will actively strive toward doing the things they find interesting or enjoyable" (p. 3) and that this creates the personal benefit of well-being (Deci & Ryan, 2009). The social environment comprising the community, workplace and educational environment is also implicated by the degree to which it influences intrinsic motivation, particularly its effect on autonomy and competence (Legault, 2016). Supportive social environments are those that acknowledge and respect autonomy through personal choice and acknowledge expertise (competency) and support efficacy (Girelli et al., 2018).

Opportunities to participate in CET may be distinct across adults may vary because of differences in their motivations. For reasons of compulsion and mandation, the level of participation in education is higher among young, employed and highly educated individuals who have both intrinsic and extrinsic reasons for participation (Berker & Horn, 2003). Less qualified and unemployed adults have a lower level of participation—they usually have more professional reasons for participating, such as getting a better job (Daehlen & Ure, 2009). Some studies show that less qualified individuals also note that participation improves their self-esteem (Valentine, 1990) and allows them to meet new people (Daehlen & Ure, 2009; Kim & Merriam, 2004). Women are less likely to participate in adult education than men, describing that participation patterns are strongly classed, raced and gendered (Leathwood & Francis, 2006). This view leads to a lifelong learning discourse which is focused on masculinist values and assumptions, and that women's skills in the workplace are less valued than those of men, with the result that women are more likely to be employed in dead-end jobs, leading to less opportunities to take place in adult learning activities (Ngo et al., 2003). Age is an important factor in adult participation in education. Perhaps not surprisingly, older adults perceive less advantage from education for their professional progression, although in the contemporary era for older workers this development, like for all others is becoming a necessity, yet they get less support from their employers (Kyndt et al., 2011). However, even when there are positive attitudes towards participation in CET, there may be barriers that can hinder the transformation of these attitudes into action.

Potential Barriers

To understand factors that inhibit participation and engagement by adults in CET, it is important to identify the main barriers to participation. One explanation is provided through Cross' model (1981, 1992) that identifies three types of barriers: Situational, dispositional, and institutional. For working age adults' participation in CET, situational barriers might refer to a lack of money and time, having too many people at home, or work responsibilities, childcare, lack of transportation, etc. A particular dispositional issue for working age adults is the conflicting demands upon their time and energy from their commitments to work, family and community life which have to be negotiated around that which they commit to participation in CET provisions, particularly when they are separated and remote from work and community life. Dispositional barriers include negative attitudes and perceptions about further education, its usefulness, and the appropriateness of engaging in learning; low self-esteem and evidence of prior poor academic performance are also dispositional barriers. Institutional barriers are usually caused by institutions of learning such as inconvenient scheduling, location, lack of interesting, practical, or relevant courses, administrative or procedural issues, the lack of information about programs and procedures, etc. (Cross, 1992). Another perspective refers to the intentionality of adults and how they position themselves and direct their energies and interests (Malle et al., 2001). While dispositional barriers are often directly related to the students themselves and issues over which they have control, institutional and situational barriers are out of the learner's personal control. Other research indicates the main reasons for non-participation of adults in education are lack of time, lack of money and family responsibilities (e.g., Leow et al., 2022; Valentine, 1990). It follows then that, currently, a critical challenge for CET is to overcome multidimensional barriers to participation provide accessible educative experiences to meet both the needs of the labour market and those of individuals who must make choices about how they use their time and resources and for what purposes. Providing high-quality guidance and assessments and implementing effective validation and recognition mechanisms of adult education may be a priority when seeking to overcome these barriers so that the decision-making can be informed as possible, and actions taken appropriately focused on working age adults needs, readiness and goals, once these are understood.

As far as worklife learning is concerned, young adults, upon graduation from their programs of initial occupational preparation and transition into employment are just commencing a journey in the ongoing development of their occupational competence that will be required to secure employability across their working lives (OECD, 2010). That is, securing the ability to be and remain employed as work practices and requirements change and be able to advance their careers premised upon the ongoing development of their occupational and personal competence. This is an imperative that working age adults need to address across working lives regardless of their occupation, as all kinds and classifications of work are subject to change. However, the motivations for working age adults for learning and participation in educational activities (e.g., CET courses/programs) may be influenced by their personal experiences and imperatives and shaped by their discretion about how they use their time and balance their commitments. Hence, they need to mediate the balance between their imperatives and intrinsic motivations and constraints of external factors, such as work, family, and community commitments. All these factors contribute to create a framework within which working age adults make decisions about if and how they engage in CET.

As indicated above, to date, there has been a plethora of research on working age adults' attitudes, motivations, and barriers for participating in CET, yet a lack of research on their experiences of CET and how CET provisions have been adjusted and enacted to accommodate these individuals' needs thus enhancing their experiences. Thus, it has been important to understand what drives and supports working age adults' participation in CET and illuminate the qualities of educational experiences that attracts and sustains their interests, and particularly the alignments with work life requirements. By examining the motivations of and affordances for working age adults, the aim is to contribute to a deeper understanding of the complex interplay amongst individual choices, societal imperatives, and the evolving demands of the workforce. This knowledge aims not only to benefit adult students, but also to inform policy and practice, ensuring that CET remains a vibrant and essential part of our educational landscape. Informing and effecting this change entails developing a future-oriented curriculum that engages students in relevant educative experiences and affords appropriate and purposeful pedagogies to assist meet these learning needs. Elaborating these practices and approaches for enacting and evaluating CET provisions stands to make helpful contributions to the implementation for policy and practice to increase both participation in CET and its efficacy.

Hence, these are the major focuses of a three-phase investigation undertaken in Singapore to identify what constitutes effective CET provisions for working age adults. The practical inquiry was enacted through interviews with CET graduates and their employers in Phase 1, followed by a survey in Phase 2 administered to Singaporean working age adults in a range of employment and industry sectors to validate and advance the interview findings. In Phase 3, the consolidated findings from the first two phases were presented to CET educators and administrators who engaged in co-construction of the implications and generation of guidelines for curriculum and pedagogic practices (*see* Chap. 4 for detailed methods and procedures). The sections below report and discuss the findings from interviews with CET graduates in Phase 1 about the motivations and affordances for their participation and engagement in CET courses/programs.

Procedures

The pre-interview survey and interview data gathered from CET graduates (n = 178) provided an opportunity to consider both extrinsic and intrinsic influences that encourage their CET participation, engagement and completion. Intrinsic motivation refers to engagement in behaviour that is inherently satisfying or enjoyable, and not conditional on an outcome that is separate to the behaviour itself (Legault, 2016). Extrinsic motivation is undertaking action that is conditional upon the attainment of an outcome that is separate from the act itself (Legault, 2016). The use of these motivational factors in considering the data about supportive mechanisms for CET students to undertake and complete CET courses/programs presents a way forward to identify their impact upon their participation and completion of CET courses/programs. A thematic analysis aligning to the six-point method described by Braun and Clarke (2006) was followed. A combination of 'theory-driven'/'analyst-driven' (i.e., deductive—producing codes relative to a pre-specified conceptual framework or codebook, such as, intrinsic, and extrinsic motivation indicators (Legault, 2016) and 'data-driven' (i.e., inductive—producing codes solely reflective of the content of the data) approaches was adopted. Two over-arching themes were identified: "Motivations for CET participation" and "Affordances for CET engagement" and these, in turn, had sub-themes that are delineated and discussed below.

Findings

As noted, unlike younger participants in education, it is working age adults who largely decide if, when they participate in CET and how they engage with it. Consequently, it is important to understand what motivates their participation and how that might be best guided and supported to maximise their participation and enhance the outcomes of it, including retaining them in CET programs. Consequently, the data and findings in relation to motivations, the degree by which the purposes for participating in CET were achieved and affordances encouraging or restricting

Findings

participation in CET participation and engagement with it are presented and discussed.

Motivations for CET Participation

From a list provided in the pre-interview survey, the informants indicated their reasons for participating in the CET program from which they had recently graduated. The findings are presented in Table 5.1. In this table, the reasons for participating in the CET courses/programs are listed on the left-hand column and their ranking based on the frequency [n] of which they were reported. The ones associated with professional reasons are *italicised* here to distinguish those from personal reasons.

Overall, most of these CET graduates reported professional and personal reasons associated with enhancing employability for participating in their CET programs (i.e., securing employment, shifting to new employment, or advancement within existing employment). It is difficult to delineate these purposes as being solely focused on their work because personal interests, emphases and goals were embedded in concerns about learning for their paid work. In addition, data was gathered from the interviews with these informants also reported responses can be further delineated into three main purposes or motivations to participate in CET: (i) personal-professional motivations, (ii) personal motivations, and (iii) professional motivations. Many of the graduates (n = 76) reported a combination of personal and professional improvements as their key motivation. Most informants' responses were associated with this category and had enrolled in the CET programs of their choice to gain professional development and appreciated the opportunity to learn for both personal and professional reasons. Many informants (n = 61) referred to

Table 5.1 Factors initiating participation in CET

Reasons to participate in CET courses/programs	n	Rank
To gain personal development	122	1
To acquire extra skills for my job	108	2
To try for a different career	71	3
To get to the next level of education	64	4
To get a better job	55	5
To fulfil a job requirement	54	6
To get a job	46	7
Government subsidies	45	8
To get a promotion	38	9
To get skills for community/voluntary work	37	10
To get into another course of study	31	11
Employer's support (e.g., study leave)	29	12

their motivation to learn, influenced by their personal beliefs about lifelong learning. Some informants enrolled in their courses for the sake of learning as they wanted either to remain relevant in their current work or to progress to the next education level. These informants reported taking a course, such as a degree after their diploma, as a natural progression and an achievement they wanted, regardless of whether it had any professional impact. Also, some informants (n = 37) reported wanting to gain knowledge for their current jobs or to enable them to have a potential career switch. Informants in this group acknowledged that recognition in terms of certification and opportunities is provided through CET courses. Hence, to achieve objective career goals, such as an increase in wage and change in job scope, it was necessary to take a CET course.

The qualitative interview data provided some elaborations of these motivations to participate in CET and illuminate their differences and offered more nuanced explanations. A few informants reported participating in their CET program mainly to learn new knowledge, to remain relevant, or to proceed to the next education level. Some informants anticipated using the outcomes of their participation to seek a different career. Their overall narratives throughout their interviews, however, suggest that they are participating for personal development and to learn new knowledge. The gender and age grouping of the informants are indicated at the end of each verbatim quote.

> I wanted to go and take a degree after my diploma. *Female, 21–29*
> So, it's really something that I add on to my personal skill sets. *Male, 40–49*

Most of the informants stated that they participated in CET to secure some kind of professional development. Consequently, they often measured their achievement based on how relevant the CET program and outcomes are to their work and how the skills helped them in their workplace or their perceived effectiveness in their future workplace.

> … it's meaningful, useful, something that is practical that I can use in my workplace. *Female, 50+*

Some other informants participated in CET to secure recognition in the form of certification and be able to pursue more opportunities. They often measured the extent of their achievements based on objective goals, such as an increase in wage and being able to do a job because they have the required certification.

> I got the cert, then I started to look for a fulltime job. So, I actually managed to get a fulltime job using the cert. *Male, 40–49*

It is also important to assess the informants' key motivation for participating in CET as it influences their expectations, preferences, and evaluation of the CET provision. This includes how the type of lecturers, course arrangements, class activities, and mode of delivery aligned with them achieving their intended outcomes. It is important again to be reminded that whereas young people who attend school compulsorily or young adults being required to attend tertiary education where the goals and elements of satisfaction are set by others, for these adults, it is their intentions, expectations and aspirations that are central to how they will judge the CET program, its teaching and outcomes. For example, if the students identify themselves as motivated to participate in CET for personal development, they may want to learn the knowledge and go through the content without many assignments. Thus, a simple introductory class or lectures could be offered to these groups, instead of engaging them in a process to assess their competency and certifying them. All the data presented in this table illustrate the significance of understanding these informants' intentions. That is, understanding the imperatives and circumstances of the working age adults who participate in CET programs is integral elements of the provisions and their needs and requirements need to be accounted for in the design, development, enactment, and evaluation of CET provisions (i.e., how they are enacted) and programs (i.e., their content and focus).

Altogether, these findings suggest that these recent CET graduates were motivated personally and professionally to take CET courses. It suggests that they value learning not only for instrumental purposes such as employability, but also learning for its own sake. Generally, it is difficult to delineate these motivations as purely professional or personal as interests, emphases, and goals were intertwined with concerns about learning for their paid work. However, it is important for educators and administrators to understand their students' motivations for participation in CET courses as it influences their decisions to participate in CET in the first place, their preferences for lectures, course arrangement, class activities, and mode of delivery.

Achievement of Purposes for CET Participation

The survey data generated prior to the interviews contained an item to capture the degree by which their purposes for participating in CET programs had been achieved. That is, to capture the relationship between why they decided to participate and whether those reasons had been fulfilled. The data indicates that within 4 years after graduating from CET courses/programs, a total of 35% reported fully achieving their purposes of participating in CET. When added to those who reported partially achieving those purposes, it equates to 87% of these informants. All this indicates that there is a high level of achievement of intended goals. This is positive outcome given that some of those goals were likely to be long-term and strategic (e.g., changing occupations). Nevertheless, whilst this is a positive finding, it also indicates that there is scope for improving the number of CET graduates who will report fully achieving their goals 4 years after completing their CET course/program. Table 5.2 provides some representative quotes against the categories of achieving their goals illustrating perspectives of the value of CET courses/programs the informants had undertaken.

Generally, the informants indicated that the outcomes of their CET course had been helpful for improving their work performance and for their personal growth. Putting aside the obtaining a certificate, which can be an inevitable outcome of completing a CET course/program, the achievement of purposes for participating were

Table 5.2 Interview quotes representing the achievement of purposes for CET participation

Value of the CET	Representative quotes
Fully achieved (n = 56)	The key thing that pushes me to take this [course] is I would like to acquire skills that I need to make my work better which is to help the students better and to understand them. [...] [the course] in a way helps me to able to handle the students better; be it before the internship or during the internship period.
Partially achieved (n = 81)	In terms of expanding the portfolio, yes it had already happened, it had already changed. In terms of rank, I'm not quite sure. But technically right now I'm the only person that is trained and in that branch that I'm supposedly not heading. [...] It's possible but I don't know but due to other constraints might not happen.
Not achieved (n = 14)	I was quite disappointed that the course. [...] I felt that we don't learn much. And we don't learn from professionals. We are learning from amateurs just like us. So, that part was actually quite disappointing.

largely well met. However, it was found that the graduates' experiences when participating in their programs differed greatly depending on the course chosen, the quality of the program and its teaching and their purposes for participating. Some reported disappointment with their courses because of perceptions of poor organisation and communication about course/program objectives. Others, however, appreciated their experience in the course/program as it provided them with the confidence and skills to perform independently at work and to share with colleagues the skills they had learnt. Thus, these findings highlight the importance of understanding the factors that promote students' engagement in the CET courses/programs, affordances for such engagement, and the contributions of their experiences during the courses/programs.

Affordances for CET Engagement

The informants provided important insights, based upon their recent experiences, of the kinds of affordances (i.e., assistance and invitations to engage) that had supported their participation in CET programs and helped make it a successful experience. In this section, those forms of guidance and support are presented through a consideration of, firstly, a set of factors that were identified as helping their engagement in their CET programs. It is these that assisted them continue to participate, enjoy success and productive outcomes and complete their programs. This included, secondly, very specific kinds of support provided by their workplaces and others that were helpful. These kinds of insights are helpful as whilst not all the informants received support from the workplace, for instance, those that did provided evidence about the effectiveness of that support when it was afforded to them. Hence, these findings are helpful for considering policies and practices associated with the contributions of workplaces and others in supporting CET provisions and aligning them with workplace goals. Then, thirdly, there are kinds of qualities of the educators that were deemed to be effective in supporting their learning in achieving the intended outcomes.

Factors Supporting Engagement

The informants, who are all graduates of CET programs reported that factors that initiated and sustained their interest in participating in their program in the first place and then the motivations to engage in the program effortfully, remain within it and complete it. These factors were found to be largely personal or those arising from close associations and interactions with other people, as presented in Table 5.3. This emphasises personal intentionality or what has been referred to here as intrinsic motivation. As presented in this table, the affordances, or provision of experiences providing (or restricting) opportunities to participate and succeed in the program are listed in the left column. In the middle column are the number of informants referring to this affordance and in the right column their ranking. As can be seen, the two most frequently reported factors are informants': (i) desire to achieve the purposes of their participation in CET and (ii) personal interest. These emphases rehearse the focus on enhancing employability as a personal project, as proposed earlier (OECD, 1996) and indicate the centrality of intrinsic motivation or personal intentionality to achieve those goals. But, also fundamentally, given the discretion that working age adults have in terms of whether they participate in CET and how, this finding reinforces the importance of student satisfaction in ways that are quite different than when students engage in education compulsorily or through mandation.

Analyses of the interview transcripts indicated that sustaining attendance was, reportedly, facilitated by friends and family, and then lastly employers. Indeed, participation in CET provisions is partially premised on their accessibility and personal, family and institutional circumstances associated with attendance. For instance, the CET programs from which the informants graduated often have compulsory attendance i.e., a minimum of 75% attendance is required to fulfil course requirements (SkillsFuture Singapore, 2021). It was discussed in the interviews that whether attendance in CET should be judged on a voluntary or compulsory basis. There were diverse perspectives on the attendance requirement. Some informants justified compulsory attendance as the courses are government subsidised and measures of compulsory attendance can monitor the expenditure of public funds. Others emphasised attendance had educational benefits through engaging directly with other students and teachers. For example, a participant stated that "I still feel that the attendance requirement is still good to get people really involved in the learning, not

Table 5.3 Factors supporting CET engagement

Affordances to engage in CET courses/programs	n	Rank
Achieving goals	134	1
Personal interest	118	2
Family	52	3
Friends	44	4
Employers	24	5

really come here to get a certificate and go out". Some female informants with children reported that compulsory attendance empowered them to demand their husbands or partners' care of their children when they needed to attend their courses. However, other informants suggested making attendance compulsory was inflexible and incompatible with busy work lives and other commitments.

Given the national emphasis on workforce skills development in Singapore, which includes sponsorship and incentives by government, the frequency by which these support mechanisms are seen to be salient have direct implications for workplaces. In all, when support by employers was perceived to be quite low, it was reported to have a deleterious impact on learning. This suggests that for national goals of a strong and currently competent workforce able to exercise discretion and make contributions to national well-being requires changes in the engagement and support from the enterprises who employ these working age adults and stand to benefit from the enhanced contributions that their employees can make through participating in CET. The lack of appropriate support for learning in workplaces jeopardises realising these workplace and national goals and places an unfair expectation of and burden upon the CET institutions. A national system of CET requires engagement by both public and private sector enterprises in supporting the ongoing development of their employees and, collectively, contributing to the development of the national workforce.

Support for Completing CET Programs

In all, these data indicate that a large proportion of these CET graduates are intrinsically motivated to complete their program. That is, they were driven to achieve their intended goals that arose from their participation in the program in the first place, and to pursue learning of their own interests and intentions for participating in those programs. A smaller number reported being influenced by their employers, friends, and family. The data also suggest that for about a quarter of these graduates, support from their employers or classmates can make a difference to their learning experience and motivation to complete the CET program in which they were enrolled. Moreover, from the interviews, three key sources of support for participating in CET programs were identified: (i) work, (ii) peer, and (iii) family, as shown in Table 5.4. This table presents responses to these three forms of support as indicated in the left-hand column. In the column to its right, the number of informants that referred to that kind of support are indicated, and an illustrative example is provided of that kind of support in the right-hand column.

In these ways, the informants described their motivations to complete the course when sponsored by their companies and when receiving support such as some time off to complete their assignments. These data offer more nuanced accounts, indicating employers' support for informants' participation in CET. Indeed, they are most frequently referred to this support and the number of utterances acknowledging that support, followed closely by peers' contributions. With the latter, they stated that when classmates were supportive and willing to share their career experience and

Findings

Table 5.4 Sources of support for CET completion

Sources of support	n	ref	Representative quotes
Work support	45	114	"They actually funded this course, even though it is not very expensive, but they were very supportive because they felt that it is good to enhance myself in whatever I do."
Peer support	40	110	"I feel the class is a very supportive class. They are very willing to share their career experience, even to the extent of some of their personal growth that are relevant to the programme."
Family support	22	40	"So, my parent takes care of my kids when I am away, even when I do business travel, my parents are very supportive to take of my kids when I am away. If they are not around, my husband will stand in. So, this is a very open environment."

support one another, it provided a collaborative and supportive learning environment. It was also helpful and appreciated when family members assisted with childcare arrangements during times when scheduled educational commitments need to be managed, such as attending face-to-face (i.e., in class) or on-line sessions or group project meetings.

Together, these data indicate a complex of personal and work factors assist and enable these informants to complete their CET programs. Whilst long working days and time to travel to attend CET courses hindered and complicated their participation, these barriers can be, to some degree, ameliorated by personal commitment and interests, and support of workplaces, peers, and family. So, the provision of CET is set amongst a range of other factors which support or inhibit participation and engagement.

Importantly, how adults come to engage the CET courses likely shapes what they learn through and from them. We know that superficial engagement in such activities lightly leads to learning of a similar kind, and often associated with meeting the requirements of the institution. This has been referred to as mastery (i.e., superficial engagement and outcomes) (Wertsch, 1998). Yet, many of the informants indicated that they engaged in enthusiastic and effortful way which has been described as appropriation by Wertsch (1998) (i.e., effortful and committed engagement and rich learning outcomes). The quality of individuals' engagement is, therefore, central to how these graduates evaluated what constitutes effective CET provisions. That is, what is perceived to be effective affordances for CET engagement. In this regard, the reported experiences with CET study are central to appraising the engagement. These included means of engagement (i.e., modes of delivery), and engaging CET educators that directly impact students' experiences thus enhancing their engagement.

In referring to preferred means of engagement, the informants reported privileging a combination of face-to-face and online over either face-to-face or just online alone (*see* Table 5.5). That preference was justified through specific references to the qualities of face-to-face encounters with both teachers and peers. The interactions with educators were deemed to be helpful in gaining their insights,

Table 5.5 Preferred means of engagement

Means	N	%
Combination of F2F and online	137	78.7
Face-to-face (F2F)	34	19.5
Online	3	1.7

responses to questions, and feedback, to seek clarifications and engage with their occupational and teaching expertise. Engaging with peers was reported as supporting learning as it provides opportunities to clarify doubts, and to draw upon their experiences and understandings while sharing theirs with peers. Overall, these working-age Singaporeans report that their learning can be best supported through engagement in a combination of online and face-to-face interactions. The combination of both modes that makes educational material readily accessible and provides opportunities to extend the content to students' goals and circumstances, and through learning from those of others. Yet, central to this engagement is how educators come to enact their roles and engage with students.

In all, experiences with educators were reported as being important for CET students to sustain their interest and effectively engage in the CET courses/programs. Central here was these teachers having experience of the occupation that they are teaching about and guiding students' learning, on the one hand, and their abilities to be empathetic, engaging and flexible in meeting the working-age adult students' needs, on the other, which is similar to what was also found in earlier studies (e.g., Billett et al., 2016; Leow et al., 2022). It is these qualities that are considered next.

Qualities of CET Educators That Promoted Engagement

Central to the quality of any educational provision is likely to be how it is implemented by teachers, and CET is no different. This includes, whether this is through the kinds of, sequencing and organisation of experiences, from which intentional learning is to be derived and how educators enact the experiences and engage with students. As noted above, there are likely to be differences between the qualities of educators who engage with younger students (i.e., school or immediate post school-age) and those whose role is to assist in the education of adults. Numerous accounts have suggested that there are differences although it would seem that the needs of, readiness to engage and contextualising what is to be learnt are important for both kinds of students (Taylor & Trumpower, 2014; Tennant, 1991). Then, there is a literature referring to the needs of adults as being self-directed and exercising a high level of autonomy and discretion in learning (Merriam & Baumgartner, 2020; Tennant, 2020). Some go as far as to say that it is the students who should be actively involved in the design and implementation of educational experiences for them, in the true spirit of the concept of self-directed education (McDonough, 2014; Tennant, 2020). However, this suggestion may overestimate adults' abilities to be competent in fields of knowledge and practice that are unfamiliar and are unable to engage in

Findings

Table 5.6 CET educators' qualities affording students' engagement

Teaching practices	n	Rank
Provide relevant experiences for learners' needs and purposes	138	1
Account for and are sensitive to students' readiness	109	2
Make applicable the concepts (e.g., theories) they are advancing (i.e., teaching)	109	2
Illustrate what is to be learnt and its purposes (e.g., examples, stories)	98	4
Demonstrate competence in the field in which are teaching	84	5
Assist meeting learners' purposes and needs by being flexible and adaptive with approaches to teaching and assessment	72	6
Engage and utilise learners' experience and agency	67	7
Engage interactively and reciprocally with learners	67	7

learning without guidance and instruction. Indeed, this is often the reason that adults have indicated that they need to participate in such a program of study to gain access to guidance, support, and instruction to gain access to knowledge that they otherwise would not come to learn.

Therefore, although there are expectations about adults being perhaps more self-directed in a range of activities than children, the reason why that is not the case equally applies to adults' learning new fields of practice, domains of knowledge or abilities that are beyond their existing experience and capacities to learn through discovery alone. Thus, it is important that we come to understand the qualities required of adult educators in guiding and supporting adults in the circumstances. In response to a very specific item about the effective qualities of these educators, the informants indicated what they constituted. The list shown in Table 5.6 is derived from a thematic analysis of the interview data of the 178 informants. In this table, the qualities are set out in the left column ranked in terms of frequency [n] indicated in the right-hand column. As a means of assisting the analysis, those practices which are the product of having relevant industry experience are *italicised*. In all, the data indicate that a combination of competent educational practices and educators having relevant industry experiences are the most desired set of qualities.

In more detail, the most frequently identified quality (i.e., ranked 1st) was educators' providing relevant and pertinent experiences for developing the capacities needed by the students. These graduates reported valuing experiences that assist learning knowledge applicable for and helpful to their intended purposes (e.g., advancement, finding work, changing work). Noteworthy is that the informants had recently completed their CET programs and were seeking to apply what they learnt to advance goals in their working lives. This corresponds to CET educators needing relevant industry experience through which they could provide advice, narratives, explanations, and procedural capacities of the kind that would assist students understand and begin to approximate kinds of practices that would be required in their occupations. Concurrently, they also acknowledged the importance of foundational teacherly qualities such as being aware of students' readiness and being flexible in responding to them (i.e., ranked 2nd). The CET educators' ability to apply what they are teaching about and to offer examples and instances to enrich the teaching process is valued (i.e., ranked 2nd, 4th, and 5th). That capacity, however, goes beyond telling stories and making links with content being taught. It included having the richness and depth of knowledge that would allow them to be responsive to questions and queries and providing contextual, professional advice to students in unrehearsed ways and not able to be predicted. More than teaching from prepared material, having demonstrated capacity to embed what is being taught through relevant examples, instances and elaborations from occupational practice is also valued. So, much of this comes from having had work experiences that are relevant to the content that students need to learn.

Motivations and Affordances for CET Participation

In sum, this chapter reports and discusses the findings about what motivates working age adults' participation in CET and the kinds of affordances for supporting their engagement in CET and achieving productive outcomes from it, including completing the program of study. In all, it is proposed that:

- The need for working age adults to access effective CET provisions to sustain workers' employability across working life has perhaps never been greater.
- Most of these CET graduates reported professional and personal reasons associated with enhancing employability for participating in their CET programs.
- Their participation in CET is likely premised on: (i) the purposes that these adults want to achieve, (ii) how these provisions are aligned with their needs in terms of accessibility and relevance, and (iii) their readiness to engage. These are factors traded off against opportunities to engage and trade-offs in terms of financial, personal and time commitments.
- So, whilst governments and enterprises can create policies and opportunities, it is ultimately the adults themselves who make decisions about and accept the responsibility to engage in CET.
- Hence, it has is important to understand what drives and supports working age adults' participation in CET and the qualities of educational experiences that attracts and sustains their interests, and alignments with work life requirements.
- Most informants reported partially or fully achieving their purposes for participating.
- These findings highlight the importance of understanding the factors that led to such outcomes.
- Together, these data indicate a complex of personal and work factors assist and enable these informants to successfully complete their CET programs.
- These working age adults reported that their learning can be best supported through engagement in a combination of online and face-to-face interactions that makes educational materials readily accessible and provides opportunities to apply the content to students' goals and circumstances, and through learning from others (e.g., peers).

- The desired set of qualities CET educators are a combination of competence in educational practices and relevant industry experiences.
- More than teaching from prepared material, having demonstrated capacity to embed what is being taught through relevant examples, instances and elaborations from occupational practice is also valued.
- Inadequate support for learning in workplaces jeopardises realising enterprises and national goals for CET and places an unfair expectation of and burden on CET institutions.

These findings indicated that the recent CET graduates were motivated personally and professionally to take CET courses/programs. That is, they value learning not only for instrumental purposes such as employability (i.e., extrinsic), but also learning for its own sake (i.e., intrinsic). Yet, there was a mix of personal and institutional factors that support as well as inhibit their participation and engagement in CET. These findings inform how a provision of CET needs to be positioned to make attractive and accessible for working age adults. There are compelling imperatives from governmental and enterprise perspectives for working-age adults to participate in CET. Yet, ultimately, whether and how adults elect to participate and engage in CET provisions is central to those imperatives being realised. That participation is shaped by a range of factors about which these adults make decisions. Unlike in compulsory education that is legislated or the mandated requirements for initial occupation preparation, adults' participation in CET is premised on their interest and imperatives. More specifically, adults' engagement with these provisions are likely premised on their interests and the kinds of purposes that they want to achieve, how these provisions are perceived to meet their needs in terms of accessibility, relevance, and opportunities to engage and trade-offs in terms of financial, personal and time commitments. Thus, the growing interest and participation in CET to secure individual employability and workplace viability across working life, and specifically in countries with ageing populations such as Singapore, realizing these imperatives is dependent upon working-ages adults' participation. Thus, understanding what drives and supports working age adults' participation in CET and illuminating the quality of educational experiences and their alignment with worklife learning requirements are important. Effecting this change entails developing a future-oriented curriculum that engages students and requires effective pedagogies to meet their learning needs.

Further, in terms of meeting the needs of national focus on workforce skills development, the effectiveness of these support mechanisms holds significant implications for workplaces. Employers' support for CET is strongly correlated and aligned to the broader goal of cultivating a highly skilled and competent workforce capable of contributing and realising national well-being and economic goals. To achieve this, it is imperative for enterprises to enhance engagement and support for working-age adults participating in CET. For a successful national CET system, other than governmental sponsorship and incentives, active participation from both public and private sector enterprises is essential to ensure ongoing employee development and collectively bolster the national workforce's competence and capability.

References

Adair, S. R., & Mowsesian, R. (1993). The meanings and motivations of learning during the retirement transition. *Educational Gerontology, 19*(4), 317–330. https://doi.org/10.1080/0360127930190404

Ahl, H. (2006). Motivation in adult education: A problem solver or a euphemism for direction and control? *International Journal of Lifelong Education, 25*(4), 385–405. https://doi.org/10.1080/02601370600772384

Ahn, Y. J., & Janke, M. C. (2011). Motivations and benefits of the travel experiences of older adults. *Educational Gerontology, 37*(8), 653–673. https://doi.org/10.1080/03601271003716010

Berker, A., & Horn, L. (2003). *Work first, study second: Adult undergraduates who combine employment and postsecondary enrolment*. U.S. Department of Education National Centre for Education Statistics.

Billett, S. (Ed.). (2006). *Work, change and workers*. Springer Netherlands.

Billett, S. (2008). Subjectivity, learning and work: Sources and legacies. *Vocations and Learning: Studies in vocational and professional education., 1*(2), 149–171.

Billett, S. (2020). Developing a skillful and adaptable workforce: Reappraising curriculum and pedagogies for vocational education. In *Vocational education and training in the age of digitization-Challenges and opportunities*, 251–272.

Billett, S. (2022). Promoting graduate employability: Key goals, and curriculum and pedagogic practices for higher education. In B. Ng (Ed.), *Graduate employability and workplace-based learning development: Insights from sociocultural perspectives* (pp. 11–29). Springer.

Billett, S., Dymock, D., & Choy, S. (2016). *Supporting learning across working life: Models, processes and practices*. Springer International Publishing.

Braun, V., & Clarke, V. (2006). Using thematic analysis in psychology. *Qualitative Research in Psychology, 3*(2), 77–101. https://doi.org/10.1191/1478088706qp063oa

Browell, S. (2000). Staff development and professional education: A cooperative model. *Journal of Workplace Learning, 12*(2), 57–65. https://doi.org/10.1108/13665620010316208

Carré, P. (2000). *Motivation in adult education: From engagement to performance*. University of British Columbia, Department of Educational Studies.

Carré, P. (2001). *De la motivation à la formation*. L'Harmattan.

Chan, S. (2013). Learning through apprenticeship: Belonging to a workplace, becoming and being. *Vocations and Learning, 6*(3), 367–383. https://doi.org/10.1007/s12186-013-9100-x

Cross, P. (1981). *Adults as learners*. Jossey-Bass.

Cross, K. P. (1992). *Adults as learners: Increasing participation and facilitating learning*. Jossey–Bass.

Daehlen, M., & Ure, O. B. (2009). Low-skilled adults in formal continuing education: Does their motivation differ from other learners? *International Journal of Lifelong Education, 28*(5), 661–674. https://doi.org/10.1080/02601370903189948

Deci, E. L., & Ryan, R. M. (2009). Self-determination theory: A consideration of human motivational universals. In P. J. Corr & G. Matthews (Eds.), *The Cambridge handbook of personality psychology* (pp. 441–456). Cambridge University Press.

Deckers, L. (2018). *Motivation: Biological, psychological, and environmental* (5th ed.). Routledge. https://doi.org/10.4324/9781315178615

Eteläpelto, A., & Saarinen, J. (2006). Developing subjective identities through collective participation. In S. Billett, T. Fenwick, & M. Somerville (Eds.), *Work, subjectivity and learning* (pp. 157–177). Springer. https://doi.org/10.1007/1-4020-5360-6_10

Girelli, L., Alivernini, F., Lucidi, F., Cozzolino, M., Savarese, G., Sibilio, M., & Salvatore, S. (2018). Autonomy supportive contexts, autonomous motivation, and self-efficacy predict academic adjustment of first-year university students. *Frontiers in Education, 3*(95). https://doi.org/10.3389/feduc.2018.00095

Havighurst, R. J. (1964). Changing status and roles during the adult life cycle: Significance for adult education. In H. Burns (Ed.), *Sociological backgrounds of adult education* (pp. 17–38). Center for the Study of Liberal Education for Adults.

Illeris, K. (2006). Lifelong learning and the low-skilled. *International Journal of Lifelong Education, 25*(1), 15–28. https://doi.org/10.1080/02601370500309451

Kim, A., & Merriam, S. B. (2004). Motivations for learning among older adults in a learning in retirement institute. *Educational Gerontology, 30*(6), 441–455. https://doi.org/10.1080/03601270490445069

Kyndt, E., Michielsen, M., Van Nooten, L., Nijs, S., & Baert, H. (2011). Learning in the second half of the career: Stimulating and prohibiting reasons for participation in formal learning activities. *International Journal of Lifelong Education, 30*(5), 681–699. https://doi.org/10.1080/02601370.2011.611905

Leathwood, C., & Francis, B. (Eds.). (2006). *Gender and lifelong learning: Critical feminist engagements*. Routledge.

Legault, L. (2016). Intrinsic and extrinsic motivation. In V. Zeigler-Hill & T. K. Shackelford (Eds.), *Encyclopedia of personality and individual differences* (pp. 1–4). Springer. https://doi.org/10.1007/978-3-319-28099-8_1139-1

Leow, A., Billett, S., Le, A. H., & Chua, S. (2022). Graduates' perspectives on effective continuing education and training: Participation, access and engagement. *International Journal of Lifelong Education, 41*(2), 212–228. https://doi.org/10.1080/02601370.2022.2044398

Lester, S. (1999). Professional bodies, CPD and informal learning: The case of conservation. *Continuing Professional Development, 2*(4), 110–121.

Malle, B. F., Moses, L. J., & Baldwin, D. A. (2001). Introduction: The significance of intentionality. In B. F. Malle, L. J. Moses, & D. A. Baldwin (Eds.), *Intentions and intentionality: Foundations of social cognition* (pp. 1–26). The MIT Press.

McDonough, D. (2014). Providing deep learning through active engagement of adult learners in blended courses. *Journal of Learning in Higher Education, 10*(1), 9–16.

Merriam, S. B., & Baumgartner, L. M. (2020). *Learning in adulthood: A comprehensive guide* (4th ed.). Jossey-Bass.

Mulenga, D., & Liang, J. S. (2008). Motivations for older adults' participation in distance education: A study at the National Open University of Taiwan. *International Journal of Lifelong Education, 27*(3), 289–314. https://doi.org/10.1080/02601370802047791

Ngo, H. Y., Foley, S., Wong, A., & Loi, R. (2003). Who gets more of the pie? Predictors of perceived gender inequity at work. *Journal of Business Ethics, 45*, 227–241. https://doi.org/10.1023/A:1024179524538

Noon, M., Blyton, P., & Morrell, K. (2013). *The realities of work: Experiencing work and employment in contemporary society*. Macmillan International Higher Education.

Organisation for Economic Co-operation and Development [OECD]. (1996). *Lifelong learning for all: Meeting of the education committee at ministerial level, 16–17 January 1996*. https://www.voced.edu.au/content/ngv:25305

Organisation for Economic Co-operation and Development [OECD]. (2010). *Synthesis report of the OECD reviews of vocational education and training: Learning for jobs*. https://www.oecd.org/edu/skills-beyond-school/Learning%20for%20Jobs%20book.pdf

Roscoe, J. (2002). Continuing professional development in higher education. *Human Resource Development International, 5*(1), 3–9. https://doi.org/10.1080/13678860110076006

Ryan, R. M., & Deci, E. L. (2000). Self-determination theory and the facilitation of intrinsic motivation, social development, and Well-being. *American Psychologist, 55*(1), 68–78. https://psycnet.apa.org/doi/10.1037/0003-066X.55.1.68

SkillsFuture Singapore. (2021). *Attendance*. Retrieved from https://www.tpgateway.gov.sg/faq/attendance

Stephenson, J. (1999). *Corporate capability: Implications for the style and direction of work-based learning*. Research Centre for Vocational Education and Training, University of Technology.

Taylor, M., & Trumpower, D. (2014). Adult high school learners: Engaging conditions in the teaching and learning process. *International Forum of Teaching and Studies, 10*(2), 3–12.

Tennant, M. (1991). The psychology of adult teaching and learning. In J. Peters, P. Jarvis, & Associates (Eds.), *Adult education evolution and achievements in a developing field of study* (pp. 191–216). Jossey Bass.

Tennant, M. (2020). *Psychology and adult learning: The role of theory in informing practice* (4th ed.). Routledge.

Valentine, T. (1990). *What motivates adults to participate in the Federal Adult Basic Education Program? Research on adult basic education* (Vol. Number 1/Series 3). Iowa State Department of Education.

Vallerand, R. J., O'Connor, B. P., & Hamel, M. (1995). Motivation in later life: Theory and assessment. *The International Journal of Aging and Human Development, 41*(3), 221–238. https://doi.org/10.2190/YLFM-DGUE-HRL2-VWLG

Wertsch, J. V. (1998). *Mind as action*. Oxford University Press. https://doi.org/10.1093/acprof:oso/9780195117530.001.0001

Chapter 6
Towards an Effective, Accessible and Scalable CET Provision: A National Survey

Abstract Having a continuing education and training (CET) provision able to be meet the needs of all kinds and classifications of workers is central to its effectiveness in sustaining the employability of the working age population. Part of that requirement is for a provision that is accessible, effective and scalable to an entire population of working age adults. To identify and offer principles and practices for such an effective CET provision, this chapter reports and discusses the second phase of a national research project on CET in Singapore. The aim of this phase was to engage with a larger sample of working age adults than the 180 CET graduates who comprised the informants in the first phase. The second phase was enacted using an online survey that gathered data on the expectations of CET and the learning needs and requirements of working age Singaporeans. The sample included both adults who had participated and those who had not engaged in any recognizable form of CET. The items selected for this survey were derived in part from the findings of the first phase of the project. The intent was to engage with as wide a range of adult age survey respondents as possible to verify and extend the findings from those interviews across a broader working age population. Furthermore, items about factors that will encourage participation, completion and inform the effectiveness of the overall experience and the contributions of teachers were included, as were those associated with the worth of government subsidies and their influence on working age adults whether these made a difference to their participation in CET programs. This quantitative approach to data gathering and analysis is particularly important for informing both governmental, educational and workplace policies about CET. Findings from the survey emphasize the importance of pre-course counselling, readiness to participate in CET programs and preparatory experiences as well as the qualities of educational experiences, adult educators and subsidies as strong incentives for participation in CET by working age Singaporeans. The findings lead to conclusions about the purposes for, practices of, and means of engaging in CET that might be considered by government, tertiary education institutions and workplaces in providing an effective CET system that is accessible and scalable for the working age population.

© The Author(s), under exclusive license to Springer Nature Singapore Pte Ltd. 2024
S. R. Billett et al., *Continuing Education and Training*, Professional and Practice-based Learning 36, https://doi.org/10.1007/978-981-97-2930-2_6

Keywords Continuing education and training · Lifelong education · Lifelong learning · Workplace experiences · Role of tertiary education institutions · Qualities of CET teachers · Qualities of CET learners · Subsidies · Working age adults · Survey data · Quantitative analysis

Provisions of Continuing Education and Training and Working Age Adults

Having a provision of continuing education and training (CET) able to be meet the needs of all kinds and classifications of workers is emerging as an important policy focus for many nation states. Central here is the ability of that provision to assist the working age population to sustain their employability, make contributions to their workplaces when faced with continual change in occupational requirements and workplace practices. Collectively, these contributions assist nation states deal with growing global competitiveness and the viability of the goods and services that are generated by the nation's public and private sector enterprises. As some states face existential challenges in an era of geopolitical tensions, the focus is turning to how they can become increasingly self-sufficient and self-reliant. Much of that ability would be vested in the quality, skillfulness and adaptability of its workforces. Consequently, an element of that requirement is for a CET provision that is effective, highly accessible and scalable for its entire working age population. For such a goal to be achieved, it is necessary to identify and validate principles and practices informing and realizing that effectiveness, accessibility and potential for scalability. Imperatives driving the search for achieving such goals include a growing concern that existing educational provisions are unsuited or unable to realize these outcomes, being attractive to engage entire working age populations and having a fit with the needs and aspirations of working age adults, but also fitted around their parallel commitments (i.e., family, work and community). There is also a concern that only some sections of the working age population might be able to access, engage and benefit from CET provisions, thereby cultivating social stratification and inequity (Hoskins & Barker, 2014). All these issues have important implications for tertiary education institutions, those who work in them, the private and public sector enterprises that employ these workers and working age adults themselves.

Unsurprisingly, these factors are leading to a need for reconsideration of the approach to how CET might be best organized and enacted. These considerations are directed to its goals, processes and the possibilities and practicalities associated with remodeling CET so it can be accessible and effective for all kinds and classifications of workers. Yet, such educational transformations necessitate accounting for both the intentionalities, capacities and interests of the individuals who comprise the workforces (Malle et al., 2001), as well as the kinds of experiences that are provided for them and their prospects for achieving those outcomes through individual's engagement with them (Cole & Engestrom, 1997). So, as with any educational provision, it is important to identify how CET can meet the needs of those to whom it is directed (i.e., working age adults). In compulsory education or immediate post-school tertiary education, students are compelled or mandated to participate and attend course(s) to secure the knowledge and certification required for occupations and enter the world of work. However, this is not always the case for CET. Instead, interest and participation in CET is often premised on working-age adults electing to engage with it. Although there are occupational requirements and workplace mandates associated with professional development, much and, likely, most working age adults' participation will be voluntary. It will be based on their personal and professional interests and discretion. As indicated, also often the commitment required to engage effectively in CET competes with work, family, and community responsibilities that are often compelling for working-age adults (Rose, 2017; Su et al., 2018). Hence, developing CET provisions that are responsive to working-age adults' needs has become a priority in many countries, as these provisions are seen as being a key source of supporting their continued employability, and being able to sustain the viability of their workplaces and underpin their further development. This concern about employability is often directed to how these adults can: i) remain employable across their lengthening working lives, ii) contribute to their workplaces' continuity and development, and iii) collectively address governmental goals of supporting a robust economic base and providing quality services (Organisation for Economic Co-operation and Development [OECD], 2006, 2010).

The need for effective CET provisions to sustain working adults' employability was highlighted during the era of COVID-19 pandemic. It exacerbated and compounded the need for learning of new work processes and ways of engaging in work. Indeed, it is estimated that around 80% of the global workforce in both developed and developing countries were affected by workplace closures and changes to work practices (International Labour Organization, 2020). In response, many countries have adopted counter-cyclical fiscal policies to fund stimulus packages to support the unemployed and to increase expenditure in key areas such as healthcare, education, and training (OECD, 2020). Yet, ultimately, each nation state's economic recovery is dependent on how well its workforce is prepared to meet the evolving needs of the changing labour market (Dikhtyar et al., 2021) and individuals' engagement with CET has shown to be strongly counter cyclical (Dellas & Sakellaris, 2003). To boost the upskilling, reskilling and CET engagement, some governments have increased funding for CET, while others have provided financial support to employers for sending their employees for CET. In the case of Singapore, with its aging population profile, the government has adopted both approaches (Tan et al., 2017). This approach seems particularly important for nation states who have workforces comprising high levels of workers from lower income groups and older working adults, who may have lesser inclinations or ability to participate in CET (Boeren et al., 2020). Consequently, unlike schooling and much of tertiary education, participation in CET is contingent on working-age adults' interests and imperatives that might be stimulated and supported in some countries with financial incentives, but not in others.

Following the advent of these kinds of initiatives in Singapore and accompanying emphases on the post-secondary education institutions (PSEIs) as providers of CET, this country offers an illustrative national case to explore these issues. These include an increased level of government interest in the transformation and professionalization of those who organize programs in and enact CET (Institute of Adult Learning, 2017, SkillsFuture Singapore, 2023). Specifically, there is increased attention on creating the opportunities for adults to upskill and reskill through CET, including learning through their work activities and in their workplaces. More than in other educational sectors, the efficacy of CET educators and providers, programs, and approaches are contingent on their links to workplaces and the CET students who work in them.

To better understand and respond effectively to these new challenges, including what needs to be learnt and how, it is necessary to identify and capture the needs and requirements of the CET students. As mentioned above, the perspectives of these students will be central to effective CET provisions and students' engagement in them. It follows then that in this chapter, the survey data with 860 working age Singaporeans who may or may not have participated in a CET program is drawn upon to illuminate and elaborate responses. That survey comprised the second phase of a research project funded by the Singaporean government (Billett et al., 2021). To foreshadow the next section, Phase 2 survey items were developed from Phase 1 interview findings with graduates (n = 180) (Leow et al., 2022) and employers (n = 40) who support their employees' engagement in CET (Leow et al., 2023b). In preview, it found that:

- There is a need for CET provisions' effectiveness, accessibility and scalability to benefit the entire working age population.
- On the-job training was claimed to be the most effective means of developing applicable skills, followed by off-site external training and mentoring, versus online education and on-site external training being the least effective.
- Online education has become highly accessible and effective mode of CET since COVID-19.
- Participation in CET programs are not highly regarded for developing employability skills.
- Off-site external training was not highly regarded by employers.
- Reasons for not participating in CET include demands of work, lack of employers' support, limited knowledge of CET provisions, suitability of available courses, the cost of those programs and eligibility.
- There is a need to consider ease of accessibility including physical accessibility.
- Work-based learning effectiveness urges the integration of CET and to address accessibility.
- Availability of subsidies is an inhibiting factor of CET participation.
- Face-to-face is the most effective CET delivery mode for their interactive and spontaneous forms of engagement.

- The challenge of CET educators' currency development to remain occupationally competent is yet to be resolved.
- Effective CET students or learners need independent and interdependent learning qualities.
- Future CET provisions need a tight alignment between the learning focuses and the workplace practices.
- Workplaces can promote learning through engagement in new tasks, innovations, and structured experiences and direct mentoring.
- Future CET models need an integration of workplace experiences in their provisions.
- Pre-course counselling is an essential feature of future CET models.

Adults' Perspectives of CET: The National Survey

To appraise the interview findings in Phase 1 and potentially extend them further, it was necessary to engage with a broader sample of working age Singaporeans. Thus, the aim of Phase 2 was to capture how CET is viewed by a larger sample of working age Singaporeans, including those who have not taken any form of CET. This capturing was enacted using an online survey that gathered data on the expectations of CET and the learning needs and requirements of working age Singaporeans. Furthermore, respondents' views on subsidies and whether these made a difference to their willingness to participate in CET were also gathered, as this is a key element of the Singaporean government's policy.

Procedures

As noted, an online survey was developed drawing on the findings of the first phase and it was administered widely and responded to fully by 860 Singaporeans who indicated a range of ages, gender, levels of educational achievement and forms of employment in a selection of industry sectors within the Singaporean working age population. The survey was administered from October 2019 to March 2020. The goal for this "national survey" was to capture the responses to a series of closed items and open questions from a reasonably representative sample of working age Singaporeans including those who had not participated in CET programs. The sample of informants was obtained through circulating an invitation through electronic means to some local databases, including the alumni list from two of the polytechnics, trade associations' contact lists, and an adult educator network, personal contacts of the team, and web announcements.

In developing and refining the survey instrument, the research team engaged in iterations of discussions, reviews, and refinements, including tentative findings and cycles of testing the instrument on colleagues, and through consultation with advisory committee membership for feedback. Only when there was consensus that the online survey was clear and accessible was it administered. To attract respondents, those who completed the entire survey and elected to provide their email addresses participated in a draw to win one of a hundred $100 shopping vouchers. In addition, to target older Singaporeans, strategies such as taking electronic tablets or hard copies to the community settings were also undertaken.

Once the survey was closed, the data were cleaned to prepare for analysis. This was enacted through consistency checks and treatment of missing responses, using the SPSS software package. Consistency checks enabled the identification of data that were duplicate entries, out of range, logically inconsistent, or having extreme values to be removed. The missing responses were treated carefully to minimize their adverse effects by assigning a suitable value (e.g., neutral or imputed) or discarding them methodically. Thereafter, frequency counts were generated using SPSS with data presented in tables and graphs. It was from these analyses that much of the initial data analyses was conducted from March 2020 onwards. However, late in that year a supplementary survey was developed and administered to ascertain if there had been any changes in the working age population's perceptions about the accessibility and effectiveness of online forms of education (Billett et al., 2022).

Supplementary Survey

Given the COVID-19 pandemic that commenced in 2020 brought changes to how people worked and communicated. There was an increased exposure to and usage of electronic forms of communication (e.g., Zoom, Teams, Skype) for work and social purposes during periods of social isolation. Consequently, a supplementary survey was developed and administered towards the end of the 'lock down' period conducted to ascertain whether there had been any changes in working age adults' perceptions about the accessibility and efficacy of online CET provisions (Billett et al., 2022). Singapore was no exception and endured long periods of 'circuit breakers' or lock downs as a preventative strategy during COVID-19. This led to Singapore's working population engaging far more extensively with electronic technologies such as Zoom, Skype and Teams. Consequently, given the uptake and use of these kinds of media, the aim was to identify whether that usage had led to any changes in working age adults' views about the accessibility and efficacy of online modes of CET than had been indicated some 9 months earlier. Therefore, a brief supplementary survey was developed and administered in December 2020 focusing on whether views about the accessibility and utility of online education provisions, and this survey was distributed to contact lists of informants from the first phase of the project and the respondents to the National Survey. The quantitative data were analyzed using frequencies and comparisons, and the qualitative data were analyzed thematically. The results of this survey are briefly rehearsed in the section "mode of delivery post-COVID-19".

Findings

The demographic and work background of the national sample is provided here first, followed by respondents' views on effective ways to acquire skills, their challenges in engaging in CET, preferred arrangements for CET, views on qualities of effective teachers and students, how future provisions of CET should be provided, what subsidies schemes they would prefer, and their views on pre-course counselling.

National Survey: Demographic and Work Background

The respondents for the national survey (n = 860) comprised 55% males (n = 466) and 45% females (n = 388) (*see* Table 6.1). The age range of the respondents was widely distributed from 21 years old to 50 years plus. As a cohort of respondents, they are more highly qualified than the average adult Singaporean population, which has a higher proportion of the older population only educated up to secondary school level of education (Department of Statistics Singapore, 2024). They also mainly reported working as professionals, managers, executives, and technicians (PMET), which is also disproportionate to the actual work roles of the population. Of these respondents, 60.7% (n = 522) reported having engaged in CET programs (i.e., CET graduates), overwhelmingly through public providers (e.g., Post Secondary Education Institutes (e.g., polytechnics); 85% of them), while 39.3% (n = 338) did not (i.e., no CET experienced). Of those who indicated that they had participated in a CET program, it is presumed they included those ranging from

Table 6.1 Demographic background of 860 respondents

Variables	Values	N	%
Gender	Male	466	54.6
	Female	388	45.4
Highest qualification	N levels	5	.6
	O levels	10	1.2
	A levels	7	.8
	NITEC	7	.8
	Higher NITEC	3	.4
	Diploma	182	21.8
	Specialist Diploma	24	2.9
	Advanced Diploma	12	1.4
	Degree	332	39.8
	Postgraduate	253	30.3
Participation in CET	Yes	522	60.7
	No	338	39.3
CET program by a public educational institution	Yes	438	85.2
	No	76	14.8

full-qualification programs (i.e., long courses leading to a certification, diploma, or degree), to short courses, lunch time talks, or other once-off provisions.

These respondents worked in a range of public and private sector enterprises with diverse kinds of work arrangements (*see* Table 6.2), but with most of them having official office hours and many of them working in the public sector (44.3%) and

Table 6.2 Employment characteristics of the survey respondents

Variables	Values	N	%
Kinds of enterprises	Public sector	381	44.3
	Private sector >200 staff	272	31.6
	Private Sector ≤200 staff	143	16.6
	Self-employed	53	6.2
Work arrangement	Office hours	614	72.2
	Self-employed	65	7.6
	Shift work	53	6.2
	Freelance	41	4.8
	Not applicable	36	4.2
	Part-time	35	4.1
	Weekends	7	0.8
Employment status	Employed full time	646	75.3
	Unemployed (not seeking for work)	93	10.8
	Self-employed	62	7.2
	Employed part time	32	3.7
	Unemployed (seeking for work)	21	2.4
	Retired	4	0.5
Industry sector	Healthcare, Education	336	39.5
	Professional Services, Information, Communication and Technology and Media, Financial Services	263	30.9
	Construction, Architecture, Engineering, Real Estate, Cleaning, Security	71	8.3
	Logistics, Air/Sea/Land/Public Transport, Wholesale Trade	67	7.9
	Food Services, Retail, Hotels, Food Manufacturing	60	7.1
	Energy & Chemicals, Precision Engineering, Marine & Offshore, Aerospace, Electronics	54	6.3
Occupational category	Professionals	287	40.6
	Administration and support workers	208	29.4
	Legislators, senior officials and managers	81	11.5
	Associate professionals and technicians	76	10.7
	Service and sales workers	43	6.1
	Plant and machine operators and assemblers	7	1
	Cleaners, labourers, and related workers	3	0.4
	Agricultural and fishery workers	2	0.3

observing normal office hours (72.2%). Most were employed full-time (75.3%), but with over a tenth of these respondents being unemployed (13.2%), which is disproportionately high for this country, but is explained by their interest in securing occupational capacities to become employed. The respondents reported working a range of industry sectors, with 39.5% in the healthcare and education sectors and 30.9% in the professional services, information, communication and technology and media and financial services sector. A small percentage worked in other sectors, such as construction, logistics, and hotel sectors. An even smaller number come from the service and sales industries. Finally, about 40% identified themselves as professionals, about 30% are administrators and support workers, and about 20% are managers, senior officials, and technicians. So, whilst not wholly representative of the working age Singaporean population, the respondents were well distributed across gender and age and represented a range of industry sectors and occupations within them.

In this way, the sample, whilst not wholly representative, provided a range of insights from the perspectives of many working age Singaporeans across gender, age category, education, employment and industry sector divides. Given the concern to understand how these adults with diverse experiences accounted for how they had learnt to sustain their employability, they were asked to indicate the most effective ways to acquire skills.

Effective Ways to Acquire Skills

The respondents were asked what they considered and report what for them was the most effective way to acquire occupational and workplace skills (i.e., those required for employability). Their responses are presented in Table 6.3, which has the list of pre-set survey responses in the left column, the frequency of mention in the middle

Table 6.3 Effective means to skill acquisition

Ways to acquire skills	N	%
On-the-job training	652	75.8
Attending external training outside the workplace	351	40.8
Mentored by my supervisor	297	34.5
Supported by a more experienced buddy	260	30.2
Attending in-house training	265	30.8
Attending team meetings/team discussions with my manager	211	24.5
Attending external training in the workplace	168	19.5
Participating in online courses	135	15.7

Note: This survey was conducted between October 2019 to March 2020, before Covid inspired lock downs)

column and percentage of responses in the right column. Respondents were able to indicate more than one way they had acquired work skills. As can be seen, 'on-the-job training' was proposed as the most effective means (76%). This was followed by 'attending external training outside the workplace' (41%) and 'being mentored by supervisors' (35%). It was reported that the least effective way to acquire skills, among the options given to them, is through participating in 'online courses', and then 'attending external training in the workplace'. As foreshadowed, perception about the former (i.e., online education) appeared to have subsequently changed through the experience of becoming more familiar and competent with the use of electronic media during the lock down as is reported elsewhere (Billett et al., 2022) and discussed below. However, and has been reported elsewhere, there is a strong pattern of support for the efficacy of learning in and through work, also mentored by supervisors and supported by other workers. So, all of this suggests that there are rich opportunities for engaging working age adults and supporting their learning in and through their everyday work, and in their work settings.

In this cohort, many respondents did not regard participating in CET programs as a highly effective means of developing skills associated with their employability, although the second ranked option was 'external training' which could obviously include the kind of CET provisions offered by the tertiary education systems. What is perhaps most noticeable is the very low ranking of online education, albeit its growing prominence. In fact, opinions on online education had become more positive, but nuanced since the advent of the COVID-19 pandemic as elaborated in the section "Mode of delivery post-COVID-19". These findings are noteworthy in so far as they differ from what the employers reported as effective ways to acquire skills (*see* Leow et al., 2022).

Employers did not rate attending 'external training outside the workplace' as highly as did these respondents. However, both equally agreed that 'on-the-job training' was an effective means of acquiring skills. The interpretation here is that this response refers to where a broad range of ways of learning through work activities and interactions can progress. Yet, unlike employers who reported that 'online education' was relatively effective, respondents to the national survey reported that it was one of the least effective ways. Either way, what these responses indicate is that there is a broader recognition of the importance of workplaces as sites in which individuals can acquire skills and continue to develop their skills in, through and across working life. However, a sizable percentage of these respondents reported not having participated in CET, so may not have informed bases to report on the contributions of these options. Hence, it was necessary to conduct a comparison of these two sub-cohorts, rather than immediately progress with a synthesis of all these respondents' contributions. A comparison between the rankings of this list between those respondents who have participated in CET (i.e., CET graduates) with those who have not (i.e., no CET experienced), as presented in Table 6.4, with those who had participated in the middle column and those who had not in the right one.

There was strong consensus across both cohorts that 'on the job training' was the most preferred and 'mentoring by supervisor' were effective means. Elsewhere, there was consensus about the relative value of the lowest three ranked options.

Adults' Perspectives of CET: The National Survey

Table 6.4 Ranking of effective means to skill acquisition by CET graduates vs No-CET experienced

Effective ways to acquire skills	CET graduates	No-CET experienced
On-the-job training	1	1
Attending external training outside the workplace	2	5
Mentored by my supervisor	3	2
Attending in-house training	4	4
Supported by a more experienced buddy	5	3
Attending team meetings/team discussions with my manager in the workplace	6	6
Attending external training in the workplace	7	7
Participating in online courses	8	8

However, there was a key difference in how the respondents rated 'attending external training outside the workplace' and 'attending in house training'. Noteworthy here is that those who have attended CET courses ranked 'external training' more highly and 'internal training' lower than those who had not attended such courses. The former item was ranked as the second most important way to acquire skills (50.4%) by CET graduates and the latter seventh, whereas those who have not attended CET ranked this item as only the seventh most important way to acquire skill (13.0%) and 'internal training' as fourth.

These findings could be interpreted in two ways. Firstly, it may reflect that those who have a positive view of 'external training', such as most of the Phase 1 informants who reported to have either achieved or partially achieved their goals for participating in their CET programs (*see* section "An Effective, Accessible and Scalable CET Provision"), might be more inclined to value external training than those who had not. It may also reflect that those who have had the experience of external training are generally more likely to view it positively, because that is what they know. But, beyond these perspectives, were those from the no-CET experienced about the challenges they confront in engaging in CET. But, regardless of which explanation is the most credible, the overall preferencing indicates the importance of learning in and through work by these respondents.

Challenges in Engaging in CET

Given that all kinds of classifications of workers need to engage in further developing their capacities across working life, it is important to understand why working age adults do not or cannot participate in CET. As approximately 40% of these respondents (n = 338) did not participate in any CET, it is helpful to find out why they did not. Of this sample, the reasons for not participating in CET are listed in Table 6.5. In this table, 11 categories of reasons for not participating in CET are presented in the left-hand column. The number of these respondents who indicated each of those categories and the non-accumulative percentage is in the right-hand

Table 6.5 Reasons for not engaging in CET

Reasons for not engaging in CET in	N	%
too busy at work	111	41.7
not familiar with the course offering available in the market	106	39.8
preferred course or program offered at an inconvenient time or place	70	26.3
no suitable course available in the market	58	21.8
lack of employer's support	56	21.1
unable to afford education or training	51	19.2
lack of time due to family commitments	47	17.7
unexpected circumstances	24	9.0
not qualified or eligible for the training	14	5.3
unseen benefit of training	12	4.5
no additional training needed	9	3.4

column. This is because the respondents can indicate more than one reason. One way of considering these responses is considering those associated with: i) workplace factors, ii) knowledge of CET provisions and iii) issues of accessibility.

In terms of workplace factors, the most frequently indicated responses refer to the demands of work (111) and lack of employers' support (56). Lack of knowledge of CET provisions (106), no suitable courses available (58), being unable to afford those programs (51) and being ineligible to participate (14) indicated how the knowledge of, availability, cost of CET provisions were reported as important factors. In terms of accessibility, 70 indications of a lack of convenience in either time or location and the requirements of these courses were inconsistent with family commitments (47). And the next three were associated with knowledge about, convenience of, and suitability of courses, all of which are about the accessibility to the kinds of programs in which these working age Singaporeans might have otherwise participated. These are issues that can be addressed by PSEIs. Only 4.5% of respondents stated they did not see any benefit from training and 3.4% reported not needing CET.

These reasons suggest that there is a need to consider ease of accessibility including whether the need to travel to a physical location can be addressed eased through having more convenient locations or through online educational provisions. Given the broad consensus on the effectiveness of work-based learning experiences, this raises the question about how work and CET can be integrated into work experiences to address issues of accessibility. It also suggests that further enquiries and possibly interventions might be required and more work must be done in promoting and marketing existing courses being offered in the market as a substantial number of workers (40%) are not aware of courses suitable for them, and identifying if there are unmet needs within the working age population.

The respondents were also asked about the challenges that they would anticipate if they were to participate in CET programs. The qualitative responses are presented in Table 6.6. In the left-hand column of this table are five sets of challenges that

Table 6.6 Expected challenges of participating in CET

Expected challenges	N	%
Course fees	589	72.4
Job responsibilities	466	57.3
Family responsibilities	404	49.7
Course requirements	351	43.2
Travel time to CET venue	344	42.3

were identified to their participation. It is noteworthy that the highest number and percentage (72%) indicated that course fees were viewed to be an anticipated challenge. However, the national context is important here and requires a brief elaboration. That is, there has been a long-standing tradition in Singapore for the government to provide subsidies to encourage individuals to engage in CET. A concern at a national level is that these subsidies have now become an expectation. That is, Singaporeans widely expect that the government will pay for or subsidize their participation in further education. Indeed, the government members of the advisory committee requested that an item about whether respondents would participate in the CET if there were no subsidies. The overwhelming response was that a lack of subsidies would inhibit respondents' participation.

Beyond the issues of cost, the key challenges that have been illuminated and discussed elsewhere (Chap. 5—*Motivations and affordances for engaging CET*) are the existing work, family and community commitments that need to be balanced out against participation in CET provisions. Also indicated here are practicalities associated with travel time, which often means attending a CET program at the end of the working day and might entail travelling across the island to a PSEI and then home after that finishes. Again, this factor is an important contextual issue that Singaporeans tend to work a long day, and even getting to attend a face-to-face CET session after work commencing at 7 PM can be a challenge.

The findings presented in Table 6.6 suggest that the provision of subsidies has not, on its own, resolved the issue of financial burden and that this sentiment may be a product of expectations that such subsidies should be universal and stronger to increase their appeal and accessibility to many working age Singaporeans. As with Phase 1, there were concerns about conflicting responsibilities (i.e., work and family) and travelling time to facilities in which CET is being provided (Leow et al., 2022). Overall, these data suggest that accessibility for working age Singaporeans who have both work and family commitments is important and flexibility in the provisions of CET may be quite central to their effective enactment and wider engagement. This requirement then leads to the question about how they should be organized and enacted, which was also requested of the respondents.

Preferred Arrangements for CET

As has been noted and discussed earlier, participation in CET programs for working age adults is usually non-compulsory, except when that participation is aligned to essential occupational certification required for licensing purposes. For perhaps most working age adults, engagement in CET is discretionary. That is, it is individuals who decide whether to participate in these programs and how they will participate. So, unlike compulsory education or that which is essentially mandated in the transition between school and working life such as initial occupational preparation through tertiary education, working age adults decide whether they will participate, for what purposes and how they will participate. Consequently, their preferences are more than catering to personal partialities, but instead the needs and requirements of a student cohort who have overlapping and competing demands upon their time and energies. Although used in another context to describe the positioning of contemporary higher education students as being 'time jealous' (i.e., a requirement to use their time strategically), rather than being 'time poor' (i.e., do not have sufficient time) (Billett, 2015), the same might apply to working age adults. That is, they need to decide what ways and how best to achieve their most important goals through the available time available to them. It follows then that the national survey respondents were asked about their preferences for the mode of delivery of CET programs and when these should best occur. In the sections below, responses to these questions are presented and discussed.

Mode of Delivery

Those respondents to the national survey undertaken in late 2019 and early 2020 who have participated in CET (n = 522) when asked to determine amongst three options—i) face-to-face, ii) online or iii) a combination of face-to-face and online, reported that the latter (i.e., combination of face-to-face and online learning modes) as being the most convenient and effective approach. But they also reported the online mode as more convenient than the face-to-face mode. However, when it comes to effectiveness of the educational experience, the face-to-face mode was preferred over the online mode (*see* Table 6.7). That table presents data on the reported convenience and effectiveness of the modes of CET. The middle column

Table 6.7 Convenient/Effective modes of delivery

	Mode of delivery	N	%
Convenience	Combination	303	60.4
	Online	110	21.9
	Face-to-face	89	17.7
Effectiveness	Combination	262	52.1
	Face-to-face	207	41.2
	Online	44	8.7

indicates the mode and those to its right the number of respondents and overall percentage of respondents. What can be seen quite clearly is that prior to the COVID era, it was acknowledged that the combination of online and face-to-face was by far the most convenient. Moreover, that combination was also viewed as being the most effective.

The quantitative rating of each of these modes of CET delivery was justified by respondents for specific reasons (*see* Table 6.8). Online CET was valued for ease of access to a range of content that is best represented through text and images and because additional materials are easily accessible through online provisions. It was also valued for structuring the CET program through its organization and capacity to revisit or engage proactively with the content. The face-to-face CET experiences were deemed to be helpful for interactions with teachers and peers, gaining their

Table 6.8 Justified strengths of different modes of CET delivery

Online		Face-to-face		Combination		Learning materials	
Strengths	%	Strengths	%	Strengths	%	Effectiveness	%
accommodates CET learners with busy work and travelling schedules	77.3	provides a supportive learning experience	74.9	caters directly to students' learning needs in class	61.5	Hardcopy notes	74.4
permits learning at a preferred pace	70.5	provides opportunities to share diverse views and experiences	74.4	assists in retention of learning through online and classroom learning	57.6	As much information as possible to learn more about the topic	61.4
makes course materials accessible at anytime	63.6	clarifies concerns and uncertainties immediately by the lecturers	54.6	utilises course materials online for preparation before class	51.9	Learning materials available online (e.g. through smartphone, tablet)	44.9
reduces disruption to family commitments	34.1	enhances peer interaction	34.3	improves communication via offline and online methods	46.6	Learning materials that are updated and relevant to the field	39.2
avoids commuting to class	34.1	allows lecturers' presentation of content and structure of lesson	31.9	permits continuation of classroom discussions online	44.7	Notes to be summarised for the purpose of assessment	38.2
		allows receipt of immediate feedback from classmates	16.9			Notes to be distributed in advance before classes start	22.9

insights, responses to questions, and feedback. That is, their interactive and spontaneous forms of engagement with the aspects of this mode of attendance that the participants reported as being most worthwhile. From the Phase 1 interviews, it had been emphasized that when these face-to-face interactions comprised the teacher merely presenting information and did not provide opportunities for students to discuss, question and relate to their own experiences, they were deemed unsatisfactory. It was the interactive sharing and collaborative aspects of the face-to-face experiences that these working age adults valued the most. In those interviews, many commented that it was those qualities that made it worthwhile to make the long journeys at the end of the working day to spend time and effort on these face-to-face engagements.

In summary, the data gathered from working Singaporeans pre-COVID suggested that effective CET can be supported by both online and face-to-face interactions and engagements, when they are able to participate in them. These respondents identified justifications for their preferences for each of these modes of engagement, with issues of convenience balanced against those of effectiveness, which often concurred with the detailed accounts provided by the Phase 1 interviewees. However, as with those interviewees, the survey respondents reported that the combination of both platforms was what made them most effective. That is, making educational materials readily accessible and providing opportunities to extend the content to students' goals and circumstances, and through learning from those of others.

It is noteworthy that online provision has become more appreciated for its convenience since the advent of the COVID-19 pandemic and the consequent more widespread use of online technology during the circuit breaker, as elaborated upon in the following section (*see* Billett et al., 2022).

Mode of Delivery Post-COVID-19

As foreshadowed, a supplementary survey was developed and administered in December 2020 after a 9-month period of lock downs (i.e., circuit breaker) during which working age Singaporeans had necessarily engaged in a heightened use of electronic technology and online platforms such as Teams, Zoom and Skype to conduct their work, and engage with each other, family members and perform a range of tasks which previously they would have conducted through face-to-face means. Hence, it was deemed expedient to ascertain whether any changes in working age adults' perceptions of the convenience and effectiveness of online provisions of CET had arisen through this heightened engagement with electronic technologies. The supplementary survey data, indeed, indicated that a statistically significant percentage of respondents appreciated the convenience of the online mode, more so than represented in the data gathered prior to the lockdown. Moreover, although not statistically significant, the percentage of those referring to its effectiveness was slightly higher. A total of 258 complete responses were received in December 2020 and this number was compared to the responses from the National Survey in 2019 discussed in the previous section. In Table 6.9, the percentage differences between

Table 6.9 Comparisons between 2019 and 2020 surveys

Variables	Values	% of responses		
		2019	2020	Difference
Convenient mode	Online	21.7	49.2	+27.5
	Face-to-face	19.9	7.8	−12.1
	Combination	58.4	43.0	−15.4
Effective mode	Online	8.4	12.0	+3.6
	Face-to-face	39.9	35.3	−4.6
	Combination	51.7	52.7	+1.0

the responses in 2019 and 2020 are presented in terms of convenience of mode of delivery and their effectiveness as an educational provision.

The 2020 respondents were also asked if they were now more open to fully online courses because of what they had experienced during the circuit breaker. An overwhelming 72.1% of the respondents responded with "Yes". A smaller percentage of 12.4% and 15.5% responded with "No" and "Unsure," respectively. What this suggests is that because of the broader use of electronic technologies by working age Singaporeans that they have become more familiar, comfortable and competent with its use and this opens up the prospect for a preference for engaging in educational provisions by these adults which was far lower prior to heightened use of electronic technologies during the lockdown period.

Together, the findings suggest that appraisals about the convenience of online education has increased. Likely, this change arises from more opportunities to experience online engagement because of the COVID-19 pandemic. To further understand this response and the challenges working age adults may face with the increased use of online education, we also examined the respondents' open comments. The 145 comments provided by survey respondents revealed a nuanced understanding of the benefits and drawbacks of online education. For instance, while it was proposed that online education was time saving and allowed for flexibility in learning, it also required more focus by students and better facilitation skills of lecturers to facilitate effective online interactions and the overall effectiveness of online provisions was also likely to be dependent on the type of course taken and accessibility and availability of technology (Billett et al., 2021).

These findings are important to consider as it is most certain that we have reached "a point of no return" for the digital transition for PSEIs in Singapore (Watermeyer et al., 2022, p. 878), and elsewhere as tertiary education transitions into a far greater use of electronic technology as means of engaging in work and in education. All of this is important to understand in the context of working age adults who are time jealous and need to spend that time effectively. Consequently, in the following section, the preference of Phase 2 national survey respondents about the arrangements of time and attendance are presented.

Table 6.10 Timing and compulsoriness of attendance

Variable	Values	N	%
Preferred timing	Flexible (e.g., online)	476	60.5
	Evening classes	376	47.8
	Daytime classes	303	38.5
	Weekends	232	29.5
	Intensive (full-day training)	221	28.1
Compulsory attendance	80%	358	75.8
	50%	111	23.5
	25%	3	0.6

Timing and Attendance

The national survey respondents also indicated their preferred times and requirements for participating in CET programs. Table 6.10 summarizes the responses to a range of options of preferred timing where the respondents were able to indicate multiple preferences. This table has two sections, the first about preferred timing (i.e., part of the day or week) for CET engagements, and secondly, whether attendance should be compulsory or not. For both, the variable is in the left-hand column, the values being responded to are in the central column and the number of responses and overall percentage are in the right-hand columns. The findings about preferred timings did not suggest any clear pattern, except to suggest that 'flexibility' in modes of attendance is most strongly supported. Least preferred are intensive all-day professional development of training sessions and also 'weekends'. In terms of the former, data from interviews with CET graduates (i.e., Phase 1) indicates that not all employers are willing to sponsor employee's participation in these kinds of all-day workshops and so they would come at a cost to employees in either lost pay or consuming precious recreational leave days. Also, for the weekend option this may be a problem for adults, particularly those with young children, given that the kinds of educational, family and community commitments are strong in this nation state.

For those working in the daytime, the orthodox provision of classes in the evenings can still be problematic, despite the strong support for this option. The evening provision of CET may not suit all working age Singaporeans because of family commitments, or the location of the courses and after a long working day. Hence, flexibility in the form of a variety of preferred times for offering CET provisions is likely required, even though this may create logistical and planning problems for tertiary education institutions. Most likely, there will be specific preferences within occupational or student cohorts that might need to be addressed. However, overall, a knowledge of students' preferences for engagement is important in advertising or promoting participation in CET.

Indeed, one of the issues raised in the survey is whether attendance should be compulsory, and if so, to what degree. Importantly, overall, this suggests that flexibility and openness to diversity in provisions of CET are most likely going to be required to meet the adult working population's needs in terms of time and commitments that need to be negotiated around. For instance, there are likely to be differences in the availability of adults with young children in their families whose weekends are taken up with cultural and educational activities and adults whose children have passed schooling years.

The key point here is that there is likely to be a requirement for tertiary education institutions to be sensitive and responsive to the needs of its adult population in providing effective and accessible CET provisions. For instance, it was concluded from the Phase 1 interviews that the orthodoxies of current models of CET provisions may need to be challenged. Instead of having either one kind of mode of engagement, hybrid arrangements might suit the needs of the course and students. For instance, there might be the need for initial face-to-face meetings followed by subsequent interactions which be conducted online. Then, if there are practical aspects of the course that require face-to-face and intense engagements, these might be done through focused and concentrated interactions, including weekend intensive activities. Whilst it might be difficult to organize family commitments around the availability every year, the occasional scheduled weekend commitment may be tolerable in terms of family needs. Fundamental here is the idea that desk education institutions and tertiary dictators need to be open to a diverse range of models of offering courses and in ways that are most accessible and engaging for the adult student cohort.

It might seem surprising and potentially contradictory that most respondents reported a preference for 80% compulsory attendance. Given the qualitative comments provided, this response most likely indicates the seriousness with which survey informants, who are most likely to be taxpayers, viewed such investments in their resources and their desire for achievement in CET. Moreover, because the subsidies are widely used in Singapore, albeit set within a Confucian heritage culture of reciprocity that is such attendance might seem as being something which is necessary to indicate commitments and return of the investment being afforded individuals by the nation state. It might also indicate perceptions of the importance of directly interacting with CET educators. Certainly, the role of these educators is paramount to the perceptions of an effective education provision by 'time jealous' working age adults. So, the following section presents and discusses the data about the respondents' views on the qualities of CET educators.

Qualities of Effective CET Teachers

A significant element of any educational provision is what is enacted by educators. Ultimately, they do much to enact and conduct the kinds of experiences that are intended to achieve the outcomes of the course. It is well understood that even the most detailed syllabus document or tightly constructed instructional design will ultimately be mediated by the educators who enact them (Lovat & Smith, 1991; Marsh, 2004). It follows then that to identify the kinds of qualities that constitute their effectiveness, the respondents were asked to indicate up to three characteristics from a listing of characteristics that were deemed to be important qualities of effective CET educators. There are similar patterns in responses for both respondent groups (i.e., those who participated in CET and those who did not) as presented in Table 6.11. In this table, those characteristics that pertain specifically to occupational experience are *italicized* to distinguish them from those that are about more general teaching capabilities. Across both groups of respondents, there is a strong emphasis in their listings of characteristics of having relevant industry experiences to inform students' needs and purposes, being responsive to students' needs and abilities, and engaging and utilizing students' experiences and interests.

These listings are aligned with and support what was found in Phase 1: an expectation of these teachers to have relevant occupational competences as well as being effective educators (Leow et al., 2022). Yet, while seemingly distinct, these qualities are likely to be compatible and interdependent. Being responsive to students and utilizing their experiences also requires an understanding of their goals and potential learning endpoints (i.e., the occupational capacities they need to learn). Similarly, having industry experience with the ability to use it effectively (i.e., instructing not impressing) is also important for educators to be able to communicate, share and engage their students effectively. Quite consistently across the samples of graduates, employers, and working age Singaporeans, the majority of whom have had

Table 6.11 Characteristics of effective CET teachers

CET teachers' characteristics	CET group	N	%
Having relevant industry experiences to inform learners' needs and purposes	CET graduate	256	52.5
	No-CET experienced	135	49.8
Being responsive to learners' needs and abilities	CET graduate	235	48.2
	No-CET experienced	145	53.5
Engaging and utilising learners' experiences and interests	CET graduate	230	47.1
	No-CET experienced	124	45.8
Adopting flexible approaches to teaching and assessment that meet learners' purposes and needs	CET graduate	174	35.7
	No-CET experienced	97	35.8
Making concepts applicable through teaching	CET graduate	163	33.4
	No-CET experienced	85	31.4
Using interactive teaching processes	CET graduate	143	29.3
	No-CET experienced	83	30.6
Illustrating what is to be learnt and its purposes	CET graduate	123	25.2
	No-CET experienced	56	20.7
Identifying and implementing effective teaching strategies for the content learnt	CET graduate	107	21.9
	No-CET experienced	55	20.3

CET experience, there is a consistent message that CET teachers need this combination of relevant industry experience and effective teaching qualities. It is these qualities that are consistently reported as being required to organize and enact effective educational experiences. And these qualities include understanding students' goals and needs not only as a pedagogue, but also from the perspective of building occupational knowledge, and from a source that students take as being credible. Also, these qualities extend to teachers being responsive to students and engaging them in activities and interactions as active participants, as the relevance of these experiences to students' goals are important. This emphasizes the need for CET teachers to be occupationally current and educationally competent. Hence, these teachers need to maintain their occupational competence, while those with industry experience need professional preparation as CET teachers. This situation is almost perennial for educators working in the field of occupational preparation and its further development. On the one hand, they need to work from, within and through the education institutions in which are employed, yet also need to remain currently competent in the occupational field. Of course, for those educators who are not competent in the specific field, the challenge is to find ways to be knowledgeable and informed about the occupational practices and requirements about which they are teaching.

However, the effectiveness of CET provisions is not just premised on what is afforded working age adults in terms of experiences and instruction or guidance. It also includes how these adults come to engage and participate in CET programs. As in any educational program, or process of learning, it is up to those who are engaging with them as students, novices or neophytes to play an active role in the learning process.

Qualities of Effective CET Students

Ultimately, any educational provision is dependent on how students engage in it, and CET is certainly no exception. These provisions are nothing more or less than invitations in the form of what students or adult learners know, can do, value and change as a legacy of their experiencing of what is provided for them. The distinction between experiences (i.e., what is afforded them) and the individual's construal and construction of what is afforded them (i.e., how they engage with what is afforded them) is central to the duality that comprises social constructivism. Hence, considerations of how working age adults elect to engage with what is provided through CET programs is salient to their effectiveness. What is most important is how CET students take up that invitation. Thus, it is important to know what respondents report as qualities of effective CET students, which they themselves, presumably, need to demonstrate.

Table 6.12 presents their responses to a set of characteristics of effective CET students that were presented in the survey. What is noteworthy about the most highly ranked characteristics is that they are strongly focused on personal dispositions (i.e., values and attitudes) that are *italicized* in this table, ahead of capabilities (i.e., being

Table 6.12 Characteristics of effective CET students

CET learner characteristics	N	%
Able to learn independently	288	38.8
Having or showing an interest in learning	248	33.2
Having a humble attitude	245	32.8
Motivated to learn for their personal development	225	30.1
Having strong workplace support	213	28.5
Motivated to learn for their professional development	212	28.3
Having good time management skills	211	28.2
Are resourceful and proactive	200	26.7
Perceiving learning as an ongoing process	170	22.7
Having strong family support	100	13.4
Having positive communication skills	90	12.0

able to achieve goals), despite the most frequently reported quality emphasizing capability (i.e., able to learn independently). As with other tables, the listing of characteristics is presented in the left column and the frequency of their mention is in the column to its right and the percentage of respondents referring to this characteristic is presented in the right column. As with some of the other tables, the ordering of the characteristics is from those most frequently mentioned at the top of the table to those least frequently mentioned at the bottom.

What these findings suggest is that, from a list of learner characteristics, readiness to be an effective CET student or learner is premised upon the capability to learn independently, and because of the need to engage with others, interdependently, as underpinned by a set of dispositions associated with interest, openness to learn, and being motivated for personal and professional purposes. The characteristics emphasized in this listing are largely personal qualities and are ranked higher than having strong work and family support or the capability of positive communication skills. These suggestions emphasize the important constructive process of meaning making by individuals as they engage in experiences. In this case, it is experiences which are intentionally directed towards specific and intended learning outcomes. What is emphasized within these responses is the importance of effortful engagement, being considerate of what can be learnt from the experiences provided and the intentionality of the meaning making process being directed towards outcomes that are important to the individual.

This set of findings, then, raises the question about the importance of the CET students' readiness to engage in these activities, and their preparedness to be independent or interdependent learners. Even if they developed these capacities earlier in compulsory or tertiary education, it might be quite a challenge for them to be independent within a new set of activities that are quite novel and potentially intimidating for them. This perhaps suggests that either an orientation about how to be an effective adult learner might be necessary before participating in CET programs, or

Adults' Perspectives of CET: The National Survey

else initial courses in those programs may quite intentionally develop those capacities. So, from these responses, again, is revisited how we view and position adults as students. Dated conceptions such as andragogy (Knowles, 1975) claiming that adults are inherently self-directed in all aspects of their life and their learning was no exception have been challenged by critics (e.g., Tennant, 1986), and that self-direction is likely to be restricted in fields of knowledge with which they are not familiar and not confident. Indeed, challenges to adults' sense of self or subjectivity can stand in the way of their effective engagement in new experiences because of these kinds of expectations. That is, because they are adults, they should be able to learn more independently than children, for instance. However, when confronted with context, content or concepts and procedures that are outside of their scope of experience, this can lead to resistance and negation of the need to learn. What this potentially emphasizes is that quite the opposite is the case and, in these circumstances, working age adults need to access guidance and counselling as much as direct interaction with educators.

Throughout the first phase of data gathering, the issue of integrating workplace experiences and learnings within CET was frequently mentioned (Leow et al., 2022). Consequently, in considering how the future for CET in Singapore might be envisaged and enacted, it seemed important to elicit responses from the informants about how future provisions of CET might be organized and elected and this included how workplace experiences consider the ways in which these experiences could be integrated into CET provisions.

Future Provisions of CET

The respondents indicated their priorities for how workplaces could support CET-related learning, based on two lists of options with which they were provided in the survey. The first focused on workplace actions that could support learning, and the second, actions by tertiary education institutions or CET educators to utilize workplaces as learning environments. The responses are presented in Table 6.13. This table comprises listings of four and five processes workplace actions and then those by CET institutions, respectively, and as responded by both cohorts (i.e., those who participated in CET and those who did not). Central here is the availability of opportunities in workplaces to apply what they have learnt from their CET programs and, vice versa. That is, the respondents reported valuing a tight alignment between the focuses for the learning in their courses and the kind of activities in which they can participate in their workplaces. We know the ability to practice, refine, hone, and integrate what has recently been learnt is a key foundation for effective learning of procedural capacities (Ericsson, 2006) required for many workplace and occupational activities. So, this request from these respondents is quite purposive, rather than being seen as being pragmatic. It also indicates the importance of having alignment between CET students' study and work activities. The next most preferred workplace action is the provision of opportunities to promote learning through

Table 6.13 Future provisions of CET

Workplace actions to support learning	CET group	N	%
Opportunities for applying what you have learnt in CET	CET graduate	373	79.7
	No-CET experienced	197	75.8
Opportunities for learning at work (new challenging tasks)	CET graduate	327	69.9
	No-CET experienced	172	66.2
Opportunities for progressive rotation of job roles	CET graduate	291	62.2
	No-CET experienced	162	62.3
Mentoring by more experienced colleagues	CET graduate	233	49.8
	No-CET experienced	129	49.6
Actions by CET to support work-based learning	CET group	N	%
Industry experts to deliver lessons	CET graduate	296	63.2
	No-CET experienced	135	51.9
Work placement/attachment opportunities related to your CET course	CET graduate	284	60.7
	No-CET experienced	173	66.5
Linking CET assessments to work-based activities	CET graduate	285	60.9
	No-CET experienced	141	54.2
Work-based educational project	CET graduate	242	51.7
	No-CET experienced	124	47.7
CET teachers coming into the workplace	CET graduate	124	26.5
	No-CET experienced	69	26.5

engagement in new tasks, and structured experiences such as progressive job rotations and direct mentoring in the workplace.

As foreshadowed, the respondents also ranked, from a listing of options, how CET provisions could support learning in and through work, as presented in Table 6.13. In their preferences, there is a very strong emphasis on integrating and making relevant CET provisions by extending them into the students' workplaces. This set of suggestions is also about workplaces reaching into the experiences provided through tertiary education institutions. This includes having industry experts engage with students through presentation, students having the opportunity to engage in workplace experiences, and work-based activities being used as the basis for effective and reliable assessment. Added here is a focus on projects based in workplaces, with 'CET teachers coming into the workplace' being the least preferred action, perhaps because of concerns about their currency. Again, noteworthy here is the emphasis on the organization of the curriculum, as well as pedagogic and assessment strategies being linked strongly to the work-related activities of CET students.

In these ways, provisions of CET for the future are seen by these respondents as having and integrating workplace experiences as part of the CET provision, its teaching, and its assessment. Further, there are consistent emphases on finding ways to integrate the two sets of experiences (i.e., in the workplace and PSEIs) to achieve effective CET outcomes. This finding is consistent with many governments' concerns and initiative to integrate and foster a stronger link between the curriculum taught in tertiary educational institutions and the needs of the workplace and industry through internships, which provide these students with authentic working and learning opportunities. So, the suggestions here are helpful in so far as they point to how experiences in the workplace can be integrated into the CET programs, and moreover, how those programs can actively reach into experiences that students are happy in their work settings.

An essential and increasingly controversial feature of the approach to promoting working age Singaporeans' engagement in CET is the provision of subsidies to participants. Next, the worth and effectiveness of subsidies is the subject of responses from the survey.

Subsidies for CET

A specific feature of the CET provision in Singapore is that government subsidies in the form of payment to cover parts or, in some cases all the fees of CET programs is a well-established practice with the intent of encouraging participation. In Singapore, two kinds of training grants' incentives are provided: i) self-sponsored training and ii) employer-sponsored training (SkillsFuture Singapore, 2024). For both schemes, depending on the course level, Singaporean citizens and permanent residents can be sponsored for up to 90% of the course fees. The acceptance and worth of these subsidies are evident in responses to the question about whether people would participate in CET if there were no subsidies. The survey included two specific questions associated with subsidies. The first was about whether they were necessary and the second concerned who or what groups of students should get priority for subsides.

When it comes to the attractiveness of subsidies in engaging adults in CET programs, there is a strong consensus among the respondents that subsidies are likely to be an important factor for individuals' decisions about CET participation. Of the CET graduates, approximately 67% agree with the proposition that they would not participate in programs without subsidies, and it was even more highly supported by those who have not yet participated in CET (77%). In this way, it seems that the practice of providing subsidies has become well entrenched and expected by working age Singaporeans. This finding complicates and challenges the earlier views about the purposes for which individuals participate in CET; that is, the degree by which they are willing to pursue personal and professional goals when this is premised upon receiving subsidies to do so. As discussed in Chap. 5—*Motivations and affordance for participation in CET*, intrinsic motivation is more likely to drive the intentional and demanding processes to learn difficult content, hence subsidies might promote extrinsic motivation to the exclusion of the intrinsic. Yet, there are also culturally derived factors that sit behind this decision-making process.

The survey respondents were then asked to indicate, from a list, the groups of people who should receive priority for CET subsidies. What is presented in Table 6.14 are the survey responses to this set of issues. In the left-hand column are the items to which both the cohorts of CET graduates and no CET experienced (*see* middle column) have responded, and then the frequency of responses to these suggestions and the overall percentages are presented in the right column. It was shown that there should be no discrimination, and that everybody listed should get the same access to subsidies. After this, respondents next prioritized individuals who were in some way disadvantaged, including those who are not able to afford CET programs without external support.

These findings suggest that subsidies are still a very strong incentive (i.e., extrinsic motivations) for the respondents to participate in CET, but respondents understand that some people need these subsidies more than others.

Across the data gathering in the first phase, evidence suggested that there is a need for the provision of advice and counselling to working age Singaporeans to

Table 6.14 Priority for use of subsidies

Priority groups for CET subsidies	CET group	N	%
No priority, everyone (Singaporeans and PRs) gets the same amount	CET graduate	130	28.4
	No-CET experienced	75	29.3
Unemployed individuals (e.g., retrenched workers, fresh graduates)	CET graduate	80	17.5
	No-CET experienced	37	14.5
Individuals who are not able to afford CET programs	CET graduate	68	14.8
	No-CET experienced	40	15.6
Those desiring to deepen their knowledge and skills in their current jobs	CET graduate	66	14.4
	No-CET experienced	50	19.5
Those who have demonstrated lifelong learning attitude	CET graduate	61	13.3
	No-CET experienced	15	5.9
Employed but changing career	CET graduate	24	5.2
	No-CET experienced	28	10.9
No priority, first-come-first-served basis	CET graduate	19	4.1
	No-CET experienced	6	2.3
Retirees and senior citizens	CET graduate	10	2.2
	No-CET experienced	5	2.0

ensure that their participation in CET was well directed and appropriate and that their selections of programs and courses were well aligned with their readiness and purposes (Leow et al., 2022; Leow et al., 2023a, b). Consequently, in the national survey, it seemed important to appraise whether pre-course counselling should be provided for new entrants.

Pre-course Counselling

Pre-course counselling is a service provided by some education institutions prior to students enrolling in a program that delivers them information and guidance about the course, so that potential students can make an informed decision on their course application. The question here is whether this type of counselling should be more broadly available and the degree by which it is important to be enacted for working age Singaporeans. Accordingly, respondents were asked to indicate whether pre-course counselling is important to them. More than 80% of the respondents agreed that it was very or slightly important to have pre-course counselling.

This suggests that respondents understand that participating in a CET program is a heavy investment of their time and effort and personal resources, and a heavy investment by the state. Therefore, decisions about participation in what kind of courses and programs should be carefully considered before a decision is made. This is an essential element of education in terms of guidance and support for students whose readiness and capabilities need to be assessed and supported and who also need to be provided with guidance about the ways they can best achieve their personal and professional goals through CET provisions.

An Effective, Accessible and Scalable CET Provision

Accessing a larger sample of working age adults through this survey enabled findings from the original and smaller cohort to be assessed, elaborated, and extended as reported through their responses. In summary, these informants proposed that:

- CET provisions need to be effective, highly accessible and scalable for its entire working age population, otherwise only some sections of that population might profit from it.
- Both employee and employer informants claimed on the-job training' was the most effective means of developing applicable skills, followed by 'attending external training and 'being mentored by supervisors'. The least effective way to acquire skills is in 'online courses', and 'attending external training in the workplace'.
- However, perceptions about the former online education changed through the Covid period and seen as highly accessible and quite an effective mode of CET.

- Participating in CET programs is not a highly regarded means of developing skills for their employability.
- Employers did not rate attending 'external training outside the workplace' highly.
- Not engaging in CET was because of demands of work, lack of employers' support, limited knowledge of CET provisions, suitability of available courses, not affording those programs and eligibility.
- These reasons suggest that there is a need to consider ease of accessibility including physical accessibility.
- Given the broad consensus on the effectiveness of work-based learning experiences, it raises questions about how work and CET can be integrated into work experiences to address issues of accessibility.
- No subsidies would inhibit respondents' participation.
- CET programs are most effective when they are face-to-face, because of their interactive and spontaneous forms of engagement providing helpful interactions with teachers and peers, access to their insights, responses to questions, and feedback.
- CET educators need relevant occupational competences as well as being effective educators, yet the challenge is to find ways to be knowledgeable and informed about the occupational practices and requirements about which they are teaching.
- Effective CET students or learners are those can learn independently and interdependently with dispositions of interest, openness to learn, and personal and professional motivations.
- Future CET provisions need a tight alignment between the focuses for the learning and the kind of activities they can participate in their workplaces.
- Workplaces provide opportunities to promote learning through engagement in new tasks, innovations, and structured experiences (e.g., job rotations) and direct mentoring in the workplace.
- Models of CET for the future comprise having and integrating workplace experiences in their teaching, and its assessment.
- Pre-course counselling is requested as an essential feature of future CET models.

So, it was found that many informants claimed on-the-job training was the most effective way to acquire skills, thereby questioning an assumption that this could best be achieved through CET provisions offered by tertiary education provisions. Nevertheless, there was seen to be great value in these kinds of provisions to promote further the development of working age adults' capacities for both personal and professional purposes, and usually a combination of both. The most frequently reported challenge in engaging in CET was the lack of time owing to work commitments and the lack of knowledge of course offerings, and sitting within this, the availability of subsidies to support and encourage their participation in these programs. The most preferred arrangement for engaging in CET provisions was one that was flexible, meaning combined online and face-to-face education that accommodates working age adults' juggling of many responsibilities, including long working days and travel time. Whilst initially reporting being hesitant to engage in wholly online education provisions, in the supplementary survey conducted among participants from Phases 1 and 2 it was found that familiarity with the use of electronic platforms during the circuit breaker in 2020 has led to greater acceptance of their ability to make CET provisions more accessible (Billett et al., 2022). Additionally, that familiarity has led to nuanced understandings on the part of working age adults about the how online education provisions can be effective. In addition, the survey respondents broadly claim that the most effective CET teachers are those with current industry knowledge and those who are skillful teachers, while the most effective CET students are independent learners with interest in learning for personal and occupational betterment. All of this emphasizes the importance of readiness to participate in CET programs and this can be addressed if pre-course counselling is enacted, and preparatory experiences are provided either before or at the commencement of their participation in CET courses. Lastly, it was found that subsidies are strong incentives for participation in CET by working age Singaporeans; however, with some understanding that certain cohorts might need it more than others.

Together, across Phase 1, the data that have been gathered, analysed, and generated into findings, which were subsequently appraised through a survey responded to by a large number of working age adults in Phase 2, led to a set of conclusions about the purposes for, practices of, and means of engaging in CET. Quite purposefully, the investigation first gathered this kind of data from those who were recipients of CET provisions. What they point to is the importance of a CET system that not only extends across the range of provisions offered through tertiary education, but which are supported by workplaces, government action and community engagement, in particular families and workplaces and in the engagement and actions of individual adults. In this way, although centred on provisions offered through tertiary education institutions, what emerges is a system that supports the provision of CET which extends far beyond what those institutions planned for, enact, and manage (Leow et al., 2023a). However, it is these institutions, through their existing provisions and prospects for change, that much of this systematic provision of CET will need to be enacted.

The systematic approach to development of CET provisions (Leow et al., 2023a) addresses three key issues we considered central to the study of effective CET provisions: First, the need to connect all CET provisions ultimately to their intended educational outcomes on working adults, and by corollary to the social and economic future of public and private sector enterprises and, collectively the nation state. Second, this approach safeguards against the individual elements of the CET system being viewed in isolation or reductively. Third, the systematic approach argues that any change in the CET system is inherently collaborative and engaging partners comprising adults, workplaces, education institutions and communities. Hence, the key finding from this project is a need for a system that can guide, support, and enact a national system of CET comprising PSEIs working collaboratively and in partnership with workplaces and working age adults.

References

Billett, S. (2015). *Integrating practice-based learning experiences into higher education*. Springer.
Billett, S., Leow, A., Chua, S., & Le, A. H. (2021). *Aligning the Polytechnic provision of CET with SkillsFuture: Meeting learners and employers' needs*. SkilsFuture Singapore.
Billett, S., Leow, A., Chua, S., & Le, A. H. (2022). Changing attitudes about online continuing education and training in the Covid-19 era: A Singapore case study. *Journal of Adult and Continuing Education., 29*, 106–123. https://doi.org/10.1177/14779714221084346
Boeren, E., Roumell, E. A., & Roessger, K. M. (2020). COVID-19 and the future of adult education: An editorial. *Adult Education Quarterly, 70*(3), 201–204. https://doi.org/10.1177/0741713620925029
Cole, M., & Engestrom, Y. (1997). A cultural-historical approach to distributed cognition. In G. Salomon (Ed.), *Distributed cognitions: Psychological and educational considerations* (pp. 1–46). Cambridge University Press.
Dellas, H., & Sakellaris, P. (2003). On the cyclicality of schooling: Theory and evidence. *Oxford Economic Papers, 55*(1), 148–172. https://doi.org/10.1093/oep/55.1.148
Department of Statistics Singapore. (2024). *Education, language spoken and literacy*. . Retrieved from https://www.singstat.gov.sg/find-data/search-by-theme/population/education-language-spoken-and-literacy/latest-data
Dikhtyar, O., Helsinger, A., Cummins, P., & Hicks, N. (2021). Adult education and the impacts of the Covid-19 pandemic: An international perspective. *Widening participation and lifelong learning, 23*(1), 201–210. https://doi.org/10.5456/WPLL.23.1.201
Ericsson, K. A. (2006). The influence of experience and deliberate practice on the development of superior expert performance. In K. A. Ericsson, N. Charness, P. J. Feltowich, & R. R. Hoffmann (Eds.), *The Cambridge handbook of expertise and expert performance* (pp. 685–705). Cambridge University Press.
Hoskins, K., & Barker, B. (2014). *Education and social mobiliy: Dreams of success*. Institute of Education Press.
Institute of Adult Learning. (2017). *Adult education professionalisation*. https://www.ial.edu.sg/join-the-community/adult-educators%2D%2Dprofessionalisation-aep-scheme/benefits.html
International Labour Organization. (2020). *COVID-19 causes devastating losses in working hours and employment*. https://www.ilo.org/global/about-the-ilo/newsroom/news/WCMS_740893/lang%2D%2Den/index.htm
Knowles, M. (1975). *Self-directed learning*. Association Press.
Leow, A., Billett, S., Le, A. H., & Chua, S. (2022). Graduates' perspectives on effective continuing education and training: Participation, access and engagement. *International Journal of Lifelong Education, 41*(2), 212–228. https://doi.org/10.1080/02601370.2022.2044398
Leow, A., Billett, S., & Le A. H. (2023a). Towards a continuing education and training eco system: A case study of Singapore. *International Journal of Training Research., 21*, 226–242. https://doi.org/10.1080/14480220.2023.2203944
Leow, A., Chua, S., Billett, S., & Le, A. H. (2023b). Employers' perspectives of effective continuing education and training in Singapore. *Higher Education, Skills and Work-Based Learning., 13*, 217–232. https://doi.org/10.1108/HESWBL-05-2022-0115
Lovat, T. J., & Smith, D. L. (1991). *Curriculum: Action on reflection*. Social Science Press.
Malle, B. F., Moses, L. J., & Baldwin, D. A. (2001). Introduction: The significance of intentionality. In B. F. Malle, L. J. Moses, & D. A. Baldwin (Eds.), *Intentions and intentionality: Foundations of social cognition* (pp. 1–26). The MIT Press.
Marsh, C. J. (2004). *Key concepts for understanding curriculum* (3rd ed.). Routledge. https://doi.org/10.4324/9780203326893
Organisation for Economic Co-operation and Development. (2006). *Live longer, work longer*. OECD Publishing.
Organisation for Economic Co-operation and Development. (2010). *Learning for jobs*. https://www.oecd.org/education/skills-beyond-school/Learning%20for%20Jobs%20book.pdf

References

Organisation for Economic Co-operation and Development. (2020). *OECD employment outlook 2020: Worker security and the Covid-19 crisis*. https://www.oecd-ilibrary.org/sites/1686c758-en/index.html?itemId=/content/publication/1686c758-en

Rose, J. (2017). 'Never enough hours in the day': Employed mothers' perceptions of time pressure. *Australian Journal of Social Issues, 52*(2), 116–130. https://doi.org/10.1002/ajs4.2

SkillsFuture Singapore. (2023). *Skills framework for training and adult education*. https://www.skillsfuture.gov.sg/initiatives/training-providers/skills-framework/tae

SkillsFuture Singapore. (2024). *Funding support for employers*. Retrieved from https://www.skillsfuture.gov.sg/funding-employers

Su, Y., Feng, L., & Hsu, C.-H. (2018). What influences teachers' commitment to a lifelong professional development programme? Reflections on teachers' perceptions. *International Journal of Lifelong Education, 37*(2), 184–198. https://doi.org/10.1080/02601370.2017.1397786

Tan, J., Yulianti, & Phan, H. V. (2017). *Aging workforce: Cost and productivity challenges of ill health in Singapore*. https://www.marsh.com/content/dam/marsh/Documents/PDF/asia/en_asia/Aging_Workforce_Cost_and_Productivity_Challenges_of_Ill_Health_in_Singapore.pdf

Tennant, M. (1986). An evaluation of Knowles' theory of adult learning. *International Journal of Lifelong Education, 5*(2), 113–122. https://doi.org/10.1080/0260137860050203

Watermeyer, R., Chen, Z., & Ang, B. J. (2022). 'Education without limits': The digital resettlement of post-secondary education and training in Singapore in the COVID-19 era. *Journal of Education Policy, 37*(6), 861–882. https://doi.org/10.1080/02680939.2021.1933198

Part III
Stakeholder Perspectives

As the section title suggests, it comprises four chapters each of which introduces, describes, and discusses the perspectives of specific categories of informants and respondents who offer particular perspectives to understanding what constitutes effective provisions of CET and how these are present in existing arrangements and, from that perspective, how they might be enhanced and advanced for the future. These are: Chap. 7—*Effective CET provisions: Perspectives from graduates and employers*; Chap. 8—*Advancing CET provisions: Perspectives of educators and practitioners*; Chap. 9—*Working women and CET: Enablers and barriers* and Chap. 10—*CET journey: Experience of 'older' working age adults*.

Chapter 7
Effective CET Provisions: Perspectives from Graduates and Employers

Abstract Considering national imperatives associated with maintaining the skills currency and adaptability of workforces, there is a need to broaden the scalability, reach, levels of engagement in and quality of continuing education and training (CET) provisions. This includes encouraging participation and informing working-age adults about it and ensuring their attendance and engagement in CET. Understanding what constitutes effective CET provisions is, thus, paramount in achieving these objectives. The perspectives of the adults who participate in CET and employers who support them is particularly salient as, unlike for younger people, participation and engagement in CET is largely the discretion of these adults (i.e., voluntary and not compulsory). The ability of CET provisions to support the achievement of the kinds of goals associated with these adults' employability are key national concerns, which includes engaging them in programs that they find worthwhile and meet their personal objectives. Hence, identifying and evaluating what constitutes effective CET through gathering data from recent CET graduates offers the bases for informing how best these provisions should be designed, enacted, and evaluated, including what constitutes effective CET teaching. Also, employers are perhaps more likely to sponsor employees' training when they believe that such investments will lead to short or long-term benefits for their enterprises. So, they are key stakeholders in deliberations about policies and practices associated with CET of the workforces. Consequently, understanding their needs and expectations may help inform about their expectations and preferences for CET programs and assist educational institutions to meet their needs as potential sponsors of such education provisions that may also benefit the society and economy. Drawing on an investigation of CET provisions in Singapore, this chapter seeks to illuminate and appraise what constitutes qualities of effective CET provisions in relation to addressing issues of relevance, accessibility, and quality of engagement with educational experiences by these stakeholders. It does this through analyses of detailed, face-to-face, and comprehensive interviews conducted with 180 CET graduates and 40 employers as informed interlocutors. The findings provide bases for understanding what constitutes effective provisions of CET in this national case study and this can inform the design, enactment, and evaluation of effective CET programs.

Keywords Continuing education and training · Participation · Engagement · Working age adults · Employers · Effective CET provisions · Modes of skill acquisition · Effective educational practices · Adult educators

Continuing Education and Training to Sustain Employability

Traditionally, much of the educational effort associated with work has always been and is currently directed at initial occupational preparation for young people transiting from schooling to working life. This is often seen as the key purpose of tertiary education. Indeed, much of its purposes historically across history and cultures has been to prepare young people for productive engagement in working life (Billett, 2011). There are often dual purposes at play here: (i) securing societal goals (i.e., strong economic capacities) and (ii) personal goals (i.e., avoiding young people becoming unemployed and not contributing to their societies (Núñez & Livanos, 2010; Snieska et al., 2015). Indeed, the key debates about occupational preparation have often been about the degree by which that preparation should be occupationally specific or of a more general kind of education (Bishop, 1998). This has led to a consideration of modes of education associated with paid work being premised upon that initial preparation variously for working life or specific occupations. For instance, whether that education should be about developing so called generic capacities, such as problem-solving and creativity, or about effective education that leads to young people being 'job ready' for specific occupations upon graduation. Yet, beyond that initial preparation is the growing realisation of a need for purposes and modes of education for supporting adults' ongoing learning and development across working lives. More than: (i) securing employment, (ii) workers need to continue developing and sustaining the capacities required to remain employable and (iii) develop the capacities for securing advancement in their workplace or occupation, or transfer to a different occupation. These three personal purposes are salient as the requirements for producing the goods and services change and the industry sectors endeavour to be responsive to transforming demands while remaining globally competitive in the production of goods and services (Organisation for Economic Co-operation and Development [OECD], 2006). It is the skilfulness of workforces that does much to achieve these kinds of goals. Consequently, that ongoing learning is important for assisting public and private sector enterprises to remain viable in the face of all these changes.

However, these constant changes in the requirements for effective work mean that, across all kinds of occupations and industry sectors, focused and sustained intentional learning is now needed by all kinds of workers across their working lives (Noon et al., 2013). Individuals' ability to secure employment, maintain it and advance their careers, requires learning across working lives as occupational practices transform and workplace requirements change (Billett & Hodge, 2016). However, the means and processes of securing that employability cannot rely upon—and may be quite distinct from—those deployed for initial occupational preparation, usually for young people transiting from school to working life. Accordingly, there is now growing interest in supporting that worklife learning. Nation states worldwide are recognising the pivotal role of Continuing Education and Training (CET). More than empowering individuals, CET can support robust economies and enable societies to profit socially and economically from having effective CET provisions. Indeed, there are growing national and global policy focuses as well as local concerns about learning, particularly as it pertains to working lives (Midtsundstad & Nielsen, 2019; OECD, 2017). Thus, the need for effective CET provisions to sustain workers' employability has perhaps never been greater in the current era because of global competition, constant changes in means of production, technologies, objects of production and services and along with geopolitical tensions are driving concerns about nation states being more self-sufficient and self-reliant.

Consequently, the overall concern is how adults' continuous learning across working life can be effectively promoted, supported, and realised in sustaining their employability and their ability to contribute to their enterprises' viability. For working-age adults, CET will likely continue to be an essential feature of their adult lives as they need to sustain their employability for longer (OECD, 1996, 2019), continually negotiate greater changes in occupational competence and workplace requirements than was required by earlier generations of workers (Billett, 2006). In sum, the effective provisions of CET are important not only to ensure workers' employability but are also necessary for enterprises to respond to changing requirements and needs of those who rely on their goods and services (Leow et al., 2022). Many occupations already acknowledge the need for ongoing CET is required for workers to perform in their jobs effectively and have in place professional development or CET provisions (Friedman & Phillips, 2004; Herschell et al., 2010). This is because there has been a recognition of what constitutes occupational competence and workplace performance is constantly changing in response to new technologies, ways of working and evolving needs of the job market.

To this end, the elements of investigation reported and discussed in this chapter aim to inform what constitutes effective CET from the perspectives of working age adults. This includes how best that these workers are able to acquire the kinds of experiences and expertise valued by workplaces. These perspectives are from a selection of diverse kinds of working age adults who have recently completed CET programs, and also a small sample of employers. These informants provided views about how such adults' employability can be sustained through participation and engagement in CET programs, including what might need to change to realise these important personal and societal goals more adequately. Employers and workers often have complementary purposes. Employers want a workforce that is occupationally current and possesses the capacities of knowing, doing, and valuing, able to meet the needs of the specific workplace or work practices for productivity and service, and employees wanting to develop the capacities to sustain their employability (Leow et al., 2022). The data indicate that there are similarities and differences in their views about how to effectively acquire and develop further occupational capacities and specific competencies required for workplace performance, what constitutes effective CET provisions, and qualities of effective educators and students. In some ways, these can be seen as complementary views about the efficacy of CET provisions. In preview, its key points are:

- Mentorship and off-site external training were perceived to be most effective to acquire work skills.
- Face-to-face and blended learning were preferred.
- Weekday evenings and weekends were perceived as suitable timings for CET attendance.
- Effective CET provisions were seen to (i) give workers contextualised knowledge and skills which are immediately applicable to their jobs; and (ii) offer employees current industry-specific knowledge.
- Work-based learning experiences were advocated by employers.
- Knowledge gained from CET is insufficient for workplace applications.
- Effective CET educators are perceived to (i) demonstrate the level of currency in the occupational areas which they are teaching, (ii) have an array of curriculum and pedagogic capacities to be able to respond to students' needs, (iii) engage with adult students in ways which are respectful and inclusive of their experiences and potential contributions, and (iv) be flexible and adapt their approaches to the organisation and enactment of educational experiences and assessment of student performance.
- Effective CET students are believed to (i) be intrinsically motivated to learn for their personal and professional development, (ii) have lifelong learning dispositions (i.e., open to learning, see learning as an ongoing process), (iii) have perseverance and self-motivation to work through the course, (iv) possess good time management skills, and (v) be proactive during educational processes to seek for the knowledge one needs.

CET Initiative: The Case from Singapore

As emphasised in this country's case study, the Singapore government recognised the importance of developing the skills of working-age adults as early as 1979 with the creation of the Skills Development Fund, which provided incentives to employers and training institutions to engage their workers in skills upgrading (National Library Board Singapore, 2024). This initiative was supplemented by the establishment of the Lifelong Endowment Fund Act in 2001 to financially support Singaporeans using CET to enhance their employability. The educational emphasis on CET is currently most evident in the launch of a nation-wide initiative to promote Singaporean workers' ongoing employability (i.e., SkillsFuture) by making it available to all working age Singaporeans. With the SkillsFuture initiative (Ministry of Manpower Singapore, 2022), there is now a renewed emphasis on ongoing skills development in Singapore (Sung et al., 2011), where participation in CET is increasingly becoming an ongoing requirement to maintain occupational competence and employability as work practices and goals transform.

Yet, it is necessary to be constructively critical about this nation state's efforts to promote the employability of working age adults. Although Singapore has been lauded for its successful implementation of a training levy scheme (Dar et al., 2003), the quality and effectiveness of CET programs to help individuals and employers make informed choices about training investments remain a perennial local and global challenge. In line with OECD's key strategy to improve the future-readiness of adult learning systems (OECD, 2019), this situation is acknowledged in Singapore by governmental concern about employees being granted greater discretion to bring about change in their workplaces (Ministry of Manpower Singapore, 2022). Together, all these factors indicate an urgent need to identify how the continuing development of working age Singaporeans' occupational capacities and workplace requirements can be realised through effective CET provisions. No longer is adults' continuing education only about cultural betterment, it now plays a central and critical role in upskilling and reskilling workforces in Singapore and around the world (OECD, 2019; UNESCO, 2022). So, this set of initiatives and governmental interest makes Singapore a worthwhile case study when considering how a national CET system might best be organised and progressed.

Investigating Effective CET Provisions: Workers' and Employers' Perspectives

What is described and discussed in this chapter is part of a larger investigation into how CET provisions could be best designed, enacted and experienced to support the ongoing employability of working-age Singaporeans (*see* Chap. 4—*Investigating effective CET provisions to promote employability: Method and procedures* for a description and justification of the method and procedures). This chapter reports and discusses the perspectives of recent CET graduates and their employers with an aim to understand and compare their perspectives of the ways to effectively acquire work skills, effective CET provisions and qualities of CET educators and working age adults as students. The findings reported and discussed here comprised those arising from the analysis of data gathered through pre-interview surveys and interviews with CET graduates (n = 178) and their employers (n = 40). The selected graduate informants were those who had completed their CET courses/programs within 4 years from the project's commencement and possessed at least 5 years of working experience. In this way, all the graduate informants were qualified to comment on the quality of the educational experience afforded to them including how the programs were taught. In this investigation, employers are defined as persons in a workplace who have decision-making power to hire employees. The employer informants were recruited from a range of industry sectors, who had been engaging their employees in CET and were interviewed to gain insights about what constitutes effective CET. The employer sample was recruited through email invitations to CET educators who were working as employers, to contact lists of our collaborators, to employers recommended by the CET graduates, and to employers on online job-search platforms.

The engagements with each of these informants, both graduates and employers were as follows. Having obtained their informed consent, they completed a pre-interview survey that gathered information about the informant, demographic as well as the educational, work background and information about their preferred modes of learning. Completing this survey took about 20 min either via hardcopy or online version which was then followed immediately by an interview, which was conducted face-to-face approximately for about 45 min with each informant and audio recorded.

The findings indicated areas of consensus[1] as well as disparities[2] in the views between graduate and employer informants about: (i) effective ways of acquiring work skills, (ii) effective CET provisions, (iii) qualities of CET educators, and (iv) qualities of CET students. That is, there were similarities and differences between graduates' and employers' perceptions of the four areas. In the sections below, each of these sets of findings are presented and briefly discussed.

Skill Acquisition

In the pre-interview survey, both categories of informants were asked to broadly indicate different ways to acquire skills for work they believed to be effective. The rankings of informants' responses are presented in Table 7.1. In this table, in the left-hand column are the survey items (i.e., ways to acquire skills), followed by employers' and graduates' rankings on the right-hand columns.

As presented in Table 7.1, there was a mix of consensus, but also disparities between employers and their workers (i.e., CET graduates) in the reported views about the effective way to acquire work skills. For instance, the employers quite consistently reported that the most effective ways to acquire workplace skills are mentorship from supervisors and through team meetings/discussions in the

Table 7.1 Rankings of effective ways to acquire work skills

Ways to acquire skills	Employers	Graduates
Mentoring by supervisors in the company	1	2
Team meetings/discussions with workplace manager/in-house trainer in the workplace	1	3
Online courses	3	7
Support by more experienced buddy	4	4
External training held in the workplace	5	6
In-house training programs	6	5
External training held outside the workplace	7	1

---

[1] the same or one rank difference

[2] two or more ranks difference

workplace (both ranked 1st). That these two items were most frequently reported suggests that employers perceived themselves to be using what they believe to be the most effective methods to develop employees' capacities. The workers, on the contrary, perceived external training outside of the workplace to be the most effective way to acquire work skills (ranked 1st). However, the workers ranked 2nd mentorship in the workplace by supervisors and senior workers (ranked 3rd). The employers indicated that external training may not be an effective approach, either on-site (ranked 5th) or off-site (bottom rank 7th). The workers, however, indicated that online courses may not be effective, assigning it the bottom rank (7th). In contrast, the employers claimed online courses to be effective (ranked 3rd), recognising the value and effectiveness of online education likely because of its cost-savings and efficiency, from their perspective. Indeed, studies have shown that a well-designed online course is not inferior to face-to-face courses. For example, the Nurse Navigator System was capable of engaging students in decision making, problem solving and reflection to prepare trainee nurses in their roles (Hayes & Graham, 2020). And, as is reported elsewhere, a large sample of working age Singaporeans had an elevated appreciation of the accessibility and, to a lesser degree, the effectiveness of online education provisions as results of them becoming more familiar with electronic means of communicating (Billett et al., 2022).

The findings in Table 7.1 also suggest that one-on-one training and support (i.e., being mentored by supervisors or more experienced worker) is the preferred method of continuing development of the workforce for many companies in Singapore. Existing research also corroborates this finding (Caplan, 2003; Parsloe & Leedham, 2017). Where it pertains to learning job-specific skills, adult workers may prefer learning on the job hands-on activities and within the workplace (Billett, 2011) to through teacher-centred classroom settings or formalised courses with assignments (Mathews & Straughan, 2014). Further, adult workers may resist learning experiences that are viewed to be remote from their work and where their own experiences are not valued or considered (Merriam & Baumgartner, 2020). It seems these employers recognise this preference and are using the preference they deem most useful to further develop their employees' capacities (Forrester & McTigue, 2004). Whilst the workers value the expertise and mentoring of their managers or senior workers, they expressed their preference for learning from external sources (i.e., online or off-site).

Altogether, it appears that, unsurprisingly, these employers value learning that is situated in the workplace as paramount and that the content and approach are closely aligned to the work that their employees undertake. This finding suggests that CET educators may benefit from being aware of their students' specific contexts and considering ways to make the learning experiences relevant not only to the students' needs, but also to those of their employers. At present, there are some courses that are specifically aligned with industry certification bodies and these kinds of CET provisions may appeal to employers because of their direct relevance and applicability to the workplace. However, most CET provisions in Singapore are wholly based within educational institutions. Thus, these findings also suggest that there is potential for developing structured learning in the workplace, and this most likely comes from the ability to tailor the content to some degree to meet the needs of the particular enterprise.

There is reported here a mismatch between existing educational practices and what is perceived to be more effective in meeting employers' needs. However, it can be the case that employers prefer particular aspects of an occupational practice utilised in their workplaces, rather than the entire occupational competence which both students and government prefer to be learnt. So, whilst the employers' perspectives are important, they need to be considered in terms of them expressing a very specific enterprise need versus those required for practising the occupation more widely. For instance, when an employee moves to another enterprise, that employer might also have specific requirements, which might be different from those of the former employer albeit in the same industry. Hence, there is a need to mediate the request from specific enterprises in terms of their specific skill needs against occupational skills more broadly. Nevertheless, where there is scope, it is often helpful to have flexibility for the content to be tailored for the work in which the working age adult is undertaking as this enriches and contextualises the learning (Merriam & Baumgartner, 2020). Moreover, employers can take up the responsibility for developing capacities associated with enterprise-specific requirements through offering more online courses with content explicitly catered to their employees and engaging more in-house trainers. The point here is that what is pertinent to a specific enterprise might not be relevant to the broader development of occupational capacities and may inhibit adaptability of workers' capacities in the longer term. As the latter is often the province of national governments (i.e., the development of courses addressing specific occupations), so to it perhaps is the province of specific enterprises to offer training provisions that meet their specific or hybrid needs.

All of this leads to a consideration of what constitutes an effective provision of CET and from whose perspective. What can be noted from above is that what is preferred and privileged by graduates, may not be equally preferred by employers, and then government has its own priority and preferences, so there are likely to be multiple perspectives on what constitutes both the processes of and outcomes of CET.

Effective CET Provisions

With regard to the modes of educational delivery, the employer informants indicated face-to-face learning was preferred, followed by the combination of face-to-face and online learning (also known as blended learning). It was the other way round for the graduates. That is, blended learning was preferred, followed by face-to-face. Table 7.2 shows the rankings of effective delivery modes from the two categories of informants. In their interviews, the graduates reported that face-to-face learning allowed students to gain immediate feedback from their lecturers and have their questions responded to immediately.

Table 7.2 Rankings of effective mode of delivery

Mode of delivery	Employers		Graduates	
	N	rank	N	rank
Face-to-face (F2F)	29	1	34	2
Combination of F2F and online	10	2	137	1
Online	1	3	3	3

Table 7.3 Rankings of preferred course timing

Course timing	Employers		Graduates	
	N	rank	N	rank
Evening classes	27	1	75	1
Weekends	18	2	27	2
Intensive (full-day training)	14	3	20	4
Self-paced	14	3	25	3
Daytime classes	7	5	18	5

These informants value classroom interactions not only with the lecturers, but also with other students through discussions and information exchange (Leow et al., 2022; Leow et al., 2023). They also reported recognising the benefits of blended education as being effective and flexible. They claimed that this mode of delivery allows for self-directed learning, on the learner's own pace and interest, yet also can benefit from guidance and mentorship from a teacher. This preference for blended learning is aligned with the current adult education sector which has adopted blended learning in response to the changes and new demand in the adult education market (Chen et al., 2021).

In terms of accessible timing, both categories of informants preferred weekday evenings, followed by weekends, as suitable timings for employees' attendance at CET institutions (*see* Table 7.3). From the employers' perspective, this preference is indicated as arising from timing that does not "eat into work hours". Yet, weekends are often difficult for working age adults, as they have family and community commitments then. Some employers reported understanding the problems involved as 'out-of-office hours' training would encroach into the workers' personal, rest, and family time. Having to attend CET programs up to three times a week on weekday evenings makes considerable demands upon individuals and their families. Yet, this is a common practice in many CET institutions in Singapore, despite it being reported in the interviews that such an intense learning (and teaching) schedule is ineffective for both students and teachers. They also questioned the value of cramming many lessons into a week, which could undermine the quality of teaching and learning.

Moreover, the survey data provided on the duration of travel to and from the tertiary education institutions to engage in face-to-face meetings was on average over one and a half hours for a return journey. Repeating this multiple times a week has a significant impact upon these adults' time commitments and always after a day's work. This prompts considerations of the use of online education provisions to obviate the need for excessive face-to-face engagement. A full-day or half-day class on weekends was proposed as it is more feasible for workers and allow them to combine both their family and community commitments with attendance at a tertiary education institution.

Together, these findings indicate employers and employees' key priority for the timing of training is that it should not affect employees' performance at work. However, as each job has a unique schedule and workload, the suitability of accessible timing is largely dependent on the practices within the industry and enterprises. This suggests that instead of asking employees to make compromises to sign up for existing courses, courses should be designed in ways with greater flexibility that will enable them to be aligned with employees' existing work, family, and community commitments for maximum participation and engagement.

Similarly to CET graduates, the employer informants valued CET provisions that gave their employees contextualised knowledge and skills which are immediately applicable to their jobs. However, unlike their employees who had participated in and experienced the CET courses/programs, employers were less interested in how CET would be conducted or the pedagogical strategies that would be deployed in the classroom. However, both sets of informants valued CET provisions that could offer employees current industry-specific knowledge. The employer informants particularly advocated work-based learning experiences. They valued contextualised learning relevant to employees' actual work, for its accessibility and not requiring time away from the workplace. Generally, these informants reported that the kinds of knowledge secured through participation in tertiary education institutional provisions are insufficient for application in their workplace. These employers' preference for work-based experiences and support provided by more experienced employees opens the prospects for more CET provisions to be enacted in the workplace. However, these would need to be conducted in ways that address the requirements of courses that may go beyond the specific needs of workplaces. This underlines the importance of incorporating the experiences of both CET educators and students in planning for the provision of experiences to achieve CET goals, being mindful of the specific context in which these adult students are engaged in their work and being able to tailor the content, assessment, and educational activities to the circumstances of their employment, where possible and educationally worthwhile. This can include allowing choice in terms of the kinds of assessment tasks and shaping those assessment tasks so that they are focused on what is relevant to the learner and their workplaces. Such practices are long-standing in many adult education courses, but negotiation might be required between the mandates of national curriculum and the needs to tailor for specific local or enterprise needs. This, of course, leads to a consideration of the qualities of CET educators and then students.

Qualities of CET Educators

Aligned with findings about the effective provision of CET are factors associated with being an effective CET educator. Central here was these educators having experience of the occupation about which they are teaching and guiding students' learning based on that competence, on the one hand, and having teacherly qualities and skills to meet the needs of working-age adult students, on the other. Similar qualities were identified in earlier studies in another country (e.g., Billett et al., 2016). A third important quality is related to positive dispositions of CET educators, which included being respectful of and inclusive of students' contributions. The importance of these qualities was highlighted and agreed by both categories of informants.

Employer Perspectives

Perhaps unsurprisingly, the employers indicated that the most effective quality of a CET educator is having relevant practical industry knowledge (*see* Table 7.4). This includes, as elaborated in the interviews, being able to share experiences from their own working lives and being current with the occupational or industry requirements. Some employers claimed that many of the CET educators' occupational capacities were redundant or not current, so they also stressed the importance of maintaining the occupational currency of these teachers.

This, however, is a perennial and global challenge, for those working in tertiary education to sustain that currency when they are outside of the workforce and also being required to be pedagogically competent as well. Most likely, some kind of compromises is required here associated with an awareness of current requirements, but not the ability to respond to all of them. The former is far easier to be developed and maintained through awareness, visits, and engagement with practitioners. Again, this raises the question of what kind of learning is best generated in what environments. There are limited possibilities of educational institutions being able to replicate what occurs within work settings and this is probably not desirable.

Table 7.4 Employers' perceived qualities of effective CET educators

Qualities of CET educators	N	Rank
Having extensive and relevant industry experience	34	1
Engaging the students actively and drawing on their expertise and experience	22	2
Being engaging and interesting in their teaching	22	3
Having in-depth theoretical knowledge of the occupational field	15	4
The ability to support students at different stages of their development	15	4
Offering learning opportunities for students to reflect and evaluate their own goals and progress	13	6
Being flexible when students encounter difficulties	6	7
Establishing and maintaining good relationship with employer	6	7

Instead, the kind of capacities that need to be generated through experiences in work are those that might best occur within work settings. Equally, the kind of understandings and practices that may not be easily learnt within work settings, such as what cannot be accessed and learnt in them, might best be addressed within dedicated educational institutions and experiences.

Graduate Perspectives

The most frequently identified preferred qualities reported by the CET graduates were educators able to provide relevant and pertinent experiences for developing the capacities the students wanted to learn (Table 7.5). These graduates reported valuing the provision of relevant experiences that are effective in learning the knowledge required for their intended employability purposes (e.g., advancement, finding work, changing work). Second ranked was the employers' first preference: CET educators' ability to apply what they are teaching about and to offer examples and instances to enrich the learning process. That capacity, however, was reported as going beyond telling stories (useful though they are) but extends to making links for the students with content being learnt. This capacity includes being responsive to questions and queries and providing contextual, professional advice in response to requests from students. So, more than teaching prepared materials, valued by the student informants is a demonstrated capacity to embed what is being taught through relevant examples, instances and elaborations from occupational practice.

Commonly, apart from having relevant industry experience and knowledge, both categories of informants acknowledged the importance of foundational teacherly qualities such as (i) engagement of students and drawing on students' experiences, and (ii) being aware of students' readiness and flexible in responding to them. The former suggests that the educators need to understand the motivations of CET students and plan their lessons accordingly to enhance the relevance of their lessons to the students. Some employers mentioned that lecturers should make the class more fun, engaging, and make dull topics interesting. This would likely be welcomed by these students, who emphasise the importance of engagement and participation in activities. This point was emphasised as employers pointed out that adult students

Table 7.5 Graduates' perceived qualities of effective CET educators

Qualities of CET educators	N	Rank
Providing relevant experiences for students' needs and purposes	138	1
Accounting for and are sensitive to students' readiness	109	2
Make applicable the concepts they are advancing	109	2
Illustrate what is to be learnt and its purposes	98	4
Demonstrate competence in the field in which are teaching	84	5
Assist meeting students' purposes and needs by being flexible and adaptive with approaches to teaching and assessment	72	6
Engage and utilise students' experience and agency	67	7

often attend their course after a long working day or week of work and need a stimulating classroom environment to be engaged during these instructional interludes. Other teaching skills mentioned included the ability to use simple examples to teach complex concepts and knowing how to teach adults. So, the emphasis here is on the CET educator providing a personalised, engaging, and relevant educational experience for adult students who have a range of experiences and, indeed, often far more extensive than their teachers.

In terms of student readiness, some graduates referred to having difficulty keeping up with the pace of the content, learning unfamiliar materials and coping with the demands of the coursework. Hence, this underlines the significance of CET educators being able to monitor and respond to students' readiness. These processes are more difficult to execute if the educator is just telling rather than interacting and when online educational provisions inhibit that monitoring. Consequently, this indicates that it is important for the educator to be familiar with the students, know their levels of readiness and provide experiences aligned with that level. Of course, there will be diverse levels of readiness within the adult student informants. This is where student collaboration and engagement by peers becomes important for collective engagement and development. The organisation of those kind of experiences is often best facilitated by the educator and providing opportunities and experiences for their students, either face-to-face or online. Regarding educators' dispositions, some employer informants mentioned that the educators should have a genuine interest in or be passionate about what they teach. Some graduates mentioned that they found the courses interesting when the educators were engaging. Some advised that they should be approachable and patient, understand that learning takes time, and continuing to provide support even after a course. The graduates reported appreciating when the educators show them some empathy like consultation outside of office hours. Other qualities mentioned under this point include educators having a good attitude and character, being open-minded and lifelong learners themselves.

Thus, these data emphasise the importance of CET educators:

(i) demonstrating the level of currency with the occupational areas about which they are teaching,
(ii) having an array of curriculum and pedagogic capacities to be able to respond to local needs (e.g., tailoring some of the content to the students' work and workplaces),
(iii) engaging with adult students in ways which are respectful and inclusive of their experiences and potential contributions, and
(iv) being flexible and engaging in their approaches to the organisation and enactment of educational experiences and assessment of student performance.

These kinds of qualities are those that might be the focus of professional development for these educators albeit in different ways and with specific focuses depending upon their experience required for and student readiness. Students are always the ultimate focus of educational processes although they are often positioned as being passive recipients rather than active participants. The latter certainly needs to be the case in the design and enactment of adult education provisions. However, this is not just about affording opportunities and experiences that meet the needs of these adults, which is important. It is also an essential focus on how these adult students can come to engage in educational provisions to direct and optimise their learning. Hence, there are qualities for these adult students which are important for them to exercise.

Qualities of CET Students

Given the emphasis on the processes and outcomes of CET as being enacted and realised, respectively, by working age adults themselves, it is also important to understand their qualities as students who effectively engage in CET. Findings from interviews with both categories of informants indicate that personal motivations to learn were reported as the most important qualities as to what constitutes effective CET students, followed by attitudes that reflected determination, and resourcefulness to learn for their professional development, and metacognitive qualities that involve self-awareness and proactiveness. Both categories of informants proposed that a disposition encompassing intentional lifelong learning attitudes makes employees effective CET students. This is consistent with findings from a study that show that lifelong learning dispositions or mindsets enhance employees' career successes (Drewery et al., 2020).

Motivation to learn was frequently mentioned as a key trait of an effective learner (*see* Table 7.6). In that table, responses to predetermined qualities (left-hand column) are presented from both employer and graduate informants. Some employers claimed the most effective students were those who had chosen their courses to attend out of genuine interest and desire to learn. Conversely, the employer informants recognised that CET provisions are ineffective when their employees are forced to attend training in which they have little interest in or desire to attend. Both sets of informants suggested that effective CET students should be goal-oriented, purposeful, and focused in participating in their CET courses/programs.

Adult students often report facing personally unique challenges as they navigate the demands of education whilst juggling work, family, and community commitments. It is claimed essential attributes for their success are discipline, coupled with effective time management. Unlike college students, adults often have work commitments, family obligations, and other responsibilities. Therefore, cultivating

Table 7.6 Top three qualities of CET students perceived by employer and graduate informants

Qualities of CET students	Employer	Graduate
Motivation to learn	33	76
Lifelong learning attitude	15	31
Metacognitive qualities (e.g., self-aware, proactive, resourceful, determined)	13	23

discipline allows them to stay focused on their educational goals amidst competing priorities. Effective time management skills are equally critical, enabling adult students to allocate dedicated periods for study, assignments, and examinations. In essence, discipline and effective time management empower adult students to optimise their learning experience and navigate the complexities of their multifaceted lives while pursuing continuing education.

The employers suggest that students particularly need to:

(i) understand why they are taking on a course/program,
(ii) the commitment required, notwithstanding the challenges, determination to complete their course/program, and, thereafter,
(iii) apply what they had learnt to their work.

While many graduate informants report long-term advantages (e.g., better job performance) of engaging in CET, juggling between work-family-study is difficult for most working adults. Withdrawal during the course/program (i.e., dropping out) was a common consideration for many graduate informants. To address this threat, they reported that they utilised coping strategies such as time management skills and perseverance. Thus, they advised that future students require resilience and self-motivation to be enduring CET students. Metacognitive qualities, such as self-awareness and proactiveness, involve knowing where one stands in the world and looking ahead to see how one should prepare for the future (Nilson, 2013), are reflected in these requirements.

In keeping with the expectations that adults are able and should be self-directed to a degree, both categories of informants referred to proactivity. The employer informants indicated their high expectations and demanded much of their employees as being active learners yet being conditional in terms of the support with which they were willing to engage. The graduate informants also recommended students be more proactive about their learning. This proactivity ranges from being prepared for their lessons (e.g., requesting for notes to be distributed in advance) to seeking out their own source of knowledge. In CET courses/programs where there are formal (e.g., from educators) and informal sources of knowledge (e.g., casual conversations with classmates and educators), the graduate informants advised that CET students need to be proactive in collaborating with classmates and educators to gain access to this informal pool of knowledge. The employer informants extend the concept of productivity to the disposition of having an open mind to learn from the educators and peers and being engaged during the course/program to contribute and ask questions as essential to being an effective CET learner. It was proposed by some of these informants that such a mindset allows them to engage with their learning proactively by asking questions and sharing their experiences and views. That is, they want and need to be active participants in a class or workplace learning situation, rather than passive participants in the educational process.

In sum, these findings show that these informants (i.e., both employers and graduates) believe that more effective adult students are those who are intrinsically motivated to learn for their personal and professional development. This suggests that individuals having awareness of their long-term career goals and the determination to follow through are valued by their employers. Helpful characteristics for adult CET students include having lifelong learning dispositions, which includes being open to learning and seeing learning as an ongoing process, having perseverance and self-motivation to work through the course, possessing good time management skills, and being proactive during educational processes to seek for the knowledge one needs. In these ways, the attitudes, actions, and ways of engagement by working age adults becomes a key element of CET provisions. Importantly, this form of education is rarely a process of mere transmission of knowledge from the teacher to students, but rather one of active meaning making and knowledge construction, by these adults. These are processes that only individuals can engage in and do so most purposefully when they have interests, imperatives, or goals to achieve. In this way, the distinction is made between the privileging of learning over that of teaching. It also suggests that understanding more about these adult students' readiness to engage, the purposes for doing so and the means by which that engagement can enhance their participation in this meaning making become important educational priorities.

Conclusions and Implications

Overall, the findings indicate that there are differences in perceptions of occupational skill acquisition between the employer and employee (graduates) informants. It is not surprising that employers prefer CET provisions that are focused upon and will directly benefit their workplaces, practically to meet employees' and workplaces' needs. They reported effective educators as those with industry experience who possess the necessary teaching skills and aptitude, and effective students as those who are motivated to learn, goal oriented, and open minded. In summary, these two informant cohorts proposed that:

- Employers consistently reported that the most effective ways to acquire workplace skills are mentorship from supervisors and by a more experienced co-worker.
- Employers perceived external training outside of the workplace to be the most effective way to acquire work skills. However, the workers ranked highly mentorship in the workplace by supervisors (ranked 2nd) and by senior workers (ranked 3rd).
- Employers indicated face-to-face learning was preferred, followed by the combination of face-to-face and online learning (also known as blended learning). It was the other way round for the graduates: blended learning was preferred, followed by face-to-face.
- Both employers and workers preferred weekday evenings, followed by weekends, as suitable timings for employees' attendance at CET institutions.
- They also questioned the value of cramming many lessons into a week, which could undermine the quality of teaching and learning.

Conclusions and Implications

- They both valued CET provisions that (i) gave workers contextualised knowledge and skills which are immediately applicable to their jobs; and (ii) could offer employees current industry-specific knowledge.
- Employers were less interested in how CET would be conducted or the pedagogical strategies that would be deployed in the classroom.
- Employers particularly advocated work-based learning experiences. They valued contextualised learning relevant to employees' actual work, for its accessibility and not requiring time away from the workplace.
- Both reported that the kinds of knowledge secured through participation in tertiary education institutional provisions are insufficient for application in their workplace.
- These lead to a consideration of what constitutes an effective provision of CET and from whose perspective. What is preferred and privileged by graduates, may not be equally preferred by employers.
- CET educators were desired to (i) have experience of the occupation about which they are teaching and guiding students' learning based on that competence, (ii) have teacherly qualities and skills to meet the needs of working-age adult students, on the other, and (iii) possess positive dispositions, including being respectful of and inclusive of students' contributions.
- CET graduates valued educators who are (i) able to provide relevant and pertinent experiences for developing the capacities the students wanted to learn, and (ii) able to apply what they are teaching about and to offer examples and instances to enrich the learning process, beyond telling stories.
- Some graduates referred to having difficulty keeping up with the pace of the content, learning unfamiliar materials and coping with the demands of the coursework. Hence, this underlines the significance of CET educators being able to monitor and respond to students' readiness.
- Effective CET students were perceived to possess qualities such as personal motivations to learn, attitudes that reflected determination, and resourcefulness to learn for their professional development, and metacognitive qualities that involve self-awareness and proactiveness.
- Both employers and workers proposed that a disposition encompassing intentional lifelong learning attitudes makes employees effective CET students.

So, the finding that employers might hold one-on-one training and support by a supervisor or more experienced worker as the best way for skills acquisition suggests that many employers value workplace learning and prefer that much of the CET learning takes place within workplaces. Perhaps to capitalise on this, one group of workers that particularly needs training are those in supervisory roles. Providing them with training and guidance on how learning can be promoted, supported, and guided in workplaces may help assist them to more effectively mentor and coach workers under their care. Additionally, it is important to create workplace environments that are conducive for that learning. For instance, this could be through having regular opportunities for workers to come together to share best practices and challenges faced at the workplace. This affordance can occur as part of work activities such as those during production meetings or other gatherings in which workers who face such challenges can share, compare, and contrast their experiences through collaborations with more experienced workers in co-creating solutions to solve problems and respond to emerging challenges.

To maintain worker employability, these employers suggest that employee training is best situated and implemented in the workplace. While this position lends credence to the affordances and agency of workplace learning, it is not without its implications and limitations. To balance the graduates' preference for off-site training, this finding suggests the need to critically evaluate the value of external educational programs in assisting employees sustain their employability. Perhaps these institutions should systematically review the current CET structure and assess their potential and capabilities to bring CET to the workplace. From these findings, it is emphasised that CET should be contextualised and applicable to the workers' workplaces and situations. This will not only enhance the relevance and effectiveness of the CET, but also enable institutions to adopt a more targeted approach to improving its quality.

Regarding the preferred mode of delivery, both categories of informants reported the benefits of diverse modes of education, i.e., face-to-face, online, or a combination of them. However, there is a stronger preference for face-to-face learning experiences emphasised by both sets of informants. The difference is that the employers want face-to-face interactions occurring in the work setting and, the graduate informants referred to a preference for face-to-face activities in the educational setting. However, despite these differences in preferences for these settings, overall, it emphasises the value of these working age adults' engaging with their peers as well as their teachers and how they can respond to requests, questions, and clarifications. Regarding the preferred timing for employees to attend training, there is variance depending on industry. Employers are generally concerned about finding the right time for their workers to attend training such that it does not affect their work performances and duties. On the other hand, the graduate informants were concerned about finding the time that can balance work, family, and personal commitments.

Both categories of informants expect an effective CET educator to have relevant industry knowledge, adroit teaching skills, and an innate passion in the topics they teach. Concurrently, they suggest that effective CET students should be self-motivated, goal-oriented, clear on their purpose for participation, committed to completing the course, and open-minded. The archetypal CET students are positioned as those who are seeking to learn from others in the classroom and the workplace, regardless of age and experience, are self-aware and proactive to know the larger milieus in which the employee and company is situated. Together, these can assist workers in maintaining their employability and the enterprise sustaining its viability.

What is important here is that the perspectives of two key stakeholders have been gathered and analysed. This was a particular focus of the research project whose findings are discussed here. That is, not to only consider curriculum as something that is intended and enacted, but to evaluate it from the perspective of how it is experienced by students and others who have investments in its outcomes. In other words, it has attempted to illuminate the 'demand-side' of educational provisions and offer perspectives which need to inform the 'supply-side' considerations. This is particularly important for an education provision that is quite distinct from both compulsory education (i.e., schooling) and from much of initial occupational preparation in tertiary education in which young people are seen to need being informed by what is intended for them in the formal syllabus and what teachers will teach them, because they are novices and naïve. This is less so the case with CET, and rather than the more homogeneous group of students in schooling and initial occupational preparation, CET students are not compelled to attend, have a wide range of abilities and experiences and levels of readiness to participate. Of course, there is no single archetype or solution for effective CET provisions from the perspective of the stakeholders. However, from the analysis here notes the centrality of: (i) adult students' purposes for participating, (ii) readiness to engage and (iii) providing means for them to participate which meet their needs in terms of the kinds of experiences provided, their accessibility and relevance to their educational goals.

References

Billett, S. (2006). *Work, change, and workers*. Springer.
Billett, S. (2011). Promoting lifelong employability for workforce aged over 45: Singaporean workers' perspectives. *International Journal of Continuing Education and Lifelong Learning, 3*(2), 57–73. https://search.informit.org/doi/10.3316/informit.367549286463139
Billett, S., & Hodge, S. (2016). Conceptualizing learning across working life, provisions of support and purposes. In S. Billett, D. Dymock, & S. Choy (Eds.), *Supporting learning across working life: Models, processes and practices* (Vol. 16, pp. 3–25). Springer International Publishing. https://doi.org/10.1007/978-3-319-29019-5_1
Billett, S., Dymock, D., & Choy, S. (Eds.). (2016). *Supporting learning across working life: Models, processes and practices*. Springer International Publishing.
Billett, S., Leow, A., Chua, S., & Le, H. A. (2022). Changing attitudes about online continuing education and training: A Singapore case study. *Journal of Adult and Continuing Education, 29*(1), 106–123. https://doi.org/10.1177/14779714221084346
Bishop, J. (1998). Occupation-specific versus general education and training. *The Annals of the American Academy of Political and Social Science, 559*(1), 24–38. https://doi.org/10.1177/0002716298559001003
Caplan, J. (2003). *Coaching for the future: How smart companies use coaching and mentoring*. Chartered Institute of Personnel and Development.
Chen, Z., Chia, A., & Bi, X. (2021). Promoting innovative learning in training and adult education—A Singapore story. *Studies in Continuing Education, 43*(2), 196–207. https://doi.org/10.1080/0158037X.2020.1772224
Dar, A., Canagarajah, S., & Murphy, P. (2003). *Training levies: Rationale and evidence from evaluations*. World Bank. Retrieved from https://documents1.worldbank.org/curated/en/705121468779070378/pdf/301290REPLACEM1iningLevies01PUBLIC1.pdf
Drewery, D. W., Sproule, R., & Pretti, T. J. (2020). Lifelong learning mindset and career success: Evidence from the field of accounting and finance. *Higher Education, Skills and Work-Based Learning, 10*(3), 567–580. Retrieved from. https://doi.org/10.1108/HESWBL-03-2019-0041

Forrester, K., & McTigue, P. (2004). Workplace learning. In G. Foley (Ed.), *Dimensions of adult learning: Adult education and training in a global era* (pp. 219–234). Open University Press.

Friedman, A., & Phillips, M. (2004). Continuing professional development: Developing a vision. *Journal of Education and Work, 17*(3), 361–376. https://doi.org/10.1080/1363908042000267432

Hayes, C., & Graham, Y. (2020). Social interactivity as driver and digital technology as vehicle: Facilitating affective domain learning for undergraduates. *Higher Education, Skills and Work-Based Learning, 10*(2), 313–324. https://doi.org/10.1108/HESWBL-05-2019-0068

Herschell, A. D., Kolko, D. J., Baumann, B. L., & Davis, A. C. (2010). The role of therapist training in the implementation of psychosocial treatments: A review and critique with recommendations. *Clinical Psychology Review, 30*(4), 448–466. https://doi.org/10.1016/j.cpr.2010.02.005

Leow, A., Billett, S., Le, A. H., & Chua, S. (2022). Graduates' perspectives on effective continuing education and training: Participation, access and engagement. *International Journal of Lifelong Education., 41*, 212–228. https://doi.org/10.1080/02601370.2022.2044398

Leow, A., Chua, S., Billett, S., & Le, A. H. (2023). Employers' perspectives of effective continuing education and training in Singapore. *Higher Education, Skills and Work-Based Learning, 13*(2), 217–232. https://doi.org/10.1108/HESWBL-05-2022-0115

Mathews, M., & Straughan, P. T. (2014). *Results from the perception and attitudes towards ageing and seniors survey* (2013/2014). Retrieved from Singapore: https://ink.library.smu.edu.sg/soss_research/2220/

Merriam, S. B., & Baumgartner, L. M. (2020). *Learning in adulthood: A comprehensive guide* (4th ed.). Jossey-Bass.

Midtsundstad, T., & Nielsen, R. A. (2019). Lifelong learning and the continued participation of older Norwegian adults in employment. *European Journal of Education, 54*(1), 48–59. https://doi.org/10.1111/ejed.12322

Ministry of Manpower Singapore. (2022). SkillsFuture. Retrieved from https://www.mom.gov.sg/employment-practices/skills-training-and-development/skillsfuture

National Library Board Singapore. (2024). *Skills Development Fund is established*. Retrieved from https://www.nlb.gov.sg/main/article-detail?cmsuuid=98e1b55f-093d-4d44-b219-d51f6a38c313#1

Nilson, L. B. (2013). *Creating self-regulated learners: Strategies to strengthen students' self-awareness and learning skills*. Routledge.

Noon, M., Blyton, P., & Morrell, K. (2013). *The realities of work: Experiencing work and employment in contemporary society* (4th ed.). Palgrave Macmillan.

Núñez, I., & Livanos, I. (2010). Higher education and unemployment in Europe: An analysis of the academic subject and national effects. *Higher Education, 59*(4), 475–487. https://doi.org/10.1007/s10734-009-9260-7

Organisation for Economic Co-operation and Development. (1996). *Lifelong learning for all: Meeting of the education committee at ministerial level*, 16–17 January 1996. OECD. Retrieved from https://www.voced.edu.au/content/ngv:25305.

Organisation for Economic Co-operation and Development. (2006). *Live longer, work longer: A synthesis report*. OECD.

Organisation for Economic Co-operation and Development. (2017). *Education at a glance 2017: OECD indicators*. OECD. Retrieved from https://www.oecd-ilibrary.org/education/education-at-a-glance-2017_eag-2017-en

Organisation for Economic Co-operation and Development. (2019). *Getting skills right: Future-ready adult learning systems*. OECD. Retrieved from https://www.oecd-ilibrary.org/education/getting-skills-right-future-ready-adult-learning-systems_9789264311756-en

Parsloe, E., & Leedham, M. (2017). *Coaching and mentoring: Practical techniques for developing learning and performance* (3rd ed.). Kogan Page.

Snieska, V., Valodkiene, G., Daunoriene, A., & Draksaite, A. (2015). Education and unemployment in European Union economic cycles. *Procedia—Social and Behavioral Sciences, 213*, 211–216. https://doi.org/10.1016/j.sbspro.2015.11.428

Sung, J., Loke, F., Ramos, C., & Ng, M. (2011). *You and your work: Skills utilisation in Singapore*. Retrieved from https://www.ial.edu.sg/getmedia/fdc73e72-88ec-40f1-8f84-31227d35f8cf/You-and-Your-Work-Skills-Utilisation.pdf

United Nations Educational, Scientific and Cultural Organization [UNESCO]. (2022). *Transforming Technical and Vocational Education and Training for successful and just transitions: UNESCO strategy 2022–2029*. Retrieved from https://unevoc.unesco.org/home/UNEVOC+Publications/lang=en/akt=detail/qs=6644

Chapter 8
Advancing CET Provisions: Perspectives of Educators and Practitioners

Abstract An effective continuing education and training (CET) system needs to extend beyond what can be provided through a range of CET institutions, but be supported by workplaces, government agencies and the community. For instance, the role of families and workplaces are ones that are less understood and central to engagement in and quality of experiences comprising CET provisions. Also, workplaces stand as being accessible and grounded circumstances in which the further development of work and skills can progress through everyday work activities. In this way, although centred on provisions offered through CET institutions, what emerges is an enhanced system that supports the provision of CET which extends far beyond what those institutions planned for, enact, and manage. However, it is these institutions, through their existing provisions and prospects for change, that much of this systematic provision of CET will need to be enacted. Drawing on data from the third and final phase of a research project about CET provisions in Singapore, this chapter reports and discusses feedback from CET educators and practitioners, identifying ways of enacting the kinds of changes being advanced by informants in the first two phases (i.e., CET graduates and employers). This phase allowed these practitioners to contribute their perspectives and understandings in response to these findings and to communicate what needs to occur for the translation of these findings into practice. This chapter concludes by providing a set of understandings and procedures that might be adopted to realize effective CET provisions.

Keywords CET system · Workplaces · Communities · CET institutions · CET educators · CET practitioners · CET administrators · Effective CET provisions · Collaboration · Contributions · Partnerships · Workshops · Strategic planning · Professional capacities · Singapore

Continuing Education and Training: A Quest for Effective Provisions

The need for effective continuing education and training (CET) provisions to sustain workers' employability has perhaps never been greater, because of the constant change in the requirements for occupational competence and workplace performance. Moreover, as nation states confront geopolitical challenges and the need for greater national self-sufficiency and self-reliance arises, a key feature will be the capacities of national workforces to be responsive and adaptive to emerging challenges. Central here is that individuals will be able to sustain their employability: to be employed, respond to changing workplace requirements and advance careers. It follows then that the employability agenda is driven by CET to achieve national priorities, in country-specific ways advanced by specific kinds of support and educational interventions required to meet those objectives. In the face of constant changes in occupational and workplace requirements, there is an added impetus to identify the kinds of educational practices and processes required to secure the ongoing employability of working age adults. Some of the country specific issues in Singapore, for instance are its ageing population and the need for working age adults to remain employable longer throughout their working lives. This focus on developing the human resource capacities of the workforce is a key tenet of Singapore's national strategy on human capital development (Osman-Gani, 2004), as the nation state has few natural resources to rely upon for its economic well-being. Consequently, the ability to provide appropriate training provisions for these workers is contingent on the identification of relevant experiences required to be provided for CET students by tertiary education institutions, and within workplaces to sustain that employability. These concerns are also rehearsed elsewhere. For example, in a report released by the UK Commission for Employment and Skills on the future of work, it was noted that as international competition for innovation continues to increase, focusing on techniques for innovation in education and training will be of great importance across all sectors (UK Commission for Employment and Skills, 2014). It also predicted that employees would need to rely increasingly on further education and lifelong learning initiatives to upgrade their skills to sustain their employability. Adults themselves know the importance of CET and desire training (European Centre for the Development of Vocational Training, 2020). This situation is acknowledged in Singapore by governmental concern about empowering employees through greater autonomy to effect change within their workplaces (Government of Singapore, 2016). Together, all these factors indicate an urgent need to identify how the continuing development of working age Singaporeans' occupational capacities and workplace requirements can be realised through effective CET provisions. No longer is adult education only about cultural betterment: it now plays a central and critical role in reskilling and upskilling national workforces and workplace viability globally.

Despite the growing emphasis on CET, there is, however, limited data on the effectiveness of these educational provisions that can enhance workers' continuing learning and employability. Yet, given the centrality of lifelong learning and lifelong education, it is pivotal that we understand more about how the policy goals associated with the development of adult learners' work skills can be realised through CET provisions. Concurrently, as the adult education sector moves towards greater professionalisation (Institute of Adult Learning, 2017; SkillsFuture Singapore, 2023), it is important to understand what roles these educators can play and how best tertiary education institutions design and enact effective provision of CET. This goal includes the development of CET educators' professional competencies. Earlier research demonstrated that continuing professional development of educators to maintain current and effective work skills can be driven by requirements of professional standards and continuing registration procedures (Friedman & Phillips, 2004). However, this impetus has been largely confined to that of healthcare professionals (Griscti & Jacono, 2006; Herschell et al., 2010; Ochieng & Ward, 2018; World Health Organization, 2013), while less is known about the CET educators in the broader reach of adult education (Chen et al., 2020) or how their work and the goals they need to achieve can be realised.

The concept of worklife learning suggests that young adults, upon graduation from their programs of initial occupational preparation and transition into the workplace is not so much an endpoint. Instead, it is commencing a journey in the development of their occupational competence that will be required to secure employability across their working lives (OECD, 2010a). That is, as foreshadowed, the adults' ability to be and remain employed as work practices and requirements change and be able to advance their careers is premised upon the ongoing development of their occupational and personal competence. This is an imperative that working age adults such as those in Singapore and globally, need to address across working lives regardless of their occupation, as all forms of work are subject to change. Within and beyond Singapore, we witnessed the commitment to and investment of considerable resources to modernise educational systems and schools towards these kinds of ends (Heng, 2014; OECD, 2010b). However, as Prensky (2012) noted, "what reformers have yet to understand is that it is not the 'system' that we need to get right; it is the education that the system provides" (p. 15). Hence, it is important to illuminate and identify the quality of effective educational experiences that includes their alignment with worklife learning requirements. Realizing this change entails developing a future-oriented curriculum that engages students and requires effective pedagogies to meet their learning needs. Within the adult education sector, recognising and accommodating the characteristics and needs of CET students and develop and enact provisions accordingly will be key to secure their educational goals and processes for securing them. This imperative is most salient for the adult education sector as the knowledge and skills required by the current CET students are not the same as initial occupational preparation were originally designed to achieve (Chen et al., 2020). To address this issue, CET curricula and educators must be transformed to create educational provisions that harness the capacities of new technologies and employ more effective pedagogies that are research informed.

Teachers are the foundational component of any education system (Beavers, 2009) and an important factor in realising student achievement (Carey, 2004), and adult educators are no exception here. However, these teachers do not drive learning. Just as teachers cannot overhaul the education system alone, the adult education sector cannot be expected to solely take on the role of equipping CET students to compete in a global economy. Instead, a systemic and system-wide approach is required, that incorporates the contributions of these educators, the experiences provided by tertiary education institutions, but also those in workplaces and from the community. Consequently, in further evolving the educational provision, tertiary education institutions might now be expected to transform from institutions that emphasize teaching to organisations that promote learning in and outside of their classrooms, including workplaces. To that end, CET courses need to be of high quality and innovative, taught by CET educators who understand contemporary industry practices, and linked to clear opportunities for further learning. The OECD (2010a) posits that workplace learning will play an increasingly important role in programs preparing individuals for working life and sustaining their employability within it. As any other, this holds true for the Singaporean adult education sector (Chen et al., 2020). For this goal to be realised, partnerships amongst CET institutions and educators, and industry partners are required to provide for experiences to secure access to the knowledge and skills acquired by CET students and that have relevance and application in their work. This means that considerations of CET provisions need to extend beyond tertiary education institutions and include workplace learning experiences.

The value of workplace as settings for learning is now well accepted (*see* Billett, 2004; Blacker, 1995; Lave, 2009; Moore, 2004). What is perhaps less established is the integration of workplace experiences within tertiary education. For instance, not only is this about the effectiveness of educational provisions but also the scalability to entire working populations. For instance, as the take-up of CET in Singapore increases from 35% in 2015 to 48.5% in 2019 and from 465,000 individuals and 12,000 enterprises in 2018 to 500,000 individuals and 14,000 enterprises in 2019 (SkillsFuture Singapore, 2020), the importance of integrating the workplace learning experiences of CET students cannot be overemphasised (Tan et al., 2023). Against the backdrop of a national agenda of continuing education, the partnering of tertiary education institutions (i.e., polytechnics and Institutes of Technical Education) with industry organisations and public and private sector enterprises assumes great significance and has direct consequences for how CET is viewed by students, employers, and the community. Consequently, partnerships bear implications for what industry organisations perceive as the worth and potential of CET and how CET educators can be equipped with the skills and knowledge to engage these CET students. As Marsick and Watkins (2002) note:

> … the rapidly changing world in which we have been living is giving birth to a host of new ways of understanding work, jobs, organisations, technology and change (p. 34).

Evans et al. (2002) further proposed that "… the workplace is a crucially important site for learning and for access to learning" (p. 1). Despite the recognition of the need for workplace learning and the potential of the workplace as a site of learning, there remain questions about the extent to which this potential can be realised in practice.

Drawing on the work of Lave and Wenger (1991), Billett (2004) urged the reconceptualization of workplaces as learning environments where learning and participation in work are inseparable. Although informed by different theoretical frameworks, Billett (2001) and Griffiths and Guile (2003) argued for the creation of strong partnerships between workplaces and educational institutions in fostering positive learning environments where knowledge is co-constructed, leading to a greater alignment between learning and what is needed in the workplace. This knowledge is often mediated and shaped by individuals' intentions and degree of engagement while shaped by their life histories and earlier learning experiences. A renewed emphasis on skills development has occurred in Singapore (Sung et al., 2011), where participation in work practices is increasingly becoming an ongoing requirement to maintain occupational competence and employability in the current policy landscape. It is also necessary to investigate these phenomena and identify the kinds of capacities and institutional practices required for CET educators to provide accessible and effective CET provisions for adult working population.

To this end, as referenced elsewhere in this volume, a three-phase research project was undertaken to investigate the perceptions of graduates of CET programs, employers, working age Singaporeans, CET educators and administrators on what constitutes accessible and effective CET provisions. This chapter reports and discusses Phase 3 of the research project. In the first phase, accounts from Singaporean worker-informants who have taken CET courses and employers who are supportive of CET were secured. In the second phase, a survey was developed from the findings of the first phase and administered to Singaporean working age adults in a range of employment and industry sectors. In the third phase, the consolidated findings from Phases 1 and 2 were presented to CET educators and administrators who engaged in identifying and co-constructing the implications and generation of guidelines for curriculum and pedagogic practices in tertiary education institutions. Overall, it was indicated a need for collaboration and engagement with different partners and between different levels of CET. Importantly, a systemic approach to such collaboration and engagement is essential for enacting effective CET provisions.

Its key points are:

- Engaging with different kinds of partners and in diverse ways is central to a responsive and effective CET system.
- There is a need to provide students with pre-course counselling for enrolment advice and then post-course guidance associated with employment.
- Support from employers and management enhances CET students' motivation and commitment to CET.
- Open and reciprocal communication between administrators and educators in CET institutions can promote constructive alignments of values and practices, and meeting stakeholders' (i.e., students and employers) needs.

- Coping with new online education provisions requires support being available (i.e., training programs and incentives) for adult educators and in ways addressing their readiness and engages their agency.
- Contemporary adult educators face diverse and unique challenges, thus requiring professional development to cope with these challenges in organising educational experiences and meeting the diverse learning needs of working age adults.

Educators' and Practitioners' Perspectives of CET: A Case from Singapore

As noted, the aim of Phase 3 of the project was to secure feedback on and identify ways of enacting the kinds of changes being advanced by informants in the first two phases from CET educators and administrators. To realise this goal, key findings from Phases 1 and 2 about what graduates from CET programs and working age Singaporeans reported as effective CET provisions were presented to CET educators and administrators who engaged in group deliberations. This phase was undertaken to allow these practitioners to contribute their perspectives and understandings in response to these findings and state what needs to occur for translating these findings into practice. In essence, the first two phases have focused on the perspectives of students, graduates and employers, as demand-side stakeholders. However, it is equally important to account for the supply-side considerations: i.e., how CET provisions need to be organised from the perspective of adult educators and those who teach in and administer the CET programs within tertiary education institutions.

From September to November 2020, six workshops and three webinars were conducted with CET educators and administrators enlisted from three sources. First, the Institute of Adult Learning sent an electronic direct mailer (EDM) to members of their Adult Educators' Network. Second, through Griffith University (GU), an EDM was sent to Singapore students who had graduated from GU's master's program operated in Singapore and those who were currently enrolled in this master program. Third, an EDM was sent to all polytechnics in Singapore. In total, 274 CET educators and administrators participated in these workshops and webinars. These events had to occur online because at that time Singapore was in a 'circuit breaker' phase in the management of the COVID pandemic and had strict rules about face-to-face meetings.

Each online workshop commenced with a 20-min presentation on the findings of Phases 1 and 2. The participants, who had been given a worksheet with three focus questions, were divided into breakout groups in which they discussed their responses to those questions. Then, the entire group reconvened to share and discuss their responses. For the webinars, the presentation of the findings of Phases 1 and 2 was prefaced with a talk on workplace learning. Subsequently, the participants shared their perspectives on the findings. The sessions were recorded through electronic means (i.e. Zoom). After the completion, the sessions were transcribed, and the transcripts were analysed thematically and organised into 10 vignettes to illustrate the data that consisted of participants' individual and collective stories. Pseudonyms were given to the vignettes to maintain the participants' confidentiality.

These vignettes capture and illuminate key aspects of the responses from the CET educators and administrators, including their struggles and successes in their roles. Some of these vignettes present individual stories, whilst others are a composite of multiple stories. They provide qualitative accounts of key issues faced by CET educators and administrators today. The vignettes were categorised into five main themes/requests: (i) Support for students before and after the course, (ii) Support from employers, (iii) Support from administrators, (iv) Coping with new online education provisions, and (v) Skills required of contemporary adult educators.

Support for Students Before and After the Course

Educators communicated observations that CET students would benefit from pre-course counselling and post-course guidance. They stated concerns of students having enrolled in courses that were not well aligned with their needs and work-related goals, leading to course regret and graduates struggling to secure employment after course completion. Some educators spoke about the potential conflicts of interest that tertiary education institutions have in marketing their courses. Vignette 1 describes this conflict from the perspective of a CET program recruitment staff member. Other educators suggested how education institutes can assist by helping graduates find jobs aligned with their study. Vignette 2 describes how a CET student experienced the benefits of a CET program that provided opportunities for networking.

Vignette 1—Sharifa
Sharifa works in a polytechnic and her role is to recruit adults for CET programs. One of her key performance indicators is the number of students she recruits. Hence, she is driven to promote the CET courses to enrol more students and additional revenue for the polytechnic. However, there were times where she counselled students and realised that her polytechnic's courses were not suitable for them and a course from another polytechnic would suit students better. She reported feeling conflicted about whether she should advise the potential students about the other courses or try to fulfil her role of promoting her host polytechnic's courses to students. She noted an independent counsellor who could advise students based on their needs would be a better arrangement for fairly advising potential CET students.

Vignette 2—Mr Lee
Mr. Lee decided to take a computing course after being retrenched as a banker. As part of the course, he was provided with networking opportunities to help students find employment. Every month, as part of the course, they visited different IT companies in Singapore and attended Zoom meetings where people from the industry share information and updates about the latest trends. During one of the company

visits, a manager was impressed by Mr. Lee's financial knowledge and his many years of experience managing teams at the bank. The manager invited Mr. Lee to apply to work as an IT manager in his company after he completes his course. Mr. Lee was thankful that his education institute had arranged for various activities that allowed him to meet people who are in hiring positions that directly increase his chances of finding a job when he graduates.

Both vignettes indicate that sometimes the challenges faced by CET educators and students are systemic in nature and a broader view should be taken to resolve issues like enrolment into inappropriate courses or inability to find jobs after graduation. In other words, more can be done to assist students in the process of course selection and to develop skills that are essential for finding jobs, such as networking and resume writing skills. Such activities broaden the scope of what is often taken as the orthodox purpose of CET provisions and that is enrolling students in courses and securing successful graduations. Whilst these are core and central, considerations of course counselling prior to enrolment and guidance to find employment upon graduation offer important augmentations to the orthodox view of CET.

Support from Employers

Educators reported that support from employers and management can increase the motivation of students who are employed in their enterprises. Vignette 3 describes how an adult educator was supported by a company manager who was personally involved in the educational progress and outcome of his staff's training. Vignette 4 describes how an institution had supported an educator by providing financial support for his course fees.

Vignette 3—Kelvin

Kelvin taught a CET course to a group of attendees from a local enterprise. He was surprised that on the first day of the training, the manager came along and emphasised to his staff the importance of the training. On the last day of the course, the manager also handed out the certificates and congratulated each of his staff. Kelvin has never previously experienced any management member being so supportive of their staff training and noted that this endorsement was a strong factor in why the students remained motivated throughout the course. Since that experience, he always encouraged management to visibly support their staff training in one way or another.

Vignette 4—Peter

Peter is an engineering lecturer at a polytechnic. When he wanted to study a Master's degree, his polytechnic paid for the program and gave him a reduced workload. They also supported him in other CET programs, often paying fully for them. Peter remained loyal to the polytechnic, working for over 15 years for them. He reported that his efforts were always recognised and appreciated by his institute's management and there were ample opportunities to succeed and grow.

These two vignettes indicate that support from employers can come in different forms. It can be monetary, where the employer financially sponsors the course for their employees, or through physical and verbal presence, where employers explicitly communicate to employees their support of their training and recognise their efforts to upgrade themselves. Either way, or in combination, educators have reported that such support enhances CET students' motivation and commitment.

Support from Administrators

Educators reported that effective communication between CET administrators and educators ensures that the needs of stakeholders (i.e., students and employers) are met. Educators reported that they want to be informed about the profiles of students and stakeholders' expectations, and to be involved in decision-making on assessment criteria and mode of delivery. Vignettes 5 and 6 describe how educators were hindered in their roles when they could not obtain information about participants or were given a list of challenging rules and regulations to abide by.

Vignette 5—Wei Ling
Wei Ling works as an adult educator for a training institute. Having been informed that she would be teaching a day course on marketing principles to a group of 20 students from a company, she inquired more about the students' profiles and abilities. However, the administration was unable to provide such information to her. At times, she reported feeling like a nuisance to be always asking administrative staff questions to which they seemed either unwilling or unable to respond. On the day of the training, Wei Ling was surprised that many students had little or no background in marketing and believed she was underprepared to teach them. She wished that there was more communication about the students' profiles prior to the commencement of the course as she had requested.

Vignette 6—Siva
Siva was engaged by a training institution to teach computer programming to a group of trainees. The administration advised him that he had to pass the entire class because they had promised all students that they would not fail the course. Siva believed his authority as a teacher was challenged. How could he agree to pass everyone if he had not even met and taught his students? Furthermore, the administration mandated a particular software to be used to teach his class. Siva preferred another software that he believed to be more suitable. Lastly, the administration told him that, to pass, all students required a minimum of 80% attendance. This requirement also troubled Siva because, from his experience, it was unreasonable to ask working adults for so much commitment. Moreover, his course would be taught online and recorded, so students could watch lessons that they missed, rather than being physically present for all lectures. Because of these expectations, Siva reported being pressured and constrained and could not teach optimally.

Both vignettes suggest that better communication and shared understanding between CET educators and administrators can enhance mutual understanding of each other's constraints and challenges and, therefore, can potentially allow for better solutions and processes that are beneficial to stakeholders. Open and reciprocal communication between administrators and educators can promote constructive alignments of values and practices. These can assist each party to understand the needs, concerns, and challenges of the other, helping them come to the best arrangements for students and staff. Having sufficient knowledge about students to provide effective learning experiences for them is critical and fundamental to educators' work and with the heterogenous nature of adult students, this is particularly crucial for CET provisions. It is hard to imagine that such information would not be available in schooling systems. Thus, given the diversity of backgrounds, readiness, and capacities of adult participants in CET, this is a requirement for that sector as well. All of this indicates the importance of having positive relations between administrators and adult educators and in ways which best serve the needs of students within CET.

Coping with New Online Education Provisions

An issue raised by many CET educators was the challenges brought about by the shift to online education. This was a particular feature of the time of the data gathering and the social distancing and lockdowns brought about by the COVID-19 pandemic. Yet, although pertaining to that pandemic, the broader issue is of how adult educators can best be prepared and assisted to respond to new challenges and circumstances and professional requirements change. Not only is this important for the competence of adult educators, but also the effective implementation of educational processes intended to enhance the experience of students. Some educators have successfully made the transition, while others struggled to do so. Educators reported appreciating assistance, whether it comes in the form of easily available and no cost courses or subsidies to attend training. Vignette 7 describes a CET educator's journey from being unfamiliar with online education to embracing online facilitation, a progression that many CET educators have undertaken in the past year because of the COVID-19 pandemic. Vignette 8 describes how a CET educator recognised that students also struggle with the transition to online education and how she designed an orientation to ease the transition for them.

Vignette 7—Sarah
Sarah has many years of teaching experience, mostly face-to-face. When the COVID-19 pandemic struck, her institution mandated a switch to online teaching via the electronic media of Zoom. Being unfamiliar with online education, she was initially uncertain whether she could manage this switch. To assist herself, she asked her colleagues for tips and attended free online training sessions on how to conduct online training. Over time, she gained confidence in online teaching and engaging

her students in this way. Her institution also informed her that it is unlikely they would return to fully face-to-face training because of considerable cost savings from not having to rent training venues. Many students have provided feedback that they enjoyed her online educational courses as they were more convenient. She realises that online education may become the standard mode of CET and hopes that more subsidies can be provided for adult educators to upgrade their online teaching skills.

Vignette 8—Rachel

Rachel realised that many of her students are unfamiliar with online education. She was able to ease their discomfort with online education by conducting an orientation about this mode of education. During the orientation, she laid out some ground rules, such as that students should turn on the video function if their situation allows for it so that she can get a sense of their understanding and attention and so students can get to know one another. She also introduced them to the online platforms and tools that she frequently uses so that students know what to expect. She found that having such an orientation reduces the anxiety and confusion for her adult students who are new to online education.

Both vignettes describe how adult educators realised that a major shift had occurred in how adult education is organised since the advent of the COVID-19 pandemic. Some educators are reportedly coping better than others with the change. The ability to become competent and confident with this form of educational engagement came through a combination of support being available (i.e., training programs and incentives), but also on the interest and agency of the adult educator. But generally, the lesson here is that more support can be offered to assist adult educators in this transition to enhance their effectiveness as teachers, to improve outcomes for educators while making educational provisions for students.

Skills Required of Contemporary Adult Educators

Some of the educators also reported realising the unique demands of CET and the challenges of teaching adults. For example, their students have different kinds and diverse levels of readiness including their knowledge and abilities, and even motivation to learn. For instance, some students may look down on lecturers and challenge their authority as they see themselves as superior in knowledge and experience. Vignette 9 describes how an educator had designed his course such that he can meet the needs of both beginner and advanced students. Vignette 10 describes how an educator facilitates her lessons to ensure maximum benefit for her students, despite being out of the industry for some years.

Vignette 9—Wei Song

Wei Song teaches investment skills. His courses are attended by students with a wide range of readiness, with some requiring handholding while others, he claimed, were even more experienced than him. To cater to his advanced students, he uploads materials for future lessons ahead of time so that they can self-study at their own pace. He reports that student diversity means the demands on the teacher are very high for adult education. Though stating that there is a need for needs to put in more effort in planning and organising the course to cater to students of different abilities, he reports feeling rewarded when he empowers his students to be independent.

Vignette 10—Rita

Rita worked in events management for over 10 years before becoming a lecturer at a polytechnic. Over time, although her teaching skills increased and improved, she has increasingly lost touch with the industry. Recently, she was given a class of CET students. On the first day, she told her students about her work history and what she knows and does not know. Her teaching style is such that she engages the students' expertise as a class resource. So, even though she is not as currently knowledgeable as some of her students, they nevertheless report enjoying and benefitting from Rita's facilitation of her lessons. Much of this is because they learn from one another and are guided to relevant resources to deepen their learning. The classroom atmosphere is reportedly warm and inclusive, and everyone is open to learning from each other as Rita guides them through the course.

These vignettes indicate that CET educators face diverse and unique challenges in organising educational experiences and meeting the diverse learning needs of working age adults. Importantly, many of them have learned to cope with these challenges and are a rich source of practical knowledge. During the workshop sessions, some educators openly shared experiences about the issues with which they have to deal and asked for solutions. It appears that professional exchanges of the kind modelled in the workshops and seminars might be broadly beneficial for educators in providing the opportunity to learn from one another on how to cope with some of the common issues faced by adult educators today.

A feature of the findings from this analysis is the salience of engaging with different kinds of partners and in different ways within a CET system. It was deemed helpful when employers engaged with employees who were also students and when administrators engaged with teachers, particularly when teachers were part-timers, to provide relevant and focused educational experiences for students and the places in which they work. Additionally, other interactions such as prospective students being provided with impartial guidance to inform their choice of courses and opportunities to engage with potential employers, peers assisting each other to deal with new technologies supporting CET, and teachers adopting strategies that engage students as partners in educational experiences and learning, were all highly beneficial. All of this points to the importance of having a CET system that seeks to secure collaboration across industry, institutions, teachers, and administrators, and extending to the working age adults who participate in these programs. It is likely to be personal institutional rivalry that will limit and inhibit development and utility of such a systemic approach.

Recommendations for Effective CET Provisions

These vignettes provide a glimpse into the complex work of CET educators and some of the challenges they face using cases from Singapore. These educators, and those who are administering CET courses and programs, reported constantly having to adapt to changes in demand for courses and the qualities required of these enactments, government policies, and priorities, and in working collaboratively with students, employers, and administrators. The key points of this analysis are:

- There is the need of support for students before and after the course (i.e., course counselling) prior to enrolment and guidance about employment upon graduation.
- CET educators are concerned about students enrolling in courses that are not well aligned with their needs and work-related goals, leading to course regret and graduates struggling to secure employment after course completion.
- There are potential conflicts of interest that tertiary education institutions have in marketing their courses and providing balanced advice.
- Support from employers were reported to increase the motivation of students who are employees. That support can come in different forms: monetary, where the employer financially sponsors the course for their employees, or through physical and verbal presence, where employers explicitly communicate to employees their support of their training and recognise their efforts to upgrade themselves.
- Support from administrators in terms of effective communication between CET administrators and educators ensures stakeholder needs (i.e., students and employers) are met.
- Educators reported want to be informed about student profiles and stakeholders' expectations, and to be involved in decision-making on assessment criteria and modes of delivery.
- Many CET educators are concerned about the challenges brought about by the shift to online education brought about by the COVID-19 pandemic.
- Some educators report coping better than others with the changes they face. The ability to become competent and confident with this form of educational engagement arose through a combination of support being available (i.e., training programs and incentives), and adult educators' interest and agency.
- CET educators face diverse and unique challenges in organising educational experiences and meeting the diverse learning needs of working age adults. Importantly, many of them have learned to cope with these challenges and are a rich source of practical knowledge for others.

The vignettes and their discussion have led to the following recommendations:

1. *Provision of informed and impartial pre- and post-course student counselling*

The provision of informed and impartial pre-and post-course counselling has emerged as an important issue for effective CET provisions and graduate employability. The findings suggest that the provision of courses for adults, alone, is insufficient in helping them attain their career goals. Many adult students need course and career guidance to help them select appropriate CET programs and find employment opportunities upon graduation. To avoid inappropriate enrolments in courses resulting in unmotivated or regretful students, an impartial provision of guidance and support prior to enrolment could assist in matching students with suitable courses. There may be a need for an independent institution or agency to play such a role to advise potential CET students. This advice might include information about the contact, focus and organisation of their CET courses and programs to facilitate job and career transitions through visits to workplaces, networking with potential employers, and other means of support to extend their course into desired employability outcomes. One consideration is to have a system-wide approach to student counselling and guidance, rather than it being premised within individual CET institutions, to overcome enrolments being based solely upon institutional student recruitment goals.

2. *Opportunities for collaborations prior to, during, and after CET programs*

The findings also suggest that, oftentimes, CET educators, administrators, and employers seem to work independently and lack opportunities for collaboration. Counter to these practices, the findings also suggest the importance of engagement amongst institutions offering CET programs, those who administer and teach them, workplaces whose employees are participants in these programs, and working age adults who commit time, resources, and personal energies to their ongoing learning across working life. Institutions offering CET can create more opportunities for CET educators, administrators, and employers to work and learn collaboratively and develop understanding about one another's needs and requirements. However, there also needs to be collaboration extending beyond the institution, reaching out to and engaging the two key principal stakeholders: (i) students and (ii) employers. So, just as teachers and administrators need to collaborate internally, it is perhaps only through this joint engagement with students and employers that the focuses of, processes for, and proposed outcomes of courses can be realised. This is done through collaboration comprising joint planning and sharing of mutual concerns to achieve effective outcomes that are mutually beneficial. In addition, an outcome here can be the development of common understandings about achieving shared goals (i.e., the provision of effective CET experiences). Whilst not doubting that much of these efforts are underway and focused on intra-institutional capacities for an effective CET system, these probably need to be extended to be inter-institutional; that is, working across individual CET institutions to establish an effective national CET system. This collaboration may provide the best mechanism for employers' needs to be fully understood and effectively catered for, and for working age adults to receive informed, impartial, and appropriate guidance for the selection of and participation in CET programs. However, such collaboration should not be seen as being reserved for interactions prior to course design, organisation, and commencement. Instead, it should be enacted in manageable ways throughout courses and even after graduation. Securing engagement inter-institutionally might be the optimum means for systemically realising collaborations amongst the three parties.

3. Expanding the professional profile of adult educators

A heightened professional profile for CET educators may assist their expertise in and contributions to educational processes as well as professional and social partnering to be recognised and enacted. Much effort has been exercised in developing effective cohorts of adult educators in Singapore, for instance through the establishment of an adult educators' professional network (Institute of Adult Learning, 2017). Yet, these educators require not only the kind of competence and profile enjoyed by Singaporean schoolteachers (OECD, 2020), but also a level of credibility that is helpful and permitting authoritative, allowing to operate and be accepted within Singaporean workplaces. Hence, just as the efforts of Singaporean schoolteachers reach into Singaporean homes, so the efforts of CET educators need to reach into Singaporean workplaces. Therefore, more resources need to be set aside to support adult educators in their roles. For example, establishing in Singapore a guild or association of adult educators that could perform a range of roles would be helpful for the competence and profile of adult educators. This could include offering professional development opportunities such as conferences, online workshops, and sharing sessions to meet the learning needs of adult educators more fully and, through these kinds of activities, elevate their professional standing. Key adult education agencies might also consider expanding their role in working with the adult educator community. Because of the diversity of adult educators (e.g., some from private institutions, others from public, and many freelancers), an organisation that oversees their professional development and learning needs may considerably benefit the adult education fraternity, regardless of whom they work for. Such an organisation might provide subsidised professional development opportunities that many adult educators reported benefiting from greatly. It can also provide opportunities for discussion sessions, such as the kind used in the research project, that was observed to be a highly beneficial model of professional development. Put plainly, as adults' worklife learning becomes increasingly important for their employability, the viability of the enterprises in which they work and the strengths of the national economy, the project for CET and adult educators is only likely to grow. Yet, those kinds of imperatives emphasise the importance of ensuring the quality of the processes and outcomes of CET provisions.

4. Regulation of the processes and outcomes of CET to ensure quality provisions

Given the importance of the role of CET and the investment by government, workplaces, and working age adults, it is important that the quality of that provision be enhanced and safeguarded. As the range of CET providers has rapidly increased, it is important that CET processes and outcomes are regulated to some degree. The findings suggest that some private education institutes do not have guidelines on best practices for matters such as assessment criteria, attendance marking, and teaching platforms. This omission may result in a disparity of the quality of education offered to students from educational institutions across the public-private divide. There may need to be some guidelines provided to educational institutes to ensure that, at the minimum, there is a reasonable standard of quality to which all of them adhere, as they are all offering the same kinds and level of certification. Perhaps an expanded kind of adult education association might play such a regulatory role to guide administrators who need help. Such an association can even play a mediating role should there be contentions between CET educators and administrators or their institutions.

Towards an Effective Provision of CET

The success and effectiveness of CET programs hinge on an orientation and approach that addresses various critical aspects of their purposes and enactments. These comprise some of the following. Firstly, the provision of informed and impartial pre- and post-course counselling can serve as a foundational element, assisting these adult students having the necessary guidance and support to make informed decisions about their educational journey. This counselling not only enhances student satisfaction but also likely contributes to the overall success and completion rates of CET programs. Such an outcome is achieved through making them aware of the requirements but also aligning their readiness to participate successfully in these programs. Collaboration opportunities before, during, and after CET programs play a pivotal role in enriching the learning experience. Consequently, fostering partnerships and strengthening the links amongst students, educators, and industry stakeholders promotes the potential for a rich, comprehensive, and encompassing set of educational experiences. This collaborative approach not only enhances the practical relevance of the education provided but also opens avenues for networking, skill application, and real-world problem-solving, and subsequent opportunities for employment.

The professionalisation of adult educators emerges as a crucial factor in ensuring the quality of CET programs. That professionalisation is premised upon these educators having both current industry sector knowledge as well as high levels of pedagogic capacities. Consequently, investing in the continuous development of educators, both in terms of occupational and pedagogical competence, serves to advance the overall standard of CET delivery. This, in turn, will positively impact the learning outcomes and the ability of adult educators to adapt to emerging educational methodologies and technologies. When sensibly and flexibly applied, regulations are helpful in maintaining the integrity and quality of CET provisions. By overseeing and regulating the processes and outcomes of CET programs, these measures can help uphold a high standard of educational provisions. For instance, if regulations demanded that students be engaged in higher-order thinking activities or in required periods of practice, such regulations can assist to achieve those outcomes. This may involve carefully auditing curriculum design, assessment methods, and the constructive alignment of CET provisions with educational requirements and the needs of the occupations and, potentially, the enterprises in which graduates will find employment and advancement. A well-regulated and cohesive CET environment may also inspire confidence among students and employers to invest their time and effort and provide guidance for educational institutions.

In essence, a comprehensive approach that integrates informed counselling, collaboration opportunities, professional competence for educators, and effective regulation contributes to potentially effective CET provisions. Such an approach not only enhances the relevance and quality of education provisions but also empowers individuals to thrive in their professional journeys, fostering a culture of lifelong learning and adaptability in the ever-evolving landscape of adult education. Beyond these provisions is the importance of how working age adults will come to engage with, participate in and contribute to these programs. As noted throughout, finding ways of securing that engagement, participation and contributions is also central to effective provisions of CET.

References

Beavers, A. (2009). Teachers as learners: Implications of adult education for professional development. *Journal of College Teaching and Learning, 6*(7), 25–30. https://doi.org/10.19030/tlc.v6i7.1122

Billett, S. (2001). *Learning in the workplace: Strategies for effective practice*. Allen and Unwin.

Billett, S. (2004). Workplace participatory practices: Conceptualising workplaces as learning environments. *Journal of Workplace Learning, 16*(6), 312–324. https://doi.org/10.1108/13665620410550295

Blacker, F. (1995). Knowledge, knowledge work and organizations: An overview and interpretation. *Organization Studies, 16*(6), 1021–1046. https://doi.org/10.1177/017084069501600605

Carey, K. (2004). The real value of teachers: Using new information about teacher effectiveness to close the achievement gap. *Thinking K-16, 8*(1), 3–42.

Chen, Z., Ramos, C., Puah, L. D., & Cheng, S. C. (2020). *Training and Adult Education landscape in Singapore: Characteristics, challenges and policies*. Retrieved February 20, 2024 from https://www.ial.edu.sg/getmedia/fa78f92c-d856-41c6-acda-896e93967a52/TAE-Landscape-Report_Final1_1.pdf

European Centre for the Development of Vocational Training. (2020). *Perceptions on adult learning and continuing vocational education and training in Europe, volume 1: Second opinion survey, member states*. Publications Office of the European Union.

Evans, K., Hodkinson, P., & Unwin, L. (Eds.). (2002). *Working to learn: Transforming learning in the workplace*. Kogan Page. https://doi.org/10.4324/9780203417164

Friedman, A., & Phillips, M. (2004). Continuing professional development: Developing a vision. *Journal of Education and Work, 17*(3), 361–376. https://doi.org/10.1080/1363908042000267432

Government of Singapore. (2016). *Formation of the council for skills, innovation and productivity*. https://www.skillsfuture.gov.sg/newsroom/formation-of-the-council-for-skills-innovation-and-productivity

Griffiths, T., & Guile, D. (2003). A connective model of learning: The implications for work process knowledge. *European Educational Research Journal, 2*(1), 56–73. https://doi.org/10.2304/eerj.2003.2.1.10

Griscti, O., & Jacono, J. (2006). Effectiveness of continuing educaion programmes in nursing: Literature review. *Journal of Advanced Nursing, 55*(4), 449–456. https://doi.org/10.1111/j.1365-2648.2006.03940.x

Heng, S. K. (2014). *Opening address by Mr Heng Swee Keat, minister for education, at the international conference of teaching and learning with technology (iCTLT)*. Ministry of Education (Singapore). Retrieved from https://www.aps.sg/files/in-the-news/opening-address-by-mr-heng-swee-keat-at-the-international-conference-of-teaching-and-learning-with-technology.pdf

Herschell, A. D., Kolko, D. J., Baumann, B. L., & Davis, A. C. (2010). The role of therapist training in the implementation of psychosocial treatments: A review and critique with recommendations. *Clinical Psychology Review, 30*(4), 448–466. https://doi.org/10.1016/j.cpr.2010.02.005

Institute of Adult Learning. (2017). *Adult education professionalisation*. Retrieved from https://www.ial.edu.sg/join-the-community/adult-educators%2D%2Dprofessionalisation-aep-scheme/benefits.html

Lave, J. (2009). The practice of learning. In K. Illeris (Ed.), *Contemporary theories of learning: Learning theorists ... in their own words* (pp. 200–208). Routledge.

Lave, J., & Wenger, E. (1991). *Situated learning: Legitimate peripheral participation*. Cambridge University Press.

Marsick, V. J., & Watkins, K. E. (2002). Envisioning new organizations for learning. In F. Reeve, M. Cartwright, & R. Edwards (Eds.), *Supporting lifelong learning* (pp. 34–50). Routledge Falmer.

Moore, D. T. (2004). Curriculum at work: An educational perspective on workplace as a learning environment. *Journal of Workplace Learning, 16*(6), 325–340. https://doi.org/10.1108/13665620410550303

Ochieng, B., & Ward, K. (2018). Safeguarding of vulnerable adults training: Assessing the effect of continuing professional development. *Nursing Management, 25*(4), 30–35. https://doi.org/10.7748/nm.2018.e1781

Organisation for Economic Co-operation and Development. (2010a). *Synthesis report of the OECD reviews of vocational education and training: Learning for jobs*. https://www.oecd.org/edu/skills-beyond-school/Learning%20for%20Jobs%20book.pdf

Organisation for Economic Co-operation and Development. (2010b). *Singapore: Rapid improvement followed by strong performance*. https://www.oecd.org/countries/singapore/46581101.pdf

Organisation for Economic Co-operation and Development. (2020). *TALIS 2018 results (volume II): Teachers and school leaders as valued professionals* (Singapore – country note). https://www.oecd.org/countries/singapore/TALIS2018_CN_SGP_Vol_II.pdf

Osman-Gani, A. M. (2004). Human capital development in Singapore: An analysis of national policy perspectives. *Advances in Developing Human Resources, 6*(3), 276–287. https://doi.org/10.1177/1523422304266074

Prensky, M. (2012). *From digital natives to digital wisdom: Hopeful essays for 21st century learning*. Corwin.

SkillsFuture Singapore. (2020). *500,000 individuals and 14,000 enterprises benefitted from SkillsFuture programmes in 2019*. Retrieved January 4, 2024 from https://www.skillsfuture.gov.sg/newsroom/500-000-individuals-and-14-000-enterprises-benefitted-from-skillsfuture-programmes-in-2019#:~:text=More%20Singaporeans%20and%20enterprises%20are,and%2012%2C000%20enterprises%20in%202018

SkillsFuture Singapore. (2023). *Skills framework for training and adult education*. https://www.skillsfuture.gov.sg/initiatives/training-providers/skills-framework/tae

Sung, J., Loke, F., Ramos, C., & Ng, M. (2011). *You and your work: Skills utilisation in Singapore*. https://www.ial.edu.sg/getmedia/fdc73e72-88ec-40f1-8f84-31227d35f8cf/You-and-Your-Work-Skills-Utilisation.pdf

Tan, N., Shien, C., Ong, C., & Billett, S. (2023). Promoting student readiness for work-life through internships: Challenges and support. *Australian Journal of Adult Education, 63*(3), 343–367.

UK Commission for Employment and Skills. (2014). *The future of work: Jobs and skills in 2030*. https://www.gov.uk/government/publications/jobs-and-skills-in-2030

World Health Organization. (2013). *Transforming and scaling up health professionals' education and training: World Health Organization guidelines 2013*. Retrieved Feb 20, 2024 from http://apps.who.int/iris/bitstream/10665/93635/1/9789241506502_eng.pdf

Chapter 9
Working Women and CET: Enablers and Barriers

Abstract The role and expectations of working women have changed dramatically in many countries due to shifts in social and economic conditions, changes of legislative requirements about work and actions against discrimination and social demands. These include such as women wanting and needing to have as fulfilling working lives as males. Working women usually have additional family responsibilities, including managing the primary care of children and extended family members and, thus, often faced with greater challenges when seeking to pursue career pathways than male counterparts. Such family commitments tend to be heightened in Asian culture, such as is the case in Singapore. When engaging in continuing education and training (CET) to sustain their employability concerns, working women/mothers usually face heightened challenges associated with (i) managing study commitments alongside work and self-care, (ii) balancing study with family commitments, and (iii) balancing study with work commitments. There is, however, a complex of personal and work factors that variously hinder or enable working women's participation and engagement in CET. So, provisions of CET are set amongst a range of other factors that support or inhibit participation and engagement of women workers. All this suggests effective CET provisions are required to meet the varied needs of these working age adults. Drawing on interviews with CET women graduates, this chapter seeks to understand their experience with CET courses in terms of enablers and barriers to their participation and engagement. Such understanding is pivotal to respond to the quest of what constitutes effective CET provisions for working women.

Keywords Working women · Study life · Family commitments · CET purposes · Successful completion · Balancing commitments · Family · Workplaces · Adult educators · Work experience · Barriers to participation

Working Women, CET and Employability

There are a range of fundamental premises for women to have the options within and for working lives in which their abilities and talents are optimized, and for which educational provisions, including continuing education and training (CET) should play a key role (United Nations Educational, Scientific and Cultural Organization [UNESCO], 2022). Firstly, it is basic right for working age adults to be able to participate in working life, secure an income and have opportunities that are as equal as for others. This is a basic democratic right that allows then to secure opportunities and develop further and optimize their capacities. Secondly, the ability to earn an income and enjoy control over it also stands as a fundamental requirement for all individuals to be able to make independent decisions about their adult lives. In relation to choices about and practicing occupations, there are very few instances in which gender is a legitimate basis for constraining employment and advancement. So, many of the orthodoxies about gender-specific work roles have been found to be ill founded, and women should be encouraged and supported to engage in the range of occupations and kinds of work that is of interest to them, suits their capacities and in which they will find fulfilment, should they wish to pursue that kind of work. Certainly, the evidence suggests that when women have incomes of their own, their wellbeing and rights are enhanced and their voice within and beyond their families are greater (Sen, 1990). Also, their independence or control over income and other economic resources plays a significant role in uplifting their dependents, especially children (UN Women, 2019). Importantly, women's participation in productive economic activities (i.e., employability) potentially contributes to the prosperity of their families, communities, broader society and, consecutively, the local or national economy (Duflo, 2012). Thus, engaging in CET to secure their preferred occupations and forms of work and sustain their employability becomes pivotal for working women. However, on becoming mothers, working women often incur additional responsibilities, which can include being the primary caregiver for children and roles in their extended families and these create barriers for and can create societal pressures that make pursuing a career path far more demanding and difficult. Moreover, as securing further education is increasingly central to remaining employable and seeking advancement, participation in it becomes increasingly essential thereby potentially creating further barriers. Indeed, for many, participation in CET means that working women with family responsibilities will likely face challenges associated with: i) managing study alongside work and self-care, ii) balancing study with family commitments, and iii) balancing study with work commitments at a heightened level than male counterparts. Therefore, provisions of CET are set amongst a range of other factors which support or inhibit participation and engagement of women workers. So, there is a strong case that provisions of CET need to be organized and enacted in ways which are sensitive to and promote these women's participation and success.

It follows then that understanding how best to assist working women maintain their employability across working lives, and what workplaces, educational institutions and government agencies can do to sustain that employability, is now central to many countries' national social and economic goals. Yet, when considering how best to promote that employability through education, training initiatives, or approaches to CET for these workers, it is necessary to include considerations of: (i) their purposes for participating, (ii) needs of readiness to engage in processes of developing further their capacities and (iii) managing and prioritizing multiple commitments. Hence, deliberations about how these outcomes can and should be realized need to be inclusive of the kinds of experiences provided through existing education and training provisions and their alignments with working women's ability to access, participate and profit from them. It is important to acknowledge that most of tertiary education provisions were established for young people's full-time engagement in initial occupational preparation and as naïve learners, who are not burdened by family, community and work commitments. This is quite a distinct orientation from engaging with adults as informed part-time students who can and often want to collaborate in their own and others' learning based upon their experiences and capacities as mature age adults and who are also balancing their study commitments with extensive work, community and family responsibilities. Accordingly, there is the need to identify the requirements for, and then design, implement and evaluate CET provisions suited to the needs and goals of working women. These will likely need to be supported by pedagogic practices appropriate to their needs as adults, readiness to engage in interdependent and dependent processes of education and in ways that accommodate working mothers.

Drawing on data from the research project investigating CET provisions in Singapore that features across this volume, this chapter seeks to illuminate and appraise the experience of working women through interviews with 61 women CET graduates. It proposes that when the goals of, purposes for, readiness to engage, capacities, and circumstances of such workers are more fully understood, effective CET provisions can be identified to meet their needs to the same extent as those who sponsor them (i.e., government and employers). The attempt here is to understand what the current circumstances in which CET is provided for these working women (i.e., 'what is') and be informed about how these provisions might best be organized and enacted to meet their needs (i.e., 'what should be') in the future.

The chapter commences by discussing factors associated with working women's participation in CET. Following this, the findings from the interview and survey data pertaining to these women are presented and then discussed. That data used to inform those findings comprises both qualitative accounts from interviews and quantitative analysis of pre-interview survey data. Overall, it was found that the working women, like their male counterparts, were driven by a range of both personal and professional reasons to participate in CET courses/programs. These informants reported that work and family commitments were key barriers to their full engagement. Insights into this cohort of CET students' perspectives and experiences offer important implications for CET provisions to enhance their quality in effectively address these students' needs and enhance the educational and practical outcomes of CET courses/programs.

Women and Participation in Continuing Education and Training

Research findings have consistently demonstrated that demographic, social, economic and technological changes have made continuing education across adult life increasingly important for working age adults. Yet, it has identified that some of these changes have created barriers for women in particular (Malhotra et al., 2007). Over recent decades, research on women's experiences in CET, workplace learning, and professional development have been a focal area in adult education, and findings have led to the consistent conclusions that a gender gap exists and persists in the provision of and engagement in CET (Hopkins et al., 2008; Howell et al., 2002; Prins et al., 2009). For example, women have had a higher rate of participation than men in CET, albeit mainly in personal interest courses, since 1978, but a lower rate in CET for work-related learning activities (Dieckhoff & Steiber, 2011; Merriam & Caffarella, 1999). Women may face more difficulties and deterrents in CET participation because of their roles and position in society. Such socially constructed gender roles often give rise to issues of gender inequality in workplaces, such as the so-called 'glass ceiling' effect (i.e., women being unable to reach the highest level of management), gender-based pay differences, and gender stereotypes about work and work roles. Hence, it has been crucial to include critical perspectives of cultural, societal, and social roles in studies of working women, their employability and CET provisions.

Gender inequality exists globally (UNESCO, 2023), in both countries that have high traditions of social democracy and those that do not. In Germany, for example, the effect of traditional gender occupational segregation has influenced women's job opportunities continually, especially for those who are over 55 years of age (Humpert, 2013). In Spain and Belgium, older women also have had fewer employment opportunities than older men or, in fact, men of any age (Del Río & Alonso-Villar, 2010; Vandenberghe, 2011). In the UK, the primary barriers to women's CET participation in the construction industry are male-dominated organizational cultures and inflexible working practices (Worrall et al., 2010). In the USA, gender bias and the intersection of work and family life have affected female faculty job satisfaction and their status in higher education as they tend to perceive more gender discrimination in promotions, salaries, space/resources, access to administrative staff, and as graduate student than male faculty (Shollen et al., 2009). In Southern Asia, Indian women still have a lower status in society, with many deterrents to entrepreneurial development, such as a male dominant social order, family obligations, lack of management and organizational skills, low levels of negotiation and bargaining skills, low levels of risk taking, and lower education, among others (Mathapati, 2013). Similarly, Malaysian working women report facing conflicts between CET participation and family obligations (e.g., childrearing responsibilities) because of cultural norms (Ariffin & Torrance, 2008). These examples provide instantiations of entrenched and global discrimination faced by working women. Gender bias in cultural expectations and in workplaces has significantly interfered with the success of working women, and childbearing and care, as well as family commitments continue to have a significant effect on women's career choices and professional development. As was also pointed out earlier by Bundy and Norris (1992), women are often more concerned about fringe benefits related to childrearing or childcare (such as employer-paid pregnancy leave and on-premises daycare facilities) when selecting a job, while men tend to focus more on office support and afterhours social activities. As such, women are likely to hold unequal positions in the economy, perform different socially shaped responsibilities, face different constraints, and respond to CET differently from male counterparts.

Compared with men, women often prefer the workplace value of 'soft issues' (e.g., relationships, respect, communication, fairness, equity, collaboration, and work-family balance) and share information to build relationships (Fapohunda, 2013), as key measures of qualities of experiences. Accordingly, women are typically associated with kindness, sensitivity, and empathy and men with aggressiveness, ambition, and competitiveness when it comes to making work appointments (Eagly & Sczesny, 2009). Yet, according to Ibarra et al. (2010), women are also deemed as 'risky appointments' and are least likely to get the sponsorship necessary to move up to leadership positions. Specifically, sponsors tend not to actively advocate their female mentees, to go beyond providing advice, and to broaden the female mentees' visibility in the company in the same way male mentees have (Ibarra et al., 2010). Eagly and Sczesny (2009) also claim that social-psychological issues have led to lower level of representation in leadership roles. The 'think manager-think male' stereotype, coined over 50 years ago by Schein (1973), is still claimed to exist contemporarily (Ryan et al., 2011). Traditional gender stereotypes are held to continually impede women to reach higher-level jobs. To examine the variations in managerial and gender stereotypes, Ryan et al. (2011) suggested that situational flexibility, such as a tendency of increased representation in particular sectors (e.g., healthcare or retail) or roles (e.g., human resources or administration) among women, should not be an oversight.

Despite women in western countries having gained more access to lower levels of management or leadership, gender equality has not yet been achieved. According to Fapohunda (2013), regardless of the significant headway women have made, men continue to dominate in the workplace and receive more promotions. For example, women account for only 16% of corporate officers in U.S. Fortune 500 companies, and an average of only 4% of the presidents of EU corporations are women (Eagly & Sczesny, 2009). In another example, according to a 2010 World Economic Forum report on corporate practices in 20 countries, although approximately 60% of companies offered mentoring and networking programs and about 28% of them provided women-specific programs, such efforts did not lead to equal opportunities for promotions and appointments (Ibarra et al., 2010). There was great concern that cultural stereotypes, as well as gender differences in personality traits and occupational preferences and unconscious bias may have contributed to these results.

Due to the broad expectations based on gender and different family and occupational roles, men and women may differ in their political attitudes, social network communication, participation in continuing education, work burnout, personality traits, gender-related occupational preferences, approach to information sharing, and methods of handling workplace conflict (Dieckhoff & Steiber, 2011; Diekman & Schneider, 2010; Lippa, 2010; Purvanova & Muros, 2010; Thompson & Lougheed, 2012). The Flemish Eurostat Adult Education Survey of 3104 respondents found that in nearly all European countries, women participation in adult education was contingent on a greater focus on inter- and intra-personal factors (e.g., having fun, gaining self-confidence, and building relationships) (Boeren, 2011).

Patterns of participation in CET are gender biased (Leathwood & Francis, 2006). Research indicates that women tend to receive fewer opportunities for CET (Blackburn & Jarman, 2006; Boeren, 2011). The factor structure of deterrents to women's participation in CET is a complex phenomenon. Reasons for non-participation (i.e., why they do not) seem more difficult to identify than participation (i.e., why they do; Cross, 1981). However, the value of identifying the effect of deterrents to adult women's engagement in CET is profound (Vaccaro & Lovell, 2010). As suggested above, working women may have different motivations and approaches to learning processes from males that require practitioners to respond to those differences pedagogically. Further, because of women's special needs in family and social roles, they must be considered as a specific target group for all developmental programs (Mathapati, 2013). For instance, Chuang (2015) conducted a review of the extant literature to explore and define key factors that deter adult women from participating in CET to promote their success in the workplace. The review identified four constraints and barriers to women's participation in CET, which are likely to be caused by women's social roles, gender inequality and gender dimensions. These comprised i) family and time constraints, ii) cost and work constraints, iii) lack of support systems, and iv) lack of career advice and resources. Whilst these factors are analogous to those reported across the working age adult informants as reported in this volume (Chap. 5—*Motivations and affordances for engaging in CET*), they are potentially likely to be heightened and more critical for working women.

However, from available and accessible policies and research studies, Singapore seems to represent a partially different scenario from some other parts of the world in terms of women's participation in CET. For example, Thangavelu et al. (2011) use the Singapore Labour Force survey data to examine the determinants of workers' participation in training programs in the island nation. The findings indicate that gender does not have any significant effect on participation at any conventional level, although the coefficient on the women dummy (i.e., manipulation of sample) is positive, suggesting women might be slightly more likely to participate in training programs. Other findings indicate that different socio-demographic and employment related characteristics influence Singaporean workers' participation in training. Well-educated and better paid workers are much more likely to participate in training programs than others. Age has a positive impact on training participation for younger workers (i.e., < 37 years), but a negative effect on older workers' participation. The findings also indicate that occupational affiliations have a significant impact on participation in CET. Further, married workers seem to be less likely to participate in training programs, but the difference between married and single is only significant at the 10% level. Indeed, this was one of the specific focuses for interview questions asked of the women participants.

To illuminate and elaborate the issue of women's participation and outcomes in Singapore, this chapter reports and discusses the perspectives and experiences of women CET graduates. It seeks to understand their experience with CET courses in terms of enablers and barriers to their participation and engagement ('what is'). Such understanding is pivotal to respond to the quest of what constitutes effective CET provisions for working women ('what should be'). The findings reported and discussed here are part of a 3-phase research project to identify the qualities of an effective CET system that is accessible, effective, and targeted to meet the needs of working age Singaporeans. In overview, it commenced by identifying factors that CET graduates and employers reported as being effective in CET provisions (Phase 1), followed by what a broader sample of working age Singaporeans report as appropriate purposes, access, and support of CET (Phase 2), and finally, how CET educators and administrators propose responding to these needs and requirements (Phase 3). The details of this investigation are reported in Chap. 4 (*Investigating effective CET provisions to promote employability: Method and procedures*) of this volume.

Women Graduates' Perspectives of CET: A Singaporean Investigation

As noted, this chapter reports on Phase 1 interview findings with a particular focus on perspectives of women CET graduate informants. Interviews were conducted with 180[1] working age graduates of CET programs at post-secondary educational institutions in Singapore. Of these graduates, 61 were women. The interview schedule included a pre-interview survey to gather demographic data and responses to sets of closed items (i.e., questions) on Likert scales from 1 to 5 regarding work and job training, and details on the CET course taken, followed by a semi-structured interview (*see* Chap. 4—*Investigating effective CET provisions to promote employability: Method and procedures*). Descriptive analysis using SPSS (i.e., a quantitative statistical software application) was performed with quantitative data from the survey. The analysis was mainly descriptive statistics, focusing on frequencies weightings and rankings. Concepts for a thematic analysis were identified initially from members of the research team reading a selection of transcripts and then that analysis was applied to the body of qualitative data using NVivo (i.e., a qualitative data analysis software application) with the interview data. The analytical process also involved identifying themes and issues that were frequently raised by informants as well as holistically assessing the interview transcripts to identify measures

---

[1] A total of 180 graduate informants were interviewed, but two refused permissions to be recorded so their transcripts could not be included in the qualitative analysis undertaken through NVivo.

of these data that were deemed to be 'positive' or 'negative' or 'neutral' based on the informants' responses. That is, an attempt of quantifying the qualitative, so that patterns of weightings from the qualitative data could be identified. Such patterning is helpful given the amount of quantitative data and the need to identify within the utterances comprising interview transcripts. Presented and discussed in the following sections are a series of data and findings relating to these female graduates' views about the CET courses/programs they had undertaken. These comprise motivations to participate in CET and barriers to that participation, factors supporting CET engagement and completion, and experiences of the CET courses/programs, including their value, lecturers and provisions. In preview, it was found that:

- Personal development through learning new knowledge was the main reason for CET participation.
- Achieving the purposes for participating in CET was measured based on: i) the relevance and practical outcomes for CET students' work, ii) the application of their learning to their workplace, and iii) the effectiveness of the processes and outcomes for future employability.
- High levels of satisfaction were reported about the value of CET course/program and the effectiveness and supportiveness of CET lecturers and provisions.
- Challenges associated with balancing study with family and work commitments reportedly inhibited CET participation.
- Effective CET teachers had: i) currency of knowledge, ii) good pedagogical and facilitation skills, and iii) who were empathetic about the challenges of adult students.
- Flexibility in course arrangements and considerations of adult students' needs in curriculum planning were most helpful to engage them as working age adults.

Motivations for CET Participation

In the pre-interview survey, informants indicated their reasons for engaging in CET, from a list provided in which they could nominate more than one reason. In Table 9.1 below, responses to the pre-interview survey on the reasons for enrolling in the CET programs are organized. The left column lists the reasons, the middle column shows rankings by female informants, and the right column indicates how often each reason was mentioned. Those reasons pertaining directly to work and working life are *italicised*. Overall, most of these CET women graduates reported reasons that were categorized as being both professional and personal reasons for taking their courses (*see* Table 9.1).

Regarding personal and knowledge development, most of the women informants reported participating in their CET courses/programs mainly to learn new knowledge associated with working life (8/13), to advanced educationally (2/13), to remain relevant (1/13), and optimize the government subsidies (1/13). So, it is noteworthy that eight of the 13 purposes are associated with these informants' working

Table 9.1 Motivations for CET participation

Reasons for enrolling in CET	Rank	N
To gain personal development	1	43
To acquire extra skills for my job	2	37
To get to the next level of education	3	26
To try for a different career	4	24
To get a job	5	23
To get a better job	6	21
Government subsidies (e.g., skills future credit)	6	21
To fulfill a job requirement (e.g., work certification)	8	20
To get skills for community/voluntary work	9	14
Employers' support (e.g., study leave)	9	14
To get a promotion	11	13
To get into another course of study	12	10
To develop or start own business	13	9

lives. Moreover, when calculated, the frequency by which these are mentioned is 161. This is compared with those associated with personal development alone (i.e., 41) and for educational related purposes (i.e., 36). Those purposes associated with working life included informants anticipating the outcomes of their participation would lead to a different career. The top ranked response of focusing on personal development was consistent with the narratives frequently advanced throughout their interviews, emphasizing that they are participating for personal development and to learn new knowledge. In terms of reasons associated with working life, most of these informants stated they participated in CET to secure some kind of advancement. Consequently, they reported measuring their achievements based on: (i) how directly relevant and pertinent the CET program and outcomes are to their work; (ii) how their newly acquired knowledge assisted them in their workplace or (iii) the perceived effectiveness of these processes and outcomes for their future employability or workplace performance. Some interviewees reported participating in CET to secure formal recognition in the form of certification to secure more opportunities. The informants often stated that they measured the extent of their achievements based on objective goals, such as an increase in wages because they have the required certification and being able to perform better at work. The degree to which they were able to achieve those outcomes through their CET program is presented in Table 9.3 and discussed below.

It is important to assess the informants' key motivation for participating in CET as it reportedly influences their preferences and evaluation of the CET provision, for instance, the type of lecturers, course arrangements, class activities, and mode of delivery. For example, if learners identify themselves as motivated to participate in CET for personal development, they tend to want to learn the knowledge, engage effort fully and engage with the course content intentionally. Thus, an introductory class or lectures could be offered to these groups to provide them with certain foundation before they enroll in the nominated course, instead of engaging them in a process to assess their competency and certifying them to assess their eligibility to meet the prerequisite of the course. All these data illustrate the significance of understanding these informants' intentions for participating in CET. In addition, provisions of CET are set amongst a range of other factors which support or inhibit participation and engagement of women workers. Understanding barriers to and enablers of participation to meet the varied needs of students is, therefore, an important consideration in terms of what constitutes effective CET provisions from these informants' perspectives.

Again, it is important to emphasize that attendance in continuing education programs is not usually compulsory, adults elect whether to engage in CET programs and complete them. These adults are not compulsory participants who lack of volition and intentions in terms of the content and approach to the teaching of the program. Instead, their participation is based upon the degree by which they believe these programs are meeting their needs. Consequently, the working age adults who participate in CET programs are an integral element of these educational provisions and their needs and requirements need to be accounted for in the design, development, enactment, and evaluation of CET provisions (i.e., how they are enacted) and programs (i.e., their content and focus) (Billett et al., 2016). Consequently, in the section below, consideration is given to the factors that either inhibit or support their participation in these programs and indicate the degree by which they have been able to meet their goals and purposes through participating in these programs.

Barriers to and Enablers for Participating in CET Programs

As noted, data were also gathered about factors that either inhibited or supported participation in their CET programs. This was completed to identify the strengths and limitations of the current education provisions (i.e., 'what is'), and to indicate what needs to happen for improvements to access these provisions (i.e., 'what should be'). The factors reportedly inhibiting participation by these informants were mainly environmental factors, such as work commitments, travel time and family commitments, that are external to the actual educational provision, but influenced participation, and were ranked in the top three of barriers to CET participation (Table 9.2). During the interviews, these informants, like their male counterparts, emphasized that the major inhibitors to their participation in their CET course are challenges associated with balancing study with family and work commitments. Hence, these findings indicate that the challenges of managing these commitments need to be considered when planning for, designing and implementing CET provisions. In Table 9.2, the left set of columns indicate 'barriers' and the right set 'enablers'. The factors that are external to the actual CET provisions and are not directly manageable by educators of educational institutes are *italicized*. In the right set, personal factors enabling student participation are also *italicized*.

Table 9.2 Barriers to and enablers of CET participation and completion

Barriers	Rank	Enablers	Rank
Job	1	*Achieving personal goals/ motivations*	1
Travel time	2	*Personal interest*	2
Family care	3	Friends	3
Venue	4	Family	4
Course fees	5	Subsidies	5
Course requirements	5	Employer	6
Childcare	7	Financial penalties	7
Use of technology	8		
Travel cost	8		

Table 9.3 Summary of women informants' views about CET courses/programs

CET features	Experience	N	%
Value	Partially achieved	33	54.1
(worth of course)	Fully achieved	22	36.1
	Not achieved	6	9.8
Lecturers (effectiveness & support)	Neutral	29	47.5
	Positive	20	32.8
	Negative	12	19.7
Provision (effectiveness & support)	Neutral	33	54.1
	Positive	21	34.4
	Negative	7	11.5

As shown in Table 9.2, the factors sustaining interest and motivation to complete are largely personal or those arising from close associations. These data indicate that a larger proportion of these women graduates are intrinsically motivated, driven to achieve their own goals and pursue learning of their own interests. A smaller number of them are influenced by their friends and family, suggesting their support can make a difference to these graduates' learning experience and motivation to complete a course. For these women informants, it was also helpful and appreciated when members of the family helped with childcare arrangements during lessons or group project meetings.

Altogether, these data indicate a complex of personal and work factors that hinder or enable these workers to complete the course. Whilst long working days and time to travel to attend CET courses hindered participation, these barriers can be ameliorated by personal desire and interests, and support of workplaces, peers, and family. So, the provision of CET is set amongst a range of other factors that support or inhibit participation. Given all of this, it is important to understand their experience of the CET courses/programs that were undertaken, firstly the degree by which the purposes for which they participated were achieved, then their perspectives and experiences of the lecturers and provisions of these CET course/programs.

Experience of CET Courses/Programs

Interview data were analyzed in relation to perspectives and experiences with the courses/programs undertaken by these women graduates. Their perspectives and experiences were categorized as being positive, neutral (i.e., a mix of positive and negative moments), and negative (i.e., concerns or issues associated with value of the courses/programs, their lecturers, and provisions). So, their responses were delineated under three categories of Value (i.e., worth of participating in their CET program), Lecturers (i.e., effectiveness and supportiveness of CET educators) and Provision (i.e., effectiveness and supportiveness of CET program) when the data were tabulated. As presented in Table 9.3, majority of the informants indicated their level of satisfaction with value of the course/program, their lecturers and provisions. That is, they expressed their experience as either positive or neutral. Whilst this is a positive finding, it also indicates that there is scope for improving the number of CET graduates who will report fully achieving their goals 4 years after completing their CET courses/programs.

Generally, regarding value of the courses/programs, over 36% of these graduates reported fully achieving their purposes of participating in their CET courses/programs, and 54.1% partially. This means that over 90% of these female graduates reported to have wholly or partially achieved their intended goals. Only around 10% indicated low levels of progress towards their intended purposes. This finding aligns with the overall findings reported by the entire cohort of informants in this project (Leow et al., 2022, 2023). Table 9.4 provides some representative quotes illustrating different perspectives of the value of CET courses/programs the informants had undertaken.

The coded data on quality of the CET lecturers was more balanced. Whilst around 80% of the informants provided either positive (32.8%) or neutral (47.5%) judgements on their CET lecturers, the 20% expressing negative view raises the concern about the qualities of the teaching experiences. Positive experiences reported were associated with certain qualities of effective CET lecturers. These informants valued CET lecturers who were empathetic and obliging towards them, were current in their knowledge, experience, and teaching pedagogy. These positive qualities included being able to draw on students' experiences of work and working life and being responsive to students' needs. These observations are consistent to those made across the gender and age categories of the entire cohort of informants in this project (Leow et al., 2022, 2023). The women graduates, just as much as the entire cohort of 180 informants, reported appreciating lecturers who were credible, engaging, and helpful facilitators. This is indicative of how pedagogic qualities go beyond content presentation and extend to its relevance to their learning and the experiences provided. So, CET lecturers who had both occupational currency and helpful teaching pedagogy were reported positively. Working towards the ideal, CET institutions may have to provide a platform for their lecturers to participate in the industry to gain more currency in occupational practice and relevance in its

Table 9.4 Interview quotes representing perspective of the value of CET undertaken

Value of the CET	Representative quotes
Partially achieved (n = 33)	How relevant… frankly speaking, I think, perhaps only half I would say. […] but for a start, as an intro, this course is very helpful. In terms of expanding the portfolio, yes it had already happened, it had already changed. In terms of rank, I'm not quite sure. But technically right now I'm the only person that is trained and in that branch that I'm supposedly not heading. […] It's possible but I don't know but due to other constraints might not happen.
Fully achieved (n = 22)	Certain problems that I encounter when dealing with my clients—how do I put it, the gaps that I faced didn't become apparent until after I took the course and after facing all these difficulties. Then when I took the course it all became apparent why I was facing those, so it helped directly for me to actually answer these gaps at work. Having achieved the master in training and development, it creates a perception by other that you are bit more professional—So because of that I've been asked to do some projects along the way. Without that master I would not have met the people or would not have created a more professional position for myself.
Not achieved (n = 6)	It's still- because for my industry that I'm in now, it's the early childhood industry. So, my diploma actually doesn't really recognised by them. […] so, the pay wise is still low. Actually, not really. Maybe is because of the change in policies and all that. So, it's about being patient. […] it [the course] wasn't directly relevant but certain aspects were in line with the organization.

application and actionable skills to impart to their students. Representative quotes about these analytical focus from the interviews were provided in Table 9.5.

Counter to those positive experiences, were those reported disconnections between the lecturers' theoretical knowledge and practical experience in the field of their teaching (Leow et al., 2022). These include the credibility of the lecturer's ability to answer students' doubts, general knowledge, current affairs, other classmates' experience, and their own experience at work. For instance, some graduates indicated their disappointment when the lecturer was not able to give them a convincing answer to their question or concern or inaccurate information in the field of work that the students had experience. This finding highlights the importance of professional preparation and development for CET lecturers in establishing their educational capacities ad maintaining their industry currency. This is particularly important and necessary for being effective CET lecturers for providing relevant and occupationally authentic experiences.

Data were also collected about the kind of provisions these informants preferred and what they believed to be helpful in terms of the organization and teaching of CET courses and programs. In all, most of these informants' experiences were categorized as positive (34.4%) or neutral (54.1%). Some examples of these kinds of experiences are presented in Table 9.6, including the frequency of their mention. In this table, the experiences (i.e., positive, neutral, negative) are represented in the left column and then representative quotes illustrating different experiences with CET

Table 9.5 Interview quotes representing experience with CET lecturers

CET Lecturers	Representative quotes
Neutral (n = 29)	Different lecturers, some of them really have actually helped us by relating to personal life examples or based on his or her job scope then it helps us to relate better. But in terms of some other areas, which when they share their personal experience or so, which is not so relevant. The quality of delivery varies according to the lecturer, varies according to their ability to make it applicable to real life situations. [...] so, it would have been nicer if let's say the examples were tailored to the course itself, then it would make me feel like, "oh okay, this is what I need to watch out for." it becomes more practical, rather than a theory.
Positive (n = 20)	They contextualise, the good facilitators I've met they conceptualise the content they want to teach to our learners' problem. So, for example if we are talking about a problem, let's say facilitation, so in your group you are allowed to actually chose a context that is more relevant to members of the group and present in a flip chart. So, when sharing right, we can also give a background of ours and we also hear about other people's work context. They were very professional, definitely adult learners. [...] they do [bring up their own experiences]. It helps when people raise up relevant examples, raise up pertaining to the course, and share insights and all that stuff. So, that is a lot of intangible value addition.
Negative (n = 12)	Generally, I feel that some of the trainers don't even seem to have a background in career counselling. [...] but the real-life experience of the trainer is less apparent. And I think the other thing you realise also from a lot of research is that a lot of time when we attend courses like that, especially for adult learners, we want to hear the trainer's experience, the real experience. Some of our classmates have actually asked them for the answers and they refused to give. And so, and sometimes you know when we are in class, the revisions tend to be very quick, I don't know why. The normal classes we feel that they are spending too much time. Meaning that we could see that they are killing time. They were not utilising the 3 h. They were just like fulfilling the 3 h. But they could have done a lot more to contribute to learning.

provisions are presented in the right column. The positive features of CET provisions reported by these women graduates are consistent with the entire 180 interviewed graduates in this project. Those features include qualities associated with flexibility, engaging, authenticity, convenience, and leniency (Leow et al., 2022, 2023). For example, the values of flexibility were reported in terms of delivery mode and assessment formats, engaging provisions in terms of teaching material and resources as well as assessment topics, and authenticity perceived in relation to educational and practical outcomes (*see* Chap. 10—*CET experience of and outcomes for 'older' working age adults*).

However, some graduates reported disappointment with their courses because of perceived poor organization and communication about course objectives that led to expectations that were not fulfilled. For example, some of these informants expressed their discomfort with certain ambiguity such as the conciseness and alignments of educational materials and learning objectives with practical outcomes. It appeared that experiences of graduates differed greatly depending on the course in which they

Women Graduates' Perspectives of CET: A Singaporean Investigation

Table 9.6 Interview quotes representing experience with CET provisions

CET provision	Representative quotes
Neutral (n = 33)	Actually, just to achieve like another field that I don't think I can go into, but I can learn something new from another industry. Because I don't have the background because FM is more like you need to have the background of engineering or mechanical or electrical background because my one is just landscape background. [...] I think it prepares but there may be more can be done.
	Not much because I think career counselling is not very mature yet. [...] I don't think the current state of the organisations; they have reached that kind of paradigm yet; so, they all look at me like, oh, okay, it's cool. Then they walk away. So, it's very difficult to practise what we have learnt. Only can do like outside law, like pro bono kind of thing. [...] so, because I think the career counselling, you need to be certified or something like that one.
	These are the top three reasons; in fact, I am still always looking for opportunities to start my own business. [...] so basically the first two has already been fulfilled already. The next is just my business, that one sees how I can start my own business.
Positive (n = 21)	I think it articulates the importance of being reflective as a practitioner, so I think the spirit of it now as I look back is trying to build the habit to reflect. Yes, it is very effective in the sense that it is the first module and when you go in to the first module you are fresh and all that and it is the first thing you encounter and remember. So, it is throughout the program it kind of builds up.
	I think that was a good [time] arrangement. [...] other provision was the location was good we had good classroom, ice setting. [...] it was convenient for me. And I drive most of the time, so it was it was alright for me.
Negative (n = 7)	They are not using LMS [learning management system]. The LMS, I think, is capable of a lot more, in terms of its contribution to learning, if well-used. But if you are using the LMS just to give us your lecture notes and give us the tutorials for example, or just resources, then you don't even need LMS. You can just put it in any of the open source for that matter.
	The online learning was quite pathetic, if my recall is right. It was like you go and do these questions. [...] I mean online learning shouldn't be this mode, isn't it? If it's online learning, there should be something that you allow us to interact with, meaning that is there something we can test ourselves, self-test, and then if we self-test, are there explanations for the answers that are right, answers that are wrong.
	In this particular course, it felt like as though the designer of the course had their own agendas and objectives. And that was more important to them than considering the students' needs. It felt like that. Especially the first term when they just plonked three modules in a week. The second term we had two modules, and it was so much more manageable. [...] if I'm in a 9 to 5 kind of work, then fine. But problem is that most of us are in the 30's and 40's, and late 40's, and you're holding on to jobs with responsibility, roles with responsibility, plus roles as parents, or, or you know, family. So, then it became very heavy-going.

had participated. Others, however, appreciated their experience in the courses as it provided them with the confidence and skills to perform independently at work and to share with colleagues the skills they had learnt.

Generally, findings from this analysis indicated that these women graduates were motivated to participate in CET for both personal and professional reasons, as was the case for the entire cohort of informants. They reported being supported in engaging in and completing the course by staying focused to achieve their goals and being genuinely interested in what they were learning. Like the other cohorts (Leow et al., 2022), these women graduates reported being hindered in engaging in and completing the course by the weight of their other responsibilities at work and home. Despite their challenges, most of them reported having fully achieved or partially achieved their purposes for participation in their courses (90.1%), but a stronger outcome could have been realized. They most appreciated lecturers who had: i) currency of knowledge, ii) good pedagogical and facilitation skills, and iii) who were empathetic about the challenges of adult students in finding time to attend courses and complete assignments during their busy lives. They also indicated that flexibility in terms of course arrangements and having their needs considered in the planning of the curriculum were most helpful in engaging them as working age adults.

Working Women's CET Experience and Outcomes

In sum, the role of working women has changed dramatically in recent years and globally because of dynamic economic conditions, changes of legislative requirements about work and discrimination and social demands, such as women wanting and needing to have fulfilling working lives. When becoming partners and mothers, working women have additional responsibilities, managing the primary care of children and extended family, thus placing greater demands and greater pressure to continue a career path. Such family commitments may be accentuated in Asian culture, as is the case in Singapore. Engaging in CET to sustain their employability concerns, working women/mothers usually face challenges associated with balancing study with family and work commitments more often than their male counterparts. Of course, there is a complex of personal and work factors that potentially hinder or enable women workers to participate and engage in CET. So, CET provisions are set amongst a range of other factors which support or inhibit working women's participation and engagement of. All this suggests effective CET provisions are deemed to meet the varied needs of students.

This analysis and discussion have provided an overview of the perceptions and experiences of the 61 working women graduates with the CET courses/programs they had completed. In all, it is proposed that:

- Most of the CET women graduates reported participating in CET for both personal and professional reasons.
- Regarding personal and knowledge development, most of them participated in CET mainly to: i) learn new knowledge associated with working life, ii) advanced educationally, iii) remain relevant, and iv) optimize government subsidies.
- Focusing on personal development was consistent with the narratives frequently advanced throughout their interviews, emphasizing they are participating for personal development and to learn new knowledge.

- Achievement of reasons for participation were measured based on: i) how directly relevant and pertinent the CET program and outcomes are to their work, ii) how their newly acquired knowledge assisted them in their workplace or iii) the perceived effectiveness of these processes and outcomes for their future employability or workplace performance.
- Major inhibitors to their CET participation are challenges associated with balancing study with family and work commitments.
- The factors sustaining interest and motivation to complete are largely personal or those arising from close personal and professional affiliations. These data indicate that a larger proportion of these graduates are intrinsically motivated, driven to achieve their own goals and to pursue learning of their own interests.
- High levels of satisfaction with value of the course/program, their lecturers and provisions were reported. Over 90% reported to have wholly or partially achieved their intended goals.
- Qualities of effective CET lecturers included being able to draw on students' experiences of work and working life and being responsive to students' needs.
- Counter to those positive experiences were disconnections between lecturers' theoretical knowledge and practical experience in the field of their teaching.
- Flexibility in terms of course arrangements and having their needs considered in the planning of the curriculum were most helpful in engaging them as working age adults.

The findings showed that these graduates were motivated both personally and professionally to participate in CET. Interestingly, the reason for CET participation reported by the majority is associated with personal development. This motivation is well aligned with long-standing goals for adult education being about cultural betterment through personal learning. Like most working age individuals (Leow et al., 2022), and working women in particular, family and work commitments have hindered their full participation in CET courses/programs. However, it was also these factors that support and enable their engagement and completion. That is, the support from family, friends, and peers and workplace affordances, including support from employers and colleagues. Noteworthily, an overwhelming number of these women graduates reported they had fully or partially achieved their goals for which they elected to participate in CET. This has important implications for CET provisions to be enhanced to achieve better outcomes for CET graduates, ensuring a higher percentage of working age, female in particular, Singaporeans would report wholly achieving their purposes for participating in CET. Also from these interviews, these informants' experiences of their CET courses/programs were appraised and understood. Overall, they expressed high level of satisfaction with value of the course/program, the effectiveness and supportiveness of their lecturers and provisions. Whilst these are positive outcomes for the CET courses/programs, concerns about credibility in terms of CET teachers' knowledge and currency, and ambiguity about the alignment between course objectives and practical outcomes provide scope for efforts to enhance the quality of CET provisions to provide more positive experiences and effectively address the practical and educational outcomes for CET students or learners. Such understanding is pivotal to respond to the quest of what constitutes effective CET provisions for working age adults overall and working women in particular.

References

Ariffin, M. H., & Torrance, J. V. (2008). Social group related entry participation motivations for continuing professional development activities among Malaysian registered quantity surveyors. *Journal of Construction in Developing Countries, 13*(2), 1–19.

Billett, S., Dymock, D., & Choy, S. (Eds.). (2016). *Supporting learning across working life: Models, processes and practices*. Springer International Publishing.

Blackburn, R. M., & Jarman, J. (2006). Gendered occupations: Exploring the relationship between gender segregation and inequality. *International Sociology, 21*(2), 289–315.

Boeren, E. (2011). Gender differences in formal, non-formal and informal adult learning. *Studies in Continuing Education, 33*(3), 333–346. https://doi.org/10.1080/0158037X.2011.610301

Bundy, P., & Norris, D. (1992). What accounting students consider important in the job selection process. *Journal of Applied Business Research, 8*(2), 1–6. https://doi.org/10.19030/jabr.v8i2.6155

Chuang, S. F. (2015). Deterrents to women's participation in continuing professional development. *New Horizons in Adult Education and Human Resource Development, 27*(2), 28–37. https://doi.org/10.1002/nha3.20104

Cross, K. P. (1981). *Adults as learners: Increasing participation and facilitating learning*. Jossey-Bass.

Del Río, C., & Alonso-Villar, O. (2010). Gender segregation in the Spanish labor market: An alternative approach. *Social Indicators Research, 98*, 337–362. https://doi.org/10.1007/s11205-009-9548-0

Dieckhoff, M., & Steiber, N. (2011). A re-assessment of common theoretical approaches to explain gender differences in continuing training participation. *British Journal of Industrial Relations, 49*, s135–s157. https://doi.org/10.1111/j.1467-8543.2010.00824.x

Diekman, A. B., & Schneider, M. C. (2010). A social role theory perspective on gender gaps in political attitudes. *Psychology of Women Quarterly, 34*(4), 486–497. https://doi.org/10.1111/j.1471-6402.2010.01598.x

Duflo, E. (2012). Women empowerment and economic development. *Journal of Economic Literature, 50*(4), 1051–1079. https://doi.org/10.1257/jel.50.4.1051

Eagly, A. H., & Sczesny, S. (2009). Stereotypes about women, men, and leaders: Have times changed? In M. Barreto, M. K. Ryan, & M. T. Schmitt (Eds.), *The glass ceiling in the 21st century: Understanding barriers to gender equality* (pp. 21–47). American Psychological Association.

Fapohunda, T. M. (2013). An exploration of gender-based differences in workplace values. *International Journal of Human Resource Studies, 3*(3), 50–61. https://doi.org/10.5296/ijhrs.v3i3.4228

Hopkins, M. M., O'Neil, D. A., Passarelli, A., & Bilimoria, D. (2008). Women's leadership development strategic practices for women and organizations. *Consulting Psychology Journal: Practice and Research, 60*(4), 348–365. https://doi.org/10.1037/a0014093

Howell, S. L., Carter, V. K., & Schied, F. M. (2002). Gender and women's experience at work: A critical and feminist perspective on human resource development. *Adult Education Quarterly, 52*(2), 112–127. https://doi.org/10.1177/0741713602052002003

Humpert, S. (2013). Age and gender differences in job opportunities. *International Journal of Human Resource Studies, 3*(1), 104–133. https://doi.org/10.5296/ijhrs.v3i1.3067

References

Ibarra, H., Carter, N. M., & Silva, C. (2010). Why men still get more promotions than women. *Harvard Business Review, 88*(9), 80–85.

Leathwood, C., & Francis, B. (Eds.). (2006). *Gender and lifelong learning: Critical feminist engagements.* Routledge.

Leow, A., Billett, S., Le, A. H., & Chua, S. (2022). Graduates' perspectives on effective continuing education and training: Participation, access and engagement. *International Journal of Lifelong Education, 41*(2), 212–228. https://doi.org/10.1080/02601370.2022.2044398

Leow, A., Billett, S., & Le, A. H. (2023). Towards a continuing education and training eco system: A case study of Singapore. *International Journal of Training Research, 21*(3), 226–242. https://doi.org/10.1080/14480220.2023.2203944

Lippa, R. A. (2010). Sex differences in personality traits and gender–related occupational preferences across 53 nations: Testing evolutionary and social–environmental theories. *Archives of Sexual Behavior, 39,* 619–636. https://doi.org/10.1007/s10508-008-9380-7

Malhotra, N. K., Shapero, M., Sizoo, S., & Munro, T. (2007). Factor structure of deterrents to adult participation in higher education. *Journal of College Teaching & Learning, 4*(12), 81–90.

Mathapati, C. M. (2013). Women entrepreneurship: A conceptual review. *International Journal of Entrepreneurship & Business Environment Perspectives, 2,* 282–287.

Merriam, S. B., & Caffarella, R. S. (1999). *Learning in adulthood: A comprehensive guide* (2nd ed.). Jossey–Bass.

Prins, E., Toso, B. W., & Schafft, K. A. (2009). "It feels like a little family to me" social interaction and support among women in adult education and family literacy. *Adult Education Quarterly, 59*(4), 335–352. https://doi.org/10.1177/0741713609331705

Purvanova, R. K., & Muros, J. P. (2010). Gender differences in burnout: A meta-analysis. *Journal of Vocational Behavior, 77*(2), 168–185. https://doi.org/10.1016/j.jvb.2010.04.006

Ryan, M. K., Haslam, S. A., Hersby, M. D., & Bongiorno, R. (2011). Think crisis–think female: Glass cliffs and contextual variation in the think manager–think male stereotype. *Journal of Applied Psychology, 96,* 470–484.

Schein, V. E. (1973). The relationship between sex role stereotypes and requisite management characteristics. *Journal of Applied Psychology, 57*(2), 95–100. https://psycnet.apa.org/doi/10.1037/h0037128

Sen, A. (1990). *Inequality and freedom.* Oxford University Press.

Shollen, S. L., Bland, C. J., Finstad, D. A., & Taylor, A. L. (2009). Organizational climate and family life: How these factors affect the status of women faculty at one medical school. *Academic Medicine, 84*(1), 87–94. https://doi.org/10.1097/ACM.0b013e3181900edf

Thangavelu, S. M., Haoming, L., Cheolsung, P., Heng, A. B., & Wong, J. (2011). The determinants of training participation in Singapore. *Applied Economics, 43*(29), 4641–4649. https://doi.org/10.1080/00036846.2010.493140

Thompson, S. H., & Lougheed, E. (2012). Frazzled by Facebook? An exploratory study of gender differences in social network communication among undergraduate men and women. *College Student Journal, 46*(1), 88–98.

UN Women (United Nations Entity for Gender Equality and the Empowerment of Women). (2019). *Progress of the World's women 2019–2020: Families in a changing world.* UN Women.

United Nations Educational, Scientific and Cultural Organization (UNESCO). (2022). *CONFINTEA VIIMarrakech framework for action: Harnessing the transformationalpower of adult learning andeducation.* UNESCO Institute for Lifelong Learning. https://unesdoc.unesco.org/ark:/48223/pf0000382306/PDF/382306eng.pdf.multi

United Nations Educational, Scientific and Cultural Organization (UNESCO). (2023). *UNESCO in action for gender equality.* UNESCO. https://unesdoc.unesco.org/ark:/48223/pf0000387300/PDF/387300eng.pdf.multi

Vaccaro, A., & Lovell, C. D. (2010). Inspiration from home: Understanding family as key to adult women's self–investment. *Adult Education Quarterly, 60*(2), 161–176. https://doi.org/10.1177/0741713609336111

Vandenberghe, V. (2011). Boosting the employment rates of older men and women. *De Economist, 159*, 159–191. https://doi.org/10.1007/s10645-011-9164-7

Worrall, L., Harris, K., Stewart, R., Thomas, A., & McDermott, P. (2010). Barriers to women in the UK construction industry. *Engineering, Construction and Architectural Management, 17*(3), 268–281. https://doi.org/10.1108/09699981011038060

Chapter 10
CET Experience of and Outcomes for 'Older' Working Age Adults

Abstract As working populations age in many countries, issues associated with older workers' employability and worklife learning arise for national economies, enterprises, communities, and these workers themselves. Understanding how best to assist these workers maintain their employability across extended working lives, and what workplaces, educational institutions and government agencies can do to sustain that employability, is now central to many countries' national social and economic goals. This is a particularly germane issue to Singapore, the site of this case study driven publication. Whilst this nation state is largely dependent upon the skills of its workforce, the workforce is one that is ageing. Indeed, this nation state has the third highest age population. Yet, it is not alone here, and many others are considering how best to retain and continue to develop the employability of its older workers. So, there are imperatives when considering how best to promote older workers' employability through education or training initiatives. Thus, the approaches to continuing education and training (CET) for these workers may need to go beyond those provided through existing tertiary education provisions. Those are often primarily established and have models associated with initial occupational preparation and position adult learners as students, rather than as collaborators in their own and others' learning. So, it is necessary to identify and enact CET provisions that are suited to the needs of older workers and are supported by pedagogic practices appropriate to their needs as adults and mature age students. Drawing on data from a research project investigating CET provisions in Singapore, this chapter seeks to illuminate and appraise the experience of and kinds of CET that meets the needs of older students. It draws on interviews with 37 CET graduates aged 50 and above. Through understanding the goals, readiness, capacities, and circumstances of these older workers, and the qualities of an effective CET provision can be identified to meet their needs.

Keywords Older workers · Employability · Working lives · Continuing education and training · Aging population · Economic goals · Societal goals · Aged over 50 · Older students

Older Workers, CET and Employability

As working populations age in many countries with both developing and developed economies, issues associated with older workers' ability to maintain their employability have come to the fore (Organisation for Economic Co-operation and Development [OECD], 2006; Yacob, 2009). This is because their ability to continue to learn to sustain their occupational and workplace performance across working life is becoming increasingly important for national economies, enterprises, communities, and these workers. These performance requirements are constantly transforming as how work is conducted, its requirements, the technologies used to undertake work and how work is undertaken constantly changes and with greater frequency and amplitude. Whilst these changes impact all kinds and classifications, given the growing duration of working life and the increasing presence in the workforce, there are likely to be specific implications for 'older workers' (e.g., those over 50 years). Yet, their needs, readiness as well as other commitments and demands on their time (i.e., work, family, community) (European Centre for the Development of Vocational Training, 2006; Schmidt, 2007), may well be quite distinct from those cohorts of young adults who typically participate in tertiary education. This is a particularly germane issue to Singapore, the source of the national investigation and case study that is reported here. Whilst this nation state is largely dependent upon the skills of its workforce, the workforce is one that is ageing. Indeed, this nation state has the third highest age population globally following Japan and South Korea (Billett, 2010). Indeed, currently, 19.1% of the population is aged 65 and above and there is an increasing trend of the median age of its citizens over the past 10 years (National Population and Talent Division, 2003). However, these nation states are not alone in being concerned about ageing populations as many others are considering how best to retain and continue to develop the employability of their older workers, and for them to have far longer working lives. This, in some countries, is a product of needing these workers to remain employed because of the shortage of young people, but also to delay them becoming reliant on the nation state through payment of pensions (e.g., Australian Bureau of Statistics, 2023). Indeed, designation of what constitutes retirement age in those countries that have state funded pensions is increasing. As the definition of what constitutes an 'older worker' is often associated with a decade before retirement even the definitions of what constitutes 'older workers' is extending. In this project we have defined these workers as being over 50 years of age.

Understanding how best to assist mature-aged or older workers maintain their employability across extended working lives, and what workplaces, educational institutions and government agencies can do to sustain that employability, is now central to many countries' national social and economic goals (Centeno, 2011; Han, 2001; Osborne & Borkowska, 2017). Yet, when considering how best to promote that employability through continuing education and training (CET) it is necessary to consider: (i) their motivations or purposes for participating, (ii) needs to do so; (iii) readiness to engage in processes of developing further their capacities; and (iv) managing and prioritising multiple commitments. It follows then that the deliberations about how CET provisions should be designed and implemented for these workers becomes imperative. As tertiary education provisions are often primarily established for young people's initial occupational preparation, these may not always align with the goals, needs and expectations of older adult students. So, there is the need to identify CET provisions that are suited to the needs and goals of older workers and are supported by pedagogic practices appropriate to their needs as adults and mature age students.

Drawing on data from a research project investigating CET provisions in Singapore, this chapter seeks to illuminate and appraise the experience of mature age or older working age adults through interviews with 37 CET graduates aged 50 and above. It proposes that when the goals of, purposes for, readiness to engage, capacities, and circumstances of such workers are more fully understood, effective CET provisions can be identified to meet their needs to the same extent as those who sponsor them (i.e., government and employers).

The chapter commences by discussing what constitutes 'older workers' and factors associated with their participation in CET. Following this, the findings from the research project that pertained to these kinds of workers are presented and then discussed. That data in those findings comprise both qualitative accounts from interviews and quantitative analysis of survey data provided by interviewees as part of their interviews, and through dedicated surveys. Overall, it was found that these graduates' participation in CET was driven by both personal and professional reasons, the mix of which were shaped by individual needs and goals. Noteworthily, the majority reported being motivated by occupational or work role changes, which is central to their sense of self as working age adults and is also important in their transitions across working life and the ability to remain employed. In preview, the key findings about these older working age adults are:

- There is a mix of professional and personal reasons for participating in CET, noteworthily professionally motivated by a change in occupational or work role.
- Most informants had wholly or partially achieved the goals for which they participated in CET.
- Work commitments, travel time, family commitments, or cost inhibited participation in CET.
- Personal factors or those arising from close associations with others sustain interest in and support CET engagement and completion.
- Experiences differed widely depending on the courses chosen and purposes for participating.
- Effective CET teachers reportedly had industry currency and were responsive to students' needs, effectively providing experiences to address those needs by drawing on the students' work/life experiences.
- Effective CET provisions comprised qualities of Flexibility, Engaging, Authenticity, Convenience, and Leniency.

Older Workers, Their Needs and Bases for Engagement in CET

Defining what constitutes 'older' workers is problematic. Such definitions are shaped by measures of age, societal factors, but also the kinds of occupations in which these individuals engage. With age as a measure of years, different jurisdictions assign terminology based upon national and institutional factors. For instance, a common approach was to nominate 10 years prior to the official retirement age as being such bases. Yet, what constitutes a retirement age differs widely across countries and, for some countries there is no specific date as there is either no pension or social welfare provision for older adults or it is not compulsory. For those countries that have such measures, e.g., far long time 60 or 65 years in European countries, when older workers might be classified by those who are either at least 50 or 55 years of age, many are now extending the age of pension entitlement to commence upwards of 70 years (Australian Bureau of Statistics, 2023; OECD, 2024). Moreover, because of the need for older workers to continue to work, the requirement for compulsory retirement in many countries is being removed. There are also differences across occupations because not all work is of the kind from which you can retire. Work that required physical strength or is of a particular demanding quality are often seen as being age intolerant and require workers to find alternative occupations or move to early retirement. Most noticeable here are military work and emergency services, such as firefighters who are not able to perform demanding and physical tasks beyond certain ages (e.g., Bennett et al., 2011; Morris & Chander, 2018). Yet, this also applies to workers in the construction industry, and industries that are constantly demanding innovations (i.e., advertising, software development) that are difficult to sustain high levels of engagement over many decades. Even particular forms of work are age intolerant such as being a short order cook or à la carte chef, which are not particularly age tolerant (Billett et al., 2011). Then, there are other forms of work that are age tolerant such as clerical, administrative and academic work, for instance. It follows therefore that it is quite difficult to define tightly what constitutes an older worker, therefore whilst using specific age categories here, the discussion needs to be open to a broader interpretation of older workers and their employability. For instance, a dentist in their 70 s would be highly employable, whereas a construction worker would not be.

Indeed, in terms of employability, earlier studies found that age was not a key factor in determining whether an individual could remain employed rather their occupation, level of education and prior work history (Billett, 2011; Billett et al., 2011; De Lange et al., 2021).

Factors Shaping Older Workers' Learning for and in Work

It is now commonly recognised that ongoing learning is required throughout working life for all kinds and classifications of workers (Billett, 2011). Given the kinds of work in which they engage, its degree and frequency of change, their background, gender, age, skill levels and support provided by their workplaces, this requirement plays out in different ways across cohorts of workers. Hence, beyond definitional issues, there are sets of factors that pertain particularly to the learning for and in work for those who are designated as 'older workers'. These factors are fourfold: (i) challenges to sense of self or subjectivity; (ii) kinds of support they need; (iii) their readiness to engage in new learning; and (iv) assumptions about self-direction, intentionality, and capacities.

Firstly, for older workers, there may be challenges arising from the redundancy of their expertise, as familiar ways of working and goals for work performance evaporate. Consequently, the new learning required by these workers sits alongside the displacement of existing capability, competence, and capacities, with its attendant risks to their confidence and well-being (Billett & Somerville, 2004; Billett & van Woerkom, 2008; Wallin et al., 2020). Central here are threats to their sense of self or subjectivity as adults. This is because much of working age adults' subjectivities is associated with the work in which they engage and changes in the kinds of work available to them can have significant impacts upon how they view themselves. For instance, studies of miners (Abrahamsson, 2006; Somerville, 2006), firefighters (Billett et al., 2005), auditors (Francis, 1994), pilots (Mavin et al., 2018) identify when confronted with changes to what they know, can do and value causes significant challenges to their sense of self. This is not to say that the new learning required to respond to these changes is necessarily wholly disempowering, alienating, or marginalising. Yet, it may be quantifiably distinct for older workers, because of the potential displacement of existing occupational competence, and/or threats to their standing in their working life and community.

Secondly, their efforts may be complicated by a lack of understanding of these impacts by government and employers and, in particular, the latter's' preference for privileging support for younger and more qualified employees over those for older workers (e.g., Billett et al., 2011; Brunello & Medio, 2001; Leuven & Oosterbeek, 1999). Consequently, older workers may not be afforded high levels of support, despite their needs being more urgent and compelling. Interestingly, in Singapore during the global financial crisis, the government intervened to provide specific support for managerial and economic staff who had been made redundant (Government of Singapore, 2024). The response, whilst welcomed and appropriate, tended to focus on financial support for and access to programs that develop new occupational competencies. However, this occurred within an environment in which filial piety (i.e., respect for elders) still plays a role. Hence, such programs while seeking to cushion the impact of employment, it positioned these workers awkwardly as novices, despite their age, which was discomforting to the subjectivity of many of these working age adults.

Thirdly, there are also the underlying beliefs about the readiness and ability of older working age adults to engage in learning and entirely new domains of knowledge and their application. That this learning can be more difficult for older people not because they are older per se, but because it represents a challenge to what their confidence and competence are aligned. This may lead to resistance and subsequent labelling (i.e., not being able to 'teach old dogs new tricks'). Despite a lack of evidence of this and much to the contrary, such societal sentiments tend to have enduring purchase. Certainly, scientifically, there are distinct and unresolved views about whether new learning is more difficult for older than younger people. For instance, studies of language acquisition conclude that the malleability of cognitive capacities and structures of younger people enables language development to occur far easier and perhaps quite distinctly from what older people are able to engage and realise (Sigelman, 1999). While this view remains to be fully proven, it is reasonable to suggest that for older workers to remain competent, it requires their effortful and focused engagement in the process of and management of their learning.

Certainly, these issues are extremely pertinent given that on the one hand there remains much that is unknown about the prospects and potentials for older workers to be competent throughout their working lives, which for many are getting longer. The literature on human development across the lifespan suggests that whereas maturation processes are helpful in expanding the competence in capacities of children and younger adults, they work against older workers (e.g., Berk, 2023; Cronin & Mandich, 2015; Peterson, 2003; Sigelman, 1999). There is an inevitable decline in a range of human functions such as speed in reaction time, processing of novel ideas and the active engagement of memory. However, the evidence also suggests that older adults have developed capacities that are highly effective in resolving problems and performing effectively in work-related roles. This can compensate for slower neural systems (Baltes & Staudinger, 1996), because the level of performance is not dependent on fast processing capacity alone. It has been shown that while typing speeds might decline of time, old typists are as efficient as younger typists, as their experience allows them to predict and execute the typing task more efficiently than the younger counterparts, because of their wealth of previous experiences (Bosman, 1993). Sigelman concluded:

> …while older adults may well experience some basic processing shortfall, they may well have developed specialised knowledge and strategies that may compensate for these losses. (Sigelman, 1999, p. 229)

Aside from what support is provided to assist their learning throughout working life, individuals' motivation, engagement, and intentionality is likely to be central to their remaining competent and extending the scope of that competence (Billett & van Woerkom, 2008). Not the least of these are their responses, either productively or unproductively, for threats to their sense of self and subjectivity as working age adults.

Fourthly, there may be unfounded societal views and perceptions about adults' need for support and guidance in their learning. That is, as mature age adults, they should be able to manage these processes themselves. This is augmented by some theories of adult learning and development that propose erroneously there are distinctions between adults and children in so far as how they come to engage in new learning. That is, the former are inherently more self-directed than children (e.g., Knowles, 1975). While this ability to self-direct may be true within their existing domains of competence and knowledge with which they have accumulated significant knowledge, when engaging in activities outside of areas in which they are competent and confident, they are far less likely to be able to be self-directed except in so far how their intentionality is directed. Such sentiments play out in at least two ways: impact upon older workers and limits and the provisions of support and guidance. The impact upon older workers might be that they should not expect or require assistance from others, and they should confront these issues individually. Of course, the exercise of personal agency and intentionality is important for learning (Malle et al., 2001) yet this places an unreasonable burden upon the adults. Then, whereas it would be seen to be quite conventional and unquestioned to provide support such as career guidance and assistance in aligning young people's capacities with appropriate educational provisions as they confront the transition from childhood to adulthood, such conventions seem more questionable for adults. Yet, when engaging in new fields of employment or educational provisions older workers might require support and guidance. Certainly, for people of all ages their agency and intentionality are central to how they engage in their learning and development, but this does not imply the need for Robinson Crusoe-like unsupported epistemological adventures.

Therefore, these four sets of factors are important in considering how we come to view older workers and their potential for learning. As learning and development is, ultimately, a process that is shaped by personal factors such as agency and intentionality, these are worth considering in the context of older workers.

Older Workers' Agency and Intentionality

Given the importance of older workers' agency and intentionality in and across their working lives, their exercise within deliberate learning efforts is for consideration for the ongoing employability. There are at least four premises for considering and making centre stage the roles of individual agency and intentionality in the ongoing competence of older workers. These are: (i) individuals' engagements in activities; (ii) their contributions to learning and development; (iii) the interactions they have with others; and (iv) the exercise of their agency.

Firstly, individuals' engagements with work activities and interactions are necessary bases for the processes of learning and development (Billett, 2004). The process of learning and everyday thinking and acting is in many ways the same. In both, the degree by which individuals engage and deploy their cognitive capacities and experiences shapes whether rich or weak learning transpires. Such outcomes are a product of the degree by which individuals elect to exercise their energy and intentionality when engaging with tasks and in interactions: goal directed activities. That is, what problems individuals identify as being worth solving (Goodnow, 1990). She noted that the social environment is important when we learn to solve problems, but we learn "what problems are considered worth solving and also what may count as an elegant solution rather than simply an acceptable solution" (Goodnow, 1990, p. 259).

Secondly, individuals' contributions to their learning and development are a product of what is suggested to them through social sources and interactions, and how they come to personally mediate those suggestions (Billett, 2009a). Yet, those social suggestions are rejected and distributed in different ways and by different degrees (Archer, 2000). The kinds of gifts that older workers sought from the workplace may not always have been afforded them in ways that are helpful and supportive (Billett et al., 2011). This suggests older workers may need to mediate more strongly and agentically what they are encountering and exercise intentionality to secure the kinds of outcomes that are not being afforded them. In some ways, this suggests that self-direction is, indeed, an important aspect of older workers' learning and development. However, the difference here is that it is not centred on an ability to learn through discovery alone (i.e., Crusoe-like epistemological adventures), but rather to engage with others and artefacts to assist the mediation of the knowledge that they need to learn. That is, intentionally engaging with social sources and identifying the kinds of knowledge they need to gain through interactions with social partners (e.g., co-workers) and social practices (e.g., observing work activities and practices). In short, the social genesis of occupational knowledge and its development in people is founded in a relational interdependence between individual and social contributions to individuals' learning and the remaking of cultural practices (Leontyev, 1981), such as those in paid work (Billett, 2006; Rogoff, 1990). From the older workers' perspective, engagement in this interdependence comprises a mediation that needs to be informed in ways that are both purposeful and agentic so that they are able to interact with the social world in ways positioning them as informed, selective, and canny participants.

Thirdly, individuals through their interactions with social partners and social practices play an important role in construing and constructing from the social experience (Billett, 2004), and older workers' circumstances are no exception. This includes how they mediate societal sentiments about older people and their ability to learn and, specifically those of employers. Some claim that there is a significant mismatch between older workers' views of their employability and effectiveness and the perceptions of those who employ them (Patrickson & Ranzijn, 2004). This is doubly problematic for older workers as their ability to be agentic in making contacts and developing further their skills are likely to be the basis of them achieving employment that reflects their capacities and contributions (Patrickson & Ranzijn, 2004). So, the societal suggestion (Archer, 2000) is not exercised and directed uniformly; it is mediated through interactions between the social experience and individuals' construction of that experience. As individual subjectivities and intentionalities are an embodiment of their agency, it remains central to the process of older workers' learning and development, including their remaking of practices in the workplace. Indeed, in a recent Singaporean study, it was found that it was largely interpersonal environment in small to medium size enterprises that shape whether workers were able to suggest, initiate and enact innovations (Billett et al., 2021). That environment was differentiated across these enterprises as was the prospect for workers' engagement in innovations. Consequently, the workplace perceptions of the abilities of older workers to learn, innovate and bring about change are central to whether these important goals can be realised through the mediation of these workers.

Fourthly, it follows that, the kinds, direction, and intensity by which older workers will exercise their interest (i.e., agency and energy) shape their learning process, what is learnt (Billett & Pavlova, 2003; Hodkinson & Hodkinson, 2004) and whether or not their full potential is able to be realised in terms of their own development and contributions to their places of employment. So, it is for these reasons that older workers' agency and intentionality stand as key elements in countering the ageing process, contested and differentiated levels of workplace affordances and in contributing to the process of maintaining their competence through negotiating self and purpose in their working lives. In particular, their sense of self is central, yet vulnerable, to the contradictory roles that older workers have to negotiate.

Singaporean Case

All of what has been proposed above is of particular relevance to Singapore and the case study advanced here. With one of the highest aged populations globally, supporting lifelong employability is a national priority for Singapore and for its national economic and social well-being. Unlike other countries who have natural resources to bolster the economy, the island nation relies alone upon its human resources. Hence, there are key national goals for lifelong employability that are retaining mature-age workers and engaging them increasingly in professional, managerial, executive, and technical (PMET) work. Moreover, the educational divide between residents aged under and over 50 years is currently significant and misaligned with the latter's lifelong employability. For instance, the findings from the survey of adult skills—a product of the OECD Program for the International Assessment of Adult Competencies—highlighted the wide gap between the most and least proficient skilled adults in Singapore. Indeed, Singapore stands out as the country in which variability in literacy is greatest, at 77 score points, compared to the OECD average of 62 score points (OECD, 2016). Whilst the report attributes the low proficiency among Singapore's older populations to the effects of age, low levels of educational attainment and language barriers, it underscored the importance of lifelong education. Legacies of age-based pay, societal views about mature-aged workers' ability to work and learn also impede their employability. Yet, in an earlier study, typically, mature-aged workers interviewed and surveyed, provided evidence of capacities for effective work, learning new tasks and work roles, use of diverse forms of learning support and being self-directed in learning for employability, claimed they do not struggle with technology, resist innovation and learning; and, overwhelmingly, were willing to engage in CET (Billett, 2011). In the following, responses to these issues are advanced over a decade after that earlier study.

Findings from CET Project

After some initial definitional comments and demographic information about the informants, the findings that are presented and discussed below address the issues of what motivated these informants to participate in CET, followed by identification of factors that might inhibit their participation in such educational provisions.

As noted, when using the term "older worker" in the investigation described and elaborated below, we refer to individuals who are over 50 years of age. The definition of what constitutes "age" has been actively discussed in literature (Weiss et al., 2022). Various age ranges and thresholds have been put forward, but there is no specific chronological age to define an older worker (Truxillo et al., 2015), instead it is socially constructed and in different ways across circumstances and cultures, including work practices. In this study, we focused on CET graduates aged 50 and older as these are the ages at which many kinds and classifications of workers become viewed as being vulnerable in or having vulnerabilities in the labour market (Marchant, 2013). It also sits with the scope of what is taken to a classification of workers of whom considerations of their ability to remain optimally employed, able to secure advancement and be deemed desirable workers are exercised.

As a means to progress, this description and elaboration commences by outlining the demographic factors of the older graduates who were interviewed (and surveyed). Following that, sections reporting and discussing data and findings on their motivations for participating in CET, barriers to that participation, factors supporting course completion, achievement of purposes, views about CET provisions and educators are advanced.

Demographic and Work Background

The older informants who completed a pre-interview survey and semi-structured interview comprised 37 individuals who had graduated from CET programs within 4 years from the time of investigation. These older graduate informants comprised 26 males (70%) and 11 females (30%), who have a range of educational backgrounds. They constitute a relatively highly educated sample of informants in the Singaporean context and in respect to the age of their age cohorts as all have at least a post-secondary qualification, albeit a diploma, degree, or postgraduate degree. It is important to note there is a significant difference in the levels of educational qualifications of the Singaporean population over 55 compared with those below that age (Billett, 2010, 2011). This difference is, in part, a product of the significant level of investment in education in this relatively young nation state of the last 40 years.

Findings from CET Project

Motivations for CET Participation

Unlike compulsory education and that which is mandated as being necessary post-schooling, participation in CET is likely premised upon individuals' decisions about whether or not they elect to participate in it. Yes, there can be workplace imperatives and occupational requirements for adults but none of these are compulsory as they are broadly discretionary for working age adults unless they are in occupations which mandate professional development requirements. Consequently, it is important to understand why older workers elect to participate in CET and for what purposes. In the interviews, the graduates were asked about their motivations and goals. In response, they reported three main purposes or motivations to participate in CET: (i) professional motivations, (ii) personal-professional motivations, and (iii) personal motivations. Each of these is now briefly discussed.

Professional motivation ($n = 18$): Most informants stated that they participated in CET to secure some kind of professional development and/or certification. That is, motivations directed towards their employability, and in particular, maintaining their ability to remain employed and employable. Consequently, they often measured their achievement based on how relevant the CET program and outcomes are to their work and how what they learnt helped them in their workplace or their perceived effectiveness in their future workplace. Many of the informants (18 out of 37) reported wanting to gain more knowledge for their current jobs or to enable them to have a potential career switch. Noteworthily was that 13 out of these 18 reported being motivated by a change in occupational or work role. Informants in this group acknowledged that recognition in terms of certification and opportunities provided through CET courses were important outcomes of their participation in these programs. Hence, to achieve their career or employability goals, such as an increase in wage and change in job scope, it was necessary to participate in a CET course. Some direct quotations that illuminate this imperative are:

> This CET course is basically Specialist Diploma in Career Counselling. And in the course of my work, I do have mentees who are students, and they are in the polytechnic. I mean these students would need guidance on career choices, so basically this is one of the factors that I am interested in this course in order to equip myself with the skills to guide the students. *Male*

> The driver was that there was an opportunity to try a new career […] to secure a change in a career or at least give me the opportunity to explore that chance […] I figure that I need a leverage to actually go in, and I see that diploma as a leverage to actually try for this new career path. *Female*

> I was out of Singapore for a good 10 years, so when I came back I realised there has been a lot of changes in the HR education sector. […] And then at the time I was trying to do a career switch and I received my first assignment to teach in a primary school. […]And I was in fact doing both at the same time, I was towards the tail-end of my MA, and then I started my RP specialist with the hope that that will help me get more teaching assignments. *Female*

> I have an opportunity to change my job role so previously I was doing programme management so then there's this facility management role that was open to me […] So I undertook this role so that is the motivation for me to try on new role and hopefully I will branch into this role, from programme management to facilities management. *Male*

> One fine day at work, I just asked myself, my earning capacity. So, I was working at a very young age and with only 'O' levels. So, I asked myself what I am doing. My earning power is not high. So, what motivated me to take the CET course was that, basically get a better job, a better pay, and a better progression in my industry. *Male*

Common across these statements are goals associated with the enabling qualities of participating in CET programs. For some, it was aimed to provide the kinds of capacities required for expansion and existing work roles, and for others it was about the ability to improve the currency of their capacities to secure opportunities and advancement, which in some instances extended to the ability to find a new form of work or occupations. So, the imperative of improving what these informants know and can do to sustain their employability was preeminent in their decisions to participate in CET and the kinds of outcomes they were seeking from it.

Personal—Professional Motivations ($n = 13$) Some of these mature age graduates reported a combination of achieving personal and professional developmental goals as their key motivation to participate in CET. Their contributions categorised in this way reported their imperatives to participate in CET programs were premised on the objective of learning for both personal and professional reasons, indicating that these were even more personally driven imperative than those demanded by the need for work currency and advancement. Some direct quotations that illuminate this dual imperative are:

> I really wanted to be informed of the latest findings or teaching methodologies. Prior to that, I was last trained in tertiary education in 1992 so I thought I wanted to just upgrade and be informed of the latest teaching skills or the new methodologies, pedagogies in teaching and I was very happy with the program. It filled me with new learning experience, which was very useful, which helped me in my deliverance in classroom. *Male*

> Although I was doing well in occupation, I felt that my skills were getting out of fashion. I did my MBA at that time about 20 years ago. And I thought that you know it is outdated and if I didn't do my [name of program] I would not be in you know going together with the trend of err new information new knowledge. […] So, I wanted to learn helping the operational practice is one thing, I wanted to get into the theories so that I can match operations and theories to become more effective in my work and to be better informed person. *Female*

In some ways, these statements reflect concerns about professional currency and standing based upon a commitment and subjectivity, and, hence a personal epistemology (i.e., how you construe, construct and utilise what you know, can do and value) (Billett, 2009b) that emphasises the importance of occupational competence to working age adults' sense of self or subjectivity as a competent professional (Billett & van Woerkom, 2008). So, the imperatives here are claimed not necessarily about just employability and seeking advancement but are more aligned with these informants' individual values. Hence, whereas the former list focused on goals associated with what those informants wanted to know and be able to do, this cohort emphasised dispositional qualities as being key motivators for participating in CET.

Personal Motivation ($n = 8$) Some informants referred to their motivation to learn, only influenced by their personal beliefs or epistemologies (Billett, 2009b) about lifelong learning. That is, they are far less concerned with immediate employability imperatives, but rather driven by personal motivations and goals that are not directly influenced by concerns about that employability. Some of these informants reported enrolling in their courses for the sake of learning per se as they wanted either to remain relevant in their current work or to progress to the next education level. They reported taking a course, such as a degree after their diploma, as a natural progression and an achievement they desired regardless of whether or not it had any professional impact. This motivation is well aligned with long-standing goals for adult education being about cultural betterment through personal learning. That is, understanding more about and able to contribute to the community in which adults live, including expanding their personal base of knowledge. Some direct quotations that illuminate this strongly personal imperative are:

> I did it out of wanting to fulfill a role to serve back the community. *Male*
>
> I think the main reason is actually self-actualisation. I was in an industry for quite a while, and I want to learn more. *Male*
>
> There's a fatigue that takes over when you have been doing something for a very long time. So, I thought the antidote for the fatigue was to take up programmes where I can put things into my brain. I felt very empty, I thought by putting things into my brain, perhaps I will recharge. […] learn the stuff and maybe overcome my fatigue and become whole-hearted again. *Female*

In all, most of these older graduates reported reasons for taking their courses that could be categorised as being both professional and personal. Yet, consistently, regardless of whether there is the direct or indirect reference to work or work roles, these are shaping the motivations and interests of these informants. Thus, the strong association between work and of working age adults' subjectivity and agency is emphasised within these data. These motivations are reported as being central to them personally and participation in CET is something which individuals have to elect to engage in and make commitments to that engagement amongst other commitments. Being aware of the centrality of this concern seems important for organising, enacting, and evaluating CET provisions for individuals who largely will have the discretion to decide whether or not they participate in these programs.

Together, these findings suggest that these older CET graduates were motivated by these imperatives to participate in CET courses. Certainly, the data suggest that these adults value learning not only for instrumental purposes such as employability, but also learning for personal purposes, including their subjectivity as adults. But it is difficult to confidently delineate these motivations as purely professional or personal as interests, emphases, and goals were intertwined with concerns about learning for their paid work. Whilst the sample of informants here is fairly small, the commitment to sustaining employability is evident throughout their responses either directly or indirectly and emphasises how important that is even for older workers who may be within the last decade of their working lives. However, it is important for educators and administrators to understand their students' motivations for participation in CET courses. There is no exception here for older age students who have had extensive work/life experiences, as it heavily influences their decisions to participate in CET in the first place, their preferences for how they come to engage in those programs and make decisions about their fit alongside other commitments.

Yet, given those other commitments, it is important to understand factors that might inhibit these older working age adults participating in CET. This is taken up in the next section.

Factors Inhibiting Participation

These older graduates also identified factors that inhibited their participation in CET. These comprised external environmental factors, such as work commitments, travel time, family commitments, or cost. Consequently, these data illuminate and elaborate the kinds of challenges faced by these working age adults as they manage their commitments across work, community and family that reportedly impact upon these informants' participation in CET. It is important to make the point again here that unlike younger students who engage in transitions from compulsory education into pre-employment education, these working age adults make decisions about whether they will participate in CET, how the participation will occur, for what purposes and outcomes. Hence, unlike those who either attend compulsorily or out of necessity, there are sets of environmental and personal factors that are quite distinct and mediate these older adults' participation in CET. For instance, the statements below illustrate some of these dimensions:

> So that means that could clash with my part-time classes, so I need to work my colleagues and see if we can reschedule the classes and all that. So that caused a little bit of sometimes tension also, because the people who are planning, they don't like changes. Like everybody else, change means stress. So, nobody wants that kind of stress, so I had to appeal with a few people and what not so that caused you know some stress for my colleagues and the relationship is affected also. *Male*

> My day starts very early five o'clock to send my younger son to catch school bus. Then, I come to work and then I finish 6:00. Then, attend class from 6:00 or 6:30, I forgot, to 9:30. By the time I go home, although I live very near, after 10:00, then it's almost time for me to go to bed. *Female*

Evident here are perspectives of the CET graduates about some of the barriers that inhibit these older Singaporeans' participation in CET, particularly those associated with work and family commitments. The time to travel to and spend in work restricts opportunities for participation in CET, and, to a lesser extent, family responsibilities and fees play key roles in inhibiting participation. This suggests that integrating study with work activities, providing study support that can be conducted whilst travelling and being flexible, but structured, about course engagement and assessment tasks are likely to be required.

Factors Sustaining Engagement and Completion

The graduates also reported factors sustaining interest and motivation to complete their courses, and these are largely personal factors or those arising from close associations with others. The data indicate that these CET graduates reported being intrinsically motivated, driven to achieve their own goals (n = 4) and to pursue learning of their own interests (n = 5), and influenced by their employers (n = 6), family (n = 6), and friends/peers/colleagues (n = 5). These data suggest that for these graduates, support from their employers, colleagues or classmates can make a difference to their learning experience and motivation to complete a CET program. These are illustrated in the following quotations:

> One thing which I really look forward to every Saturday is to come for class. Because there's such a camaraderie there, and it's like family. It's more like family. So that helped you a lot. So, until today we still text each other, in fact some of them are still texting. So, we've been family in that sense, so that helped a lot. So, once you build the relationship the stress factor is more manageable. *Male*

> I have opportunity for, to manage my work and my time. And then the organisation is the kind of the policies allow for us to go for study. And they have also got study leave where you can take study leave and study for your exam and things like that. *Male*

> I'm able to manage my work and my studies because I don't work too late into the night, and I have supportive colleagues who would help to cover me if necessary. So, I think that helps me a lot. *Male*

So, ability to manage time and reserve the time dedicated to study is central here in terms of these older workers' motivations to continue and complete their courses. In addition, they stated that when their peers in study programs were supportive and willing to share their career experience and support one another, it provided a collaborative and supportive learning environment. All of this is particularly important in a situation where these adults would come to engage in their study with very different kinds and levels of readiness to participate. If circumstances were different than those described above, there is likely to be a high level of attrition. Moreover, direct support from family was cited as being helpful for continuing and completion. Altogether, these data indicate a complex of personal and work factors that variously hinder or enable these older students in completing their CET programs. Much of that commitment and motivation to complete are aligned with achieving the purposes for which these individuals collected to participate in CET.

Achievement of Purposes

Of these 37 older graduates, nine reported fully achieving their purposes of participating in their CET program, and 21 reported partially achieving those purposes, and 7 informants indicated low levels of progress towards their intended purposes. In one way, this can be taken as a positive finding, given that the interviews were taken within a relatively short period of time after the completion of the courses and that some of the stated goals could only be achieved over a longer period. The data also provided indications that there was scope for improving the number of CET graduates who will report fully achieving their goals 4 years after completing their CET program. In the interviews, however, some graduates reported disappointment with their courses owing to its poor organisation and communication about course objectives. It also was found that the graduates' experiences when participating in their programs differed greatly depending on the course chosen and their purposes for participating. Others, however, appreciated their experience in the courses as it provided them with the confidence and skills to perform independently at work and to share with colleagues the skills they had learnt. Given the central role of educators in CET programs, it is important to capture their contributions to and influence on the experiences of these older graduates and their educational outcomes.

CET Teachers

In the analysis of the interview data about experiences with CET teachers, eight of the 37 older graduates expressed these as 'positive', 19 being 'neutral' experience (i.e., a mix of positive and negative moments), and 10 expressing concerns they experienced with the teachers in their CET courses/programs. Table 10.1 provides some quotes from the interviews regarding the graduates' experiences with the CET teachers in the courses/programs they were enrolled categorised in terms of whether their experiences were viewed to be positive, neutral, or negative.

Overall, these older graduates reported that their positive experiences with CET teachers included these teachers having relevant industry experience, being responsive to students' needs and being effective in providing experiences to address those needs, including drawing on the students' experiences of work and working life. These observations are similar to those made across the age and gender categories of informants in this project (Leow et al., 2022; Leow & Billett, 2023). That is, these teachers needing to be flexible in approach and interactive in their teaching. This is reported as being particularly important for older students who have had extensive experience across their working life and in a situation in which the exercise of their ability to be active, agentive, and effortful is essential to acquire the kinds of knowledge that is needed to succeed in their programs.

Like the entire cohort of 180 informants, these older students, appreciated teachers who had the currency of knowledge, with good pedagogical and facilitation skills, and who were empathetic about the challenges of adult students in finding time to attend courses and complete assignments in the midst of their busy lives (Leow et al., 2022, Leow & Billett, 2023).

Counter to those positive experiences were the reported disconnections between the teachers' theoretical knowledge and practical experience in the field of their teaching (Leow et al., 2022). Most associate teachers (i.e., part-time and not professionally prepared teachers) are still working in the occupations and industry about

Table 10.1 Experiences with CET teachers

Experience	Representative quotes
Positive (n = 8)	The instructors, the lecturers were wonderful in terms of clearing my doubts and helping me to comprehend all the new information. They managed to do a lot of task scaffolding and then there were a lot of group discussions. (Male) They gave us a detailed insight into the course, helping us to comprehend the subject matter and then at the same time they pose a lot of questions which enable us to reflect, to ponder on and which was quite good. There were a lot of questions that were posed that helped us to think, helped us to improve as teachers. (Male) We were very well connected, they were very patient, and they never fail to attend to even the simplest question and I think you know sometimes for persons who come as adults, there was always the fear, the angst of not wanting to look silly. (Female) I would say most of the lecturers, they are experienced. And each has their own expertise area, and they try to convey the message to us in a very clear and positive manner. And then they allow time for interaction, time for sharing and things like that. (Female)
Neutral (n = 19)	The interaction with us depends on whether the polytechnic is employing the full-time lecturers, or they are getting the adjunct lecturers from the industries. (Male) The teachers—we have a fair share of effective teachers. We also have a fair share of not so effective teachers or rather engaging teachers. I mean as an educator, I guess you see some educators—they are very academy inclined, but they are not engaging the students enough where you see some who are good in—they're equally good but I think the difference is they are able to engage the students. (Female)
Negative (n = 10)	As someone with a strong counselling background, we all have a different understanding of like, how a counselling should be, and so a lot of things that is taught in class might be oversimplified until the facts might be not very correct, I would say. [...] Like for example, they gotten a clinical psychologist to teach positive psychology module, where he doesn't really have the experience and qualification to do that, and then after that, we are kind of get it and don't get it... things being taught, and so we found there is a disconnect between the lecturer and the syllabus itself. [...] They also struggle in giving us real life example like how this thing is going to match over and to help us in our understanding of the particular topic or help us to understand certain theory. (Male) A few of the lecturers they just present the notes that are not explained in detail, and I have to go online to dig further about the subject. This takes more time for us to learn about the subject correctly. I mean for working adults, sometimes we have a lack of time and if the notes are more clearly presented, it saves us some time in terms of digging for information, ease our learning. (Female) Sometimes because of the short hours, I realised that lecturers usually tend to speed up what they are teaching us, and I didn't have a chance to really explore the concepts. Discuss with my group mates. It is very brief. Every time when there is a discussion, we don't do it anymore. We have to go back to the theories. They will have to run through the slides. So, I didn't find that there was enough engagement in terms of us sharing our experiences, hearing from other people. (Female)

which they teach. So, they reportedly have more relevant and up-to-date industry experience as compared to full-time teachers and are able to make contributions to enhancing the students' learning on that basis. However, unlike full-time teachers, associate teachers may be less well equipped with teaching pedagogy, and thus may not be able to deliver their content and message succinctly. These data advance the importance of professional development for CET teachers. That is, more occupational and workplace currency on the part of the full-time teachers, and more pedagogic preparation for the associate lecturers. In fact, there is a mixture of associate teachers and full-time teachers teaching in the CET programs in Singapore. Both types of teachers have their own strengths and weaknesses. This suggests then that part-time teachers might be encouraged to extend their educational competence, and arrangements might be provided to assist full-time teachers remain current in their understandings and practices of the occupations and industry sectors about which they teach.

CET Provisions

Data were also collected about the kind of provisions these informants preferred and experienced in terms of the organisation and teaching of CET courses and programs. As noted, effective CET goes beyond what is provided or afforded to working age adults; it is also about how they come to engage with it and learn through and from those provisions. The three categories of experience (i.e., positive, neutral, and negative) and their associated representative quotes are summarised in Table 10.2.

In all, the positive features of these graduates' experiences with CET provisions included the qualities categorised as Flexibility, Engaging, Authenticity, Convenience, and Leniency. Whilst the former three refer to pedagogies and activities associated with education, the latter are directed towards provisions of organisation and management.

First and foremost, these older graduates reported the values of flexibility in terms of delivery mode (i.e., hybrid—combination of face-to-face and online) and assessment formats. For the latter, exams were perceived unhelpful and impractical. Beyond being flexible, engaging provisions were essential, particularly when it applies to teaching materials and resources such as lectures' video recording and online learning resources. Assessment format and topic were also mentioned as an aspect that was reported as being important. As noted, these older age students often take pride in their prior knowledge and worklife experience. Hence, they tend to assess the credibility of the information provided on this basis, appraising highly the practicality and application of the knowledge presented to them. This suggests the importance of authenticity feature of the provisions associated with education. Rehearsed here is the experience of assessment reported by these informants. Examinations, for instance, were deemed as 'unauthentic' as they were considered

Table 10.2 Experiences with CET provisions

Experience	Representative quotes
Positive (n = 7)	The good thing is that I think the new technology—quite a lot of new pedagogies. There was a lot of group work which was very good, so we learn from our fellow course members. (Male)
	The model [course arrangement] is really good because first and foremost it free us and then it was very interactive, and we learned from the lecturers and from our fellow course mates. So that was very good and modelled—I really enjoyed the classroom discussion—there were very, very intellectual, so that was really good. (Male)
	The notes are good, it's well organised, and also the time is well organised, and the notes are very relevant, yeah. And the strategy, teaching strategy is multi modal, in the sense that you're online learning, you're using technology in class. So, I think overall it is quite a holistic kind of experience, teaching experience, or learning experience. (Female)
Neutral (n = 27)	I think doing the projects and assignments are okay but exams I think really should do away with that and maybe assess us in other ways. Maybe just like classroom participation or things like that. Yeah. Maybe assessments for learning—just assess us like short tests, 10- or 15-min short tests or just a quick summary and from there they can kind of see whether we comprehend the topic for the day. (Male)
	So now you don't have to memorise verbatim, but you just have to remember all these concepts and what it's how it's supposed to be applied and you just apply it based on the scenario that they give you. So… I guessed it worked ah in a way. So, the work is effective, but it's just that in general nobody… everybody not quite enjoy it. (Male)
	Other features are helpful but what is not practiced across is the video recording. So, when we are absent, we actually can review the particular lesson. The not helpful part is depending on what type of platform they use, if it's something that is so complicated. So, the blended learning is very helpful, but still some of the programs they're not able to go to blended because it comprises 40% of counselling online. It's always face to face. (Female)
Negative (n = 3)	[Assessment criteria] Useful in a way but I thought exams were a bit too time consuming because we are all adults and we had to work in the day, so it was quite difficult in a sense to really prepare well for the exams I feel, although it was an open book exam, but the questions were quite challenging, requires a bit of thinking. So sometimes it's not just a matter of just pulling out information to fit the question. We had to process. It was quite challenging, the questions. (Male)
	The system, especially to connect online can be a problem. Because you see we are supposed to learn about teaching with technology, but the technology when we brought our laptop here, it doesn't connect. […] Another nuisance, but I want to highlight those areas, the password. Every 3 months you've got to change the password. So, it becomes very disruptive because sometimes in the course of changing you cannot get through. So, there's a bit problem with it. (Male)
	I actually join online course before and I'm not able to complete them. One of the challenges that I've faced with online course right like private online course is you don't you are not close to your other peers, your lecturers and things like that you feel this disconnect. You don't feel very close to them so that's the problem I had with the online. (Female)

not to test understanding and application of the knowledge gained. Many of these graduates were seeking recognition for their competency for professional development or career progression, thus emphasising learning materials/resources and assessment with practical outcomes.

Apart from those relating to educational aspects, the provisions of organising and managing the courses/programs were considered when evaluating the effectiveness of CET provisions. These included convenience and accessibility of locations, learning management platforms, and processes. These graduates also appreciated the leniency from the teachers and the course arrangements. The latter comprise of requirement, assessment intensity, and grading rubrics. The leniency that accommodates the needs and demands of working age students' commitments across family and working life was accentuated.

Older Working Age Adults' Experiences and Outcomes in Sum

In sum, this analysis and discussion has provided an overview of the perceptions and experiences of the 37 older age graduates with the CET courses/programs they had completed. In all, it is proposed that for these older working age adults:

- The motivations to participate in CET are professional, personal-professional, and personal.
- Amongst those professionally driven, the majority reported being motivated by a change in occupational or work role. They acknowledge that recognition in terms of certification and opportunities were important outcomes of their participation in these programs.
- Common across these statements are goals associated with enabling qualities of participating in CET programs. For some, it was aimed to provide the kinds of capacities required for expansion and existing work roles, and for others it was about the ability to improve the currency of their capacities to secure opportunities and advancement, including the ability to find a new form of work or occupations.
- Some reported enrolling in their courses for the sake of learning per se, as they wanted either to remain relevant in their current work or to progress to the next education level.
- Inhibiting participation in CET was reportedly caused by external environmental factors, such as work commitments, travel time, family commitments, or cost.
- Sustaining interest and motivation to complete their courses are largely personal factors or those arising from close associations with others.
- Most informants reported fully or partially achieving their purposes of participating in their CET program.

- Experiences when participating in CET programs differed widely depending on the course chosen and their purposes for participating. Some reported disappointment with their courses owing to its poor organisation and communication about course objectives. Others appreciated their experience in the courses as it provided them with the confidence and skills to perform independently at work and to share with colleagues the skills they had learnt.
- Positive experiences with CET teachers included (i) having relevant industry experience, (ii) being responsive to students' needs and (iii) being effective in providing experiences to address those needs, including drawing on students' experiences of work and working life.
- Positive features of experiences with CET provisions included the qualities categorised as Flexibility, Engaging, Authenticity, Convenience, and Leniency. Whilst the former three refer to pedagogies and activities associated with education, the latter are directed towards provisions of program organisation and management.

The findings indicate that these graduates' participation in CET was driven by both personal and professional reasons, the mix of which were shaped by individual needs and goals. Noteworthily, the majority reported being motivated by occupational or work role changes, which is central to their sense of self as working age adults and is also important in their transitions across working life and the ability to remain employed. Like the other cohorts (Leow et al., 2022), for these adult students, family and work commitments were the key barriers for them to fully engage in CET. Simultaneously, it was these personal and work factors that also support their participation and completion of CET courses/programs in which they were enrolled. Overwhelmingly, these older CET graduates reported partially or wholly achieving the purposes for which they participated in CET. The key question henceforth is to enhance the quality of provisions and outcomes to ensure that a higher percentage of working age, older age in particular, Singaporeans would report wholly achieving their purposes for participating in CET programs. These graduates reported that effective CET teachers should possess relevant industry experience, be responsive to students needs and be effective in providing experiences to address those needs, including drawing on the students' experiences of work and working life. These qualities include being flexible in approach and interactive in teaching. Whilst online CET provisions are reported assisting with flexibility and accessibility, their preference was face-to-face contact with lecturers and with peers which contributed to positive CET experiences. Whilst content could be presented online through text, interactions with teachers and peers were essential for clarifying, engaging, discussing, and evaluating the experiences. These experiences were reported as assisting exposure to new ideas and practices, their evaluation, and contributions to practice. Similarly, and consistently reported was the importance of engaging with peers and provisions of these opportunities are helpful for gaining a range of perspectives, constructive interactions, ability to compare and contrast experiences and testing the knowledge being generated through the course.

References

Abrahamsson, L. (2006). Exploring constructions of gendered identities at work. In S. Billett, T. Fenwick, & M. Somerville (Eds.), *Work, subjectivity and learning* (pp. 105–121). Springer. https://doi.org/10.1007/1-4020-5360-6_7

Archer, M. S. (2000). *Being human: The problem of agency*. Cambridge University Press.

Australian Bureau of Statistics. (2023). *Education and Work, Australia*. Retrieved from https://www.abs.gov.au/statistics/people/education/education-and-work-australia/may-2023

Baltes, P. B., & Staudinger, U. M. (Eds.). (1996). *Interactive minds: Life-span perspectives on the social foundation of cognition*. Cambridge University Press.

Bennett, A. I., Hanley, J., Buckle, P., & Bridger, R. S. (2011). Work demands during firefighting training: Does age matter? *Ergonomics, 54*(6), 555–564. https://doi.org/10.1080/00140139.2011.582540

Berk, L. E. (2023). *Development through the lifespan* (7th ed.). Sage Publications.

Billett, S. (2004). Co-participation at work: Learning through work and throughout working lives. *Studies in the Education of Adults, 36*(2), 190–205. https://doi.org/10.1080/02660830.2004.11661496

Billett, S. (2006). Relational interdependence between social and individual agency in work and working life. *Mind, Culture, and Activity, 13*(1), 53–69. https://doi.org/10.1207/s15327884mca1301_5

Billett, S. (2009a). Conceptualizing learning experiences: Contributions and mediations of the social, personal, and brute. *Mind, Culture, and Activity, 16*(1), 32–47. https://doi.org/10.1080/10749030802477317

Billett, S. (2009b). Personal epistemologies, work and learning. *Educational Research Review, 4*(3), 210–219. https://doi.org/10.1016/j.edurev.2009.06.001

Billett, S. (2010). *Promoting and supporting lifelong employability for Singapore's workers aged 45 and over*. Institute of Adult Learning. https://www.ial.edu.sg/getmedia/be7bf9c8-4534-465d-8088-29a077a4440b/Promoting-and-Supporting-Lifelong-Employability.pdf

Billett, S. (2011). Promoting lifelong employability for workforce aged over 45: Singaporean workers' perspectives. *International Journal of Continuing Education and Lifelong Learning, 3*(2), 57–73.

Billett, S., & Pavlova, M. (2003). Learning through working life: Individuals' agentic action, subjectivity and participation in work. In *11th Annual International conference on post-compulsory education and training: Enriching learning cultures*.

Billett, S., & Somerville, M. (2004). Transformations at work: Identity and learning. *Studies in Continuing Education, 26*(2), 309–326. https://doi.org/10.1080/158037042000225272

Billett, S., & van Woerkom, M. (2008). Personal epistemologies and older workers. *International Journal of Lifelong Education, 27*(3), 333–348. https://doi.org/10.1080/02601370802047833

Billett, S., Smith, R., & Barker, M. (2005). Understanding work, learning and the remaking of cultural practices. *Studies in Continuing Education, 27*(3), 219–237. https://doi.org/10.1080/01580370500376564

Billett, S., Dymock, D., Johnson, G., & Martin, G. (2011). Overcoming the paradox of employers' views about older workers. *International Journal of Human Resource Development, 22*(6), 1248–1261. https://doi.org/10.1080/09585192.2011.559097

Billett, S., Yang, S., Chia, A., Tai, J. F., Lee, M., & Alhadad, S. (2021). Remaking and transforming cultural practices: Exploring the co-occurrence of work, learning and innovation. In K. Collin, V. Glaveanu, S. Lemmetty, & P. Forsman (Eds.), *Creativity and learning: Contexts, processes and impact* (pp. 219–244). Palgrave Macmillan.

Bosman, E. A. (1993). Age-related differences in in the motoric aspects of transcription typing skills. *Psychology and Aging, 8*(1), 87–102. https://psycnet.apa.org/doi/10.1037/0882-7974.8.1.87

Brunello, G., & Medio, A. (2001). An explanation of international differences in education and workplace training. *European Economic Review, 45*(2), 307–322. https://doi.org/10.1016/S0014-2921(99)00065-3

References

Centeno, V. (2011). Lifelong learning: A policy concept with a long past but a short history. *International Journal of Lifelong Education, 30*(2), 133–150. https://doi.org/10.1080/02601370.2010.547616

Cronin, A., & Mandich, M. B. (2015). *Human development and performance throughout the lifespan* (2nd ed.). Cengage Learning.

De Lange, A. H., Van der Heijden, B., Van Vuuren, T., Furunes, T., De Lange, C., & Dikkers, J. (2021). Employable as we age? A systematic review of relationships between age conceptualizations and employability. *Frontiers in Psychology, 11*, 605684. https://doi.org/10.3389/fpsyg.2020.605684

European Centre for the Development of Vocational Training. (2006). *Promoting lifelong learning for older workers: An international overview*. Publications Office of the European Union. Retrieved from https://www.cedefop.europa.eu/files/3045_en.pdf

Francis, J. R. (1994). Auditing, hermeneutics, and subjectivity. *Accounting, Organizations and Society, 19*(3), 235–269. https://doi.org/10.1016/0361-3682(94)90034-5

Goodnow, J. J. (1990). The socialization of cognition: What's involved? In J. W. Stigler, R. A. Shweder, & G. Herdt (Eds.), *Cultural psychology: Essays on comparative human development* (pp. 259–286). Cambridge University Press. https://psycnet.apa.org/doi/10.1017/CBO9781139173728.008

Government of Singapore. (2024). *Speech by PM Lee Hsien Loong at the Singapore Tripartism Forum on 22 February 2009 at NTUC Centre*. https://www.pmo.gov.sg/Newsroom/we-will-do-more-middle-income-pmets-pm-lee.

Han, S. (2001). Creating systems for lifelong learning in asia. *Asia Pacific Education Review, 2*(2), 85–95. https://doi.org/10.1007/BF03026293

Hodkinson, P., & Hodkinson, H. (2004). The significance of individuals' dispositions in workplace learning: A case study of two teachers. *Journal of Education and Work, 17*(2), 167–182. https://doi.org/10.1080/13639080410001677383

Knowles, M. (1975). *Self-directed learning: A guide for learners and teachers*. Association Press.

Leontyev, A. N. (1981). *Problems of the development of the mind*. Progress Publishers.

Leow, A., Billett, S., & Le, A. H. (2023). Towards a continuing education and training eco system: A case study of Singapore. *International Journal of Training Research, 21*(3), 226–242. https://doi.org/10.1080/14480220.2023.2203944

Leow, A., Billett, S., Le, A. H., & Chua, S. (2022). Graduates' perspectives on effective continuing education and training: Participation, access and engagement. *International Journal of Lifelong Education, 41*(2), 212–228. https://doi.org/10.1080/02601370.2022.2044398

Leuven, E., & Oosterbeek, H. (1999). The demand and supply of work-related training: Evidence from four countries. *Research in Labor Economics, 18*, 303–330. https://doi.org/10.1016/S0147-9121(99)18026-9

Malle, B. F., Moses, L. J., & Baldwin, D. A. (2001). Introduction: The significance of intentionality. In B. F. Malle, L. J. Moses, & D. A. Baldwin (Eds.), *Intentions and Intentionality: Foundations of Social Cognition* (pp. 1–26). The MIT Press.

Marchant, T. (2013). Keep going: Career perspectives on ageing and masculinity of self-employed tradesmen in Australia. *Construction Management and Economics, 31*(8), 845–860. https://doi.org/10.1080/01446193.2013.808353

Mavin, T. J., Kikkawa, Y., & Billett, S. (2018). Key contributing factors to learning through debriefings: Commercial aviation pilots' perspectives. *International Journal of Training Research, 16*(2), 122–144. https://doi.org/10.1080/14480220.2018.1501906

Morris, C. E., & Chander, H. (2018). The impact of firefighter physical fitness on job performance: A review of the factors that influence fire suppression safety and success. *Safety, 4*(4), 60. https://doi.org/10.3390/safety4040060

National Population and Talent Division. (2003). *Population in brief 2023*. Prime Minister's Office: Singapore. https://www.population.gov.sg/files/media-centre/publications/population-in-brief-2023.pdf

Organisation for Economic Co-operation and Development (OECD). (2016). *Singapore PIAAC data* [Data set]. https://www.oecd.org/skills/piaac/data/

Organisation for Economic Co-operation and Development (OECD) (2024). *Working age population (indicator)*. doi:https://doi.org/10.1787/d339918b-en. Accessed on 22 February 2024.

Organisation for Economic Co-operation and Development [OECD]. (2006). *Live longer, work longer: A synthesis report of the ageing and employment policies project*. OECD. https://doi.org/10.1787/9789264035881-en

Osborne, M., & Borkowska, K. (2017). A European lens upon adult and lifelong learning in Asia. *Asia Pacific Education Review, 18*(2), 269–280. https://doi.org/10.1007/s12564-017-9479-4

Patrickson, M., & Ranzijn, R. (2004). Bounded choices in work and retirement in Australia. *Employee Relations, 26*(4), 422–432. https://doi.org/10.1108/01425450410544515

Peterson, C. C. (2003). Lifespan human development. In J. P. Keeves & R. Watanabe (Eds.), *International handbook of educational research in the Asia-Pacific Region: Part One* (pp. 379–394). Springer. https://doi.org/10.1007/978-94-017-3368-7_27

Rogoff, B. (1990). *Apprenticeship in thinking: Cognitive development in social context*. Oxford University Press.

Schmidt, B. (2007). Older employee behaviour and interest in continuing education. *Journal of Adult and Continuing Education, 13*(2), 156–174. https://doi.org/10.7227/JACE.13.2.4

Sigelman, C. K. (1999). *Life-span human development* (3rd ed.). Brooks/Cole Publishing Company.

Somerville, M. (2006). Subjected bodies, or embodied subjects: Subjectivity and learning safety at work. In S. Billett, T. Fenwick, & M. Somerville (Eds.), *Work, subjectivity and learning* (pp. 37–52). Springer. https://doi.org/10.1007/1-4020-5360-6_3

Truxillo, D. M., Cadiz, D. M., & Hammer, L. B. (2015). Supporting the aging workforce: A review and recommendations for workplace intervention research. *Annual Review of Organizational Psychology and Organizational Behavior, 2*(1), 351–381. https://doi.org/10.1146/annurev-orgpsych-032414-111435

Wallin, A., Pylväs, L., & Nokelainen, P. (2020). Government workers' stories about professional development in a digitalized working life. *Vocations and Learning, 13*(3), 439–458. https://doi.org/10.1007/s12186-020-09248-y

Weiss, M., Weiss, D., & Zacher, H. (2022). All set in stone? How essentialist beliefs about aging affect older workers' motivation to continue working beyond retirement age. *Journal of Organizational Behavior, 43*(8), 1446–1461. https://doi.org/10.1002/job.2647

Yacob, H. (2009, November 5). Opening address by Mdm Halimah Yacob, deputy secretary general of the National Trades Union Congress, at the 2nd IAL Adult Learning Symposium, Singapore.

Index

A
Adaptiveness, 4
Adult educator, 26, 33, 41, 47, 49, 57, 62, 64, 78, 86, 87, 91, 99, 100, 119, 129, 184, 186–193, 195, 196
Aged over 50, 82, 112
Aging population, 127

B
Balancing commitments, 33
Barriers to participation, 108

C
Case study, 1, 6, 16, 17, 47–49, 52, 64, 71, 75–78, 162, 163, 220, 227
CET administrator, 189, 193
CET educator, 5, 18, 19, 26, 33–36, 38, 39, 41, 47, 51, 54, 56–58, 62, 63, 75, 77–79, 86, 87, 89–91, 105, 110, 117–121, 128, 129, 143, 144, 147, 152, 162–165, 168–172, 175, 176, 183–188, 190, 192–196, 205, 210
CET institution, 27–28, 32, 34, 35, 47, 105, 116, 121, 147, 167, 174, 184, 185, 194, 210
CET practitioner, 182–197
CET purpose, 6–17, 30, 188, 201, 205, 206, 210, 215, 220, 232, 233, 239
CET system, 5, 13, 17, 26–29, 32–41, 47, 49, 50, 62, 75, 88, 90–92, 121, 153, 163, 185, 192, 194, 205
Collaboration, 15, 19, 27, 28, 35, 39, 41, 47, 56, 63, 91, 171, 176, 185, 192, 194, 196, 197, 203

Community, 1, 6–8, 12, 13, 15, 24, 26–30, 32, 34, 48, 51–53, 55, 59, 63, 74, 83, 91, 98, 106–109, 111, 126, 127, 130, 137, 142, 153, 167, 168, 172, 184, 195, 200, 201, 207, 220, 223, 231, 232
Continuing education and training (CET), 4, 24, 46, 74, 104, 126, 161, 182, 200, 220
Contribution, 1, 4, 6, 8, 17–19, 24, 26, 28–36, 40, 41, 47, 53–63, 80, 87–89, 92, 109, 114, 116, 126, 134, 162, 169, 171, 175, 184, 195, 197, 213, 225–227, 230, 234, 236, 239

D
Data analysis, 75, 80, 92, 130, 205

E
Economic goal, 4, 12, 17, 47, 52, 121, 201, 220
Educational engagement, 191, 193
Educational process, 8, 15, 34, 37, 55, 162, 171, 173, 174, 190, 195
Educational purpose, 9, 13, 38
Education system, 1, 5, 10, 49, 134, 183, 184
Effective CET provision, 1, 4–19, 26, 28, 29, 32, 33, 36–38, 41, 46–48, 50, 52, 56, 58, 62–64, 71, 74–92, 105, 109, 117, 120, 127, 128, 153, 157, 160–177, 182, 185, 186, 193–197, 201, 205, 208, 214, 216, 221

Effectiveness, 4, 7, 16, 28, 41, 48, 52–54, 58, 63, 77, 83, 84, 112, 114, 121, 126, 128, 130, 136, 138–141, 143, 145, 149, 152, 163, 165, 176, 182, 184, 191, 196, 206, 207, 209, 210, 215, 226, 229, 238

Effective provision, 1, 4–6, 8, 12, 13, 17, 26, 33, 46–64, 80, 90, 157, 161, 166, 169, 175, 182–186, 196–197

Employability, 4–8, 12, 13, 16–18, 24–35, 37, 40, 41, 46–56, 59, 62, 64, 71, 74–92, 104, 105, 107, 109, 111, 113, 115, 120, 121, 126–128, 133, 134, 152, 160–177, 182–185, 193–195, 200–202, 205–207, 214, 215, 220–222, 225–227, 229–231

Employer, 5, 6, 17, 18, 28, 32, 35–39, 41, 49–51, 54, 56, 64, 71, 74, 75, 77–82, 84, 87–92, 105, 108, 110, 111, 115, 116, 121, 127, 128, 134, 136, 142, 144, 151, 152, 157, 160–177, 184–189, 192–194, 197, 201, 205, 207, 209, 215, 221, 223, 226, 233

Employment, 4, 7–9, 11, 13–15, 18, 19, 24–30, 32–38, 40, 41, 46, 47, 52, 54–57, 60, 62, 63, 74–77, 79, 83–85, 88, 90–92, 99, 104–111, 114–121, 127–129, 132, 133, 137, 138, 140–143, 146–149, 152, 153, 160, 161, 164, 168–171, 174, 182, 185, 187, 188, 193, 194, 196, 197, 200–202, 204–206, 208, 214, 215, 221–228, 231–233, 235

Engagement, 8, 26, 46, 75, 105, 127, 160, 185, 200, 221

Extrinsic motivation, 110, 150

F

Family, 13, 24, 48, 74, 107, 126, 167, 200, 220
Family commitment, 19, 76, 136, 137, 139, 142, 143, 200, 201, 203, 208, 214, 221, 232, 238

G

Geopolitical tension, 4, 7, 25, 126, 161
Global competition, 25, 161
Global competitiveness, 126
Governmental goal, 52, 63, 127
Graduate, 6, 16–19, 30–32, 41, 53, 71, 75, 78, 80–83, 86–92, 99, 105, 110, 111, 113–117, 119–121, 128, 131, 134, 135, 142, 144, 148–150, 157, 160–177, 185–188, 193, 196, 201, 202, 205–215, 221, 228–234, 236, 238, 239

Guideline, 18, 19, 79, 86, 88, 98, 110, 185, 195

I

Informant, 6, 19, 28, 80–83, 86–90, 92, 106, 111–117, 119, 120, 129, 130, 135, 143, 147, 151, 152, 157, 161, 163, 164, 166–174, 176, 186, 201, 204–212, 214, 215, 221, 228–234, 236, 238
Innovative, 25, 27, 35, 184
Intentionality, 14, 30, 40, 108, 115, 126, 146, 223–227
Interdependence, 27, 32, 35, 226
Intrinsic motivation, 107, 109, 110, 115, 150

L

Lifelong education, 53, 77, 183, 227
Lifelong learning, 37, 46, 47, 50–52, 63, 76, 77, 89, 108, 112, 150, 162, 172, 174, 175, 182, 183, 197, 230

M

Method, 6, 18, 64, 71, 74–92, 105, 110, 139, 163, 165, 196, 204, 205
Modes of skill acquisition, 133, 135, 164–166

N

National priority, 46, 74, 182, 227
National sustainability, 53

O

Occupational currency, 39, 47, 51, 53, 55, 58, 63, 169, 210
Older student, 233, 234
Older worker, 6, 8, 28, 51, 108, 204, 220–229, 231, 233

P

Participation, 7, 26, 48, 75, 104, 127, 161, 185, 200, 221
Partnership, 18, 27, 32, 54, 55, 62, 153, 184, 185, 196
Private enterprise, 24
Procedure, 6, 13, 18, 38, 57, 60, 61, 64, 71, 74–92, 105, 108, 110, 129–130, 147, 163, 183, 205

Provision of goods and services, 7, 25
Public enterprise, 4

Q

Qualitative, 79, 80, 83, 87, 90, 112, 130, 136, 143, 187, 201, 205, 206, 221
Quality of CET learners, 129, 131, 145–147
Quality of CET teachers, 143–145
Quantitative, 79, 82, 90, 92, 130, 139, 205, 221
Quantitative analysis, 201, 221

R

Respondent, 6, 28, 82–86, 89, 92, 129–153, 157, 204
Role of tertiary education institutions, 126, 143, 147, 183

S

Scalability, 6, 26, 126, 128, 184
Singapore, 1, 4–7, 9, 10, 16–18, 24, 25, 28, 29, 40, 41, 47–52, 54, 64, 71, 75–77, 79, 81–83, 85, 86, 88, 89, 91, 92, 99, 109, 115, 116, 121, 127, 128, 130, 131, 137, 141, 143, 147, 149, 162–163, 165, 167, 182–193, 195, 201, 204, 205, 214, 220, 221, 223, 227, 229, 236
Singaporean, 6, 17, 18, 26, 33, 35, 41, 48–52, 64, 71, 75–83, 86–91, 105, 110, 118, 128–131, 133, 136, 137, 140–142, 144, 149–151, 153, 162, 163, 165, 182, 184–186, 195, 204–215, 226–228, 232, 239
Social goal, 4, 24, 26, 41

Societal goal, 18, 160, 161
Subsidy, 56, 82, 89, 100, 111, 128, 129, 131, 137, 143, 149–153, 190, 191, 206, 207, 209, 214
Successful completion, 37, 90
Survey, 6, 17, 18, 28, 33, 50, 51, 71, 75, 77, 79, 80, 82–86, 90–97, 110, 111, 113, 126–153, 163, 164, 167, 185, 201, 204–206, 221, 227, 228
Survey data, 86, 113, 128, 140, 167, 201, 204, 221

W

Work experience, 37, 38, 120, 136, 152
Working-age adult, 4–8, 12–19, 24–41, 46–49, 51–64, 74–80, 88–92, 104–110, 113, 115, 116, 118, 120, 121, 126–130, 134, 135, 138, 140, 141, 143, 145, 147, 151–153, 157, 161–163, 166, 167, 169, 172, 174–176, 182, 183, 185, 186, 192–195, 197, 200, 202, 204, 206, 208, 212, 214–216, 220–239
Working life, 1, 4–19, 24, 26, 28, 29, 31, 40, 41, 46–54, 57, 59, 61–63, 74, 75, 79, 80, 86, 88, 91, 104, 106, 109, 119–121, 127, 134, 135, 138, 160, 161, 169, 182–184, 194, 200, 206–207, 210, 214, 215, 220, 221, 223–225, 227, 231, 234, 238, 239
Working women, 19, 157, 200–216
Workplace, 4, 24, 46, 74, 104, 126, 160, 182, 200, 220
Workplace experiences, 56, 61–62, 129, 147–149, 152, 184
Workshop, 17, 79, 86, 98–101, 142, 186, 192, 195

Printed in the United States
by Baker & Taylor Publisher Services